A WORLD BANK COUNTRY STUDY

Pacific Island Economies

Building a Resilient Economic Base for the Twenty-First Century

The World Bank
Washington, D.C.

Manufactured in the United States of America
First printing April 1996

World Bank Country Studies are among the many reports originally prepared for internal use as part of the continuing analysis by the Bank of the economic and related conditions of its developing member countries and of its dialogues with the governments. Some of the reports are published in this series with the least possible delay for the use of governments and the academic, business and financial, and development communities. The typescript of this paper therefore has not been prepared in accordance with the procedures appropriate to formal printed texts, and the World Bank accepts no responsibility for errors. Some sources cited in this paper may be informal documents that are not readily available.

The World Bank does not guarantee the accuracy of the data included in this publication and accepts no responsibility whatsoever for any consequence of their use. The boundaries, colors, denominations, and other information shown on any map in this volume do not imply on the part of the World Bank Group any judgment on the legal status of any territory or the endorsement or acceptance of such boundaries.

The complete backlist of publications from the World Bank is shown in the annual *Index of Publications*, which contains an alphabetical title list (with full ordering information) and indexes of subjects, authors, and countries and regions. The latest edition is available free of charge from the Distribution Unit, Office of the Publisher, The World Bank, 1818 H Street, N.W., Washington, D.C. 20433, U.S.A., or from Publications, The World Bank, 66, avenue d'Iéna, 75116 Paris, France.

ISSN: 0-0253-2123

Library of Congress Cataloging-in-Publication Data

Pacific Island economies : building a resilient economic base for the twenty-first century.
p. cm. — (A World Bank country study, 0253-2123)
The report includes economic profiles of eight Pacific Island countries : Fiji, Federated States of Micronesia, Kiribati, Marshall Islands, Solomon Islands, Tonga, Vanuatu, and Western Samoa ; it was prepared by a team led by Hilarian Codippily.
Includes bibliographical references (p.).
ISBN 0-8213-3554-5
1. Oceania—Economic conditions. 2. Oceania—Commerce.
I. Codippily, Hilarian M. A., 1938– . II. International Bank for Reconstruction and Development. III. Series.
HC681.P276 1996 95-48482
338.99— dc20 CIP

CONTENTS

List of Tables

List of Figures

List of Boxes

ABSTRACT

This report presents a selection of topics of special interest and relevance to eight Pacific Island countries that are members of the World Bank (PMCs)—Fiji, Federated States of Micronesia, Kiribati, Marshall Islands, Solomon Islands, Tonga, Vanuatu, and Western Samoa. The themes selected are: the impact of recent changes in the external trading environment of the PMCs; economic diversification into tourism; improving the management of and getting better returns for natural resources, i.e. fisheries and forestry; and regional cooperation. The report also includes eight country profiles.

ACKNOWLEDGMENTS

The World Bank wishes to express its appreciation to all member Governments, bilateral donor agencies, the Asian Development Bank, the Forum Secretariat, The South Pacific Forum Fisheries Agency, the South Pacific Commission, the United Nations Development Programme, Institut Francais de Recherche Scientifique Pour le Developpement en Cooperation (ORSTOM), the University of the South Pacific, International Center for Living Aquatic Resources Management, South Pacific Forestry Development Programme, and several research organizations, non-governmental organizations and individuals for their cooperation in preparing this report. The World Bank acknowledges, in particular, the valuable support for the study provided by the Australian Agency for International Development (AusAID).

This report was prepared by a team led by Hilarian Codippily and was based on field work carried out in mid-1994. The core team included Irene Davies, Cyrus Talati, Monique Garrity, Farrukh Iqbal, Sofia Bettencourt, Eduardo Loayza, Jay Blakeney, Steven Tabor, Sonia Pahwa and Peter Osei. Geoffrey Waugh, Richard Bramley, Jesse Floyd, Robert Johannes, Carolyn Wiltshire, Thorsten Block, and Joan Curry made major contributions. The report was prepared under the guidance of Mr. Ajay Chhibber and Mrs. Marianne Haug. Ms. Phyllis Williams provided administrative support and coordinated the processing of the report.

ACRONYMS AND ABBREVIATIONS

A$	=	Australian Dollar
ACP	=	African, Caribbean and Pacific States
ADB	=	Asian Development Bank
AIDAB	=	Australian International Development Assistance Bureau (now AusAID)
APEC	=	Asia Pacific Economic Cooperation
ATC	=	Australian Tourist Commission
AusAID	=	Australian Agency for International Development
CER	=	Closer Economic Relations
CMT	=	Customary Marine Tenure Systems
CO_2	=	Carbon Dioxide
CPUE	=	Catch Per Unit of Effort
DP7	=	Development Plan 7
EEZ	=	Exclusive Economic Zone
EU	=	European Union
FAO	=	Food and Agriculture Organization
FDI	=	Foreign Direct Investment
FFA	=	Forum Fisheries Agency
FFI	=	Fiji Forest Industries
FIJ	=	Fiji
FIT	=	Frequent Independent Travel
FJS	=	Fishery Judicial System
FORSPA	=	Forestry Research Support Program for Asia and the Pacific
FMR	=	Fisheries Management Regime
FMS	=	Fishery Management System
FRIM	=	Forest Research Institute of Malaysia
FSM	=	Federated States of Micronesia
FSP	=	Foundation for the Peoples of the South Pacific
GATT	=	General Agreement on Tariffs and Trade
GDP	=	Gross Domestic Product
GNP	=	Gross National Product
GRT	=	Gross (registered) Tonnage
GSP	=	Generalized System of Preferences
GTZ	=	German Technical Cooperation
HMTA	=	Harmonized Minimum Terms and Conditions of Access
IFC	=	International Finance Corporation
ITQs	=	Individual Transferable Quotas
ITTO	=	International Tropical Timber Organization
IUCN	=	The World Conservation Union
KFPL	=	Kolombangara Forest Plantation Ltd.
KIR	=	Kiribati
LDC	=	Less Developed Country
MEY	=	Maximum Economic Yield
MFN	=	Most Favored Nation
MOU	=	Memorandum of Understanding
MSY	=	Maximum Sustainable Yield
MT	=	Metric Tons
NAFTA	=	North American Free Trade Agreement
NGO	=	Non-Government Organization
NLTB	=	Native Lands Trust Board
NTO	=	National Tourism Organization
NZ$	=	New Zealand Dollar
NZFS	=	New Zealand Forest Service
NZODA	=	New Zealand Overseas Development Assistance

ODA	=	Overseas Development Assistance
OECD	=	Organization for Economic Cooperation and Development
PIMRIS	=	Pacific Islands Marine Resource Information System
PMC	=	Pacific Island Member Country
PNG	=	Papua New Guinea
REER	=	Real Effective Exchange Rate
RER	=	Regional Economic Report
RERF	=	Revenue Equalization Reserve Fund
RIL	=	Reduced Impact Logging
RMI	=	Republic of Marshall Islands
SI$	=	Solomon Islands Dollar
SOL	=	Solomon Islands
SPARTECA	=	South Pacific Regional Trade and Economic Cooperation Agreement
SPC	=	South Pacific Commission
SPC/OFP	=	South Pacific Commission, Oceanic Fisheries Programme
SPFDP	=	UNDP/FAO South Pacific Forestry Development Program
STABEX	=	Export Earning Stabilization System
TC	=	Total Cost
TCSP	=	Tourism Council of the South Pacific
TON	=	Tonga
TR	=	Total Revenue
U.K.	=	United Kingdom
U.S.	=	United States
UN-ESCAP	=	United Nations-Economic and Social Commission for Asia and the Pacific
UNDP	=	United Nations Development Programme
US$	=	United States Dollar
USA	=	United States of America
USAID	=	United States Agency for International Development
USP	=	University of the South Pacific
VAN	=	Vanuatu
VAT	=	Value Added Tax
WS$	=	Western Samoa Dollar
WSM	=	Western Samoa
WSVB	=	Western Samoa Visitors Bureau
WTO	=	World Trade Organization
WWF	=	World Wildlife Fund

CURRENCY EQUIVALENTS

FEDERATED STATES OF MICRONESIA (FSM)

(The US Dollar is the official currency of exchange)

FISCAL YEAR

October 1 - September 30

FIJI

Annual Averages

1991	F$1.00	=	US$0.68
1992	F$1.00	=	US$0.67
1993	F$1.00	=	US$0.65

FISCAL YEAR

January 1 - December 31

KIRIBATI

Annual Averages

(The Australian dollar is the official currency and the main medium of exchange)

1991	A$1.00	=	US$0.78
1992	A$1.00	=	US$0.74
1993	A$1.00	=	US$0.68

FISCAL YEAR

January 1 - December 31

MARSHALL ISLANDS

(The US Dollar is the official currency of exchange)

FISCAL YEAR

October 1 - September 30

SOLOMON ISLANDS

Annual Averages

1991	US$1.00	=	SI$2.7148
1992	US$1.00	=	SI$2.9281
1993	US$1.00	=	SI$3.1877

Fiscal Year

January 1 to December 31

TONGA

Annual Averages

1991	US$1.00	=	T$1.2961
1992	US$1.00	=	T$1.3471
1993	US$1.00	=	T$1.3841

Fiscal Year

July 1 - June 30

VANUATU

Annual Averages

1991	US$1.00	=	Vt 111.68
1992	US$1.00	=	Vt 113.39
1993	US$1.00	=	Vt 121.58

Fiscal Year

January 1 - December 31

WESTERN SAMOA

Annual Averages

1991	WS$1.00	=	US$0.4171
1992	WS$1.00	=	US$0.4056
1993	WS$1.00	=	US$0.3894

Fiscal Year

July 1 - June 30

EXECUTIVE SUMMARY

With so many of East Asia's economies now poised to leap onto the economic center stage and become full-fledged competitors in the world market. the next century has been dubbed the "Century of the Pacific". Yet for the Pacific Islands—hovering at the edges of this whirlwind of activity—how best to participate in it is less certain.

Small and remote, scattered across the Pacific Ocean, these Island nations face many development challenges. The heritage of the Pacific Islands, however, rests in their unique cultures, their natural beauty, their forests, and their fish. They will have to work together to protect, conserve, and make the most of these rare gifts. Can the Pacific Islands ensure that the Century of the Pacific will be one of economic opportunity and prosperity for all their people?

Favorable physical environments, and rich cultural traditions including the extended family system, customary land ownership and benefit sharing practices, have endowed their populations with a relatively safe and secure lifestyle. By world standards, the average life expectancy of over 60 years is high. But while life is safe and secure in the Pacific Islands, economic growth has been slow. Unless the Islands achieve moderate sustainable economic growth, improvements in the quality of life may not be possible.

Throughout the past decade, the Pacific Island Member Countries (PMCs) have invested an average of 29 percent of GDP in their economy, yet economic growth has remained at a low 2 percent a year. As a recent study showed, this may reflect the lumpiness and long gestation periods of public investments, which accounted for 17 percent of GDP, as well as some unproductive investments. The 12 percent of GDP provided by private investment, on the other hand, was positively correlated with growth, confirming the importance of the role of the private sector in economic growth, as emphasized in previous reports.

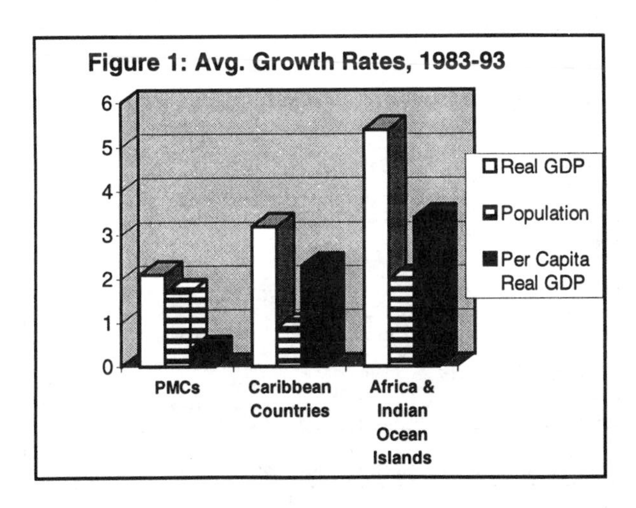

The PMCs need to change course and rely on a more effective private and public investment oriented growth strategy. Change is all the more essential because of external vulnerability and rising demands for modern goods and services within the PMCs. As elaborated below, an outward oriented investment-led growth strategy is needed—but not necessarily the path of labor intensive agriculture and manufacturing witnessed in the early stages of East Asian growth. Achieving such a strategy would depend on evolving a more effective development partnership between the state and the private sector. In such a partnership, the state should focus on ensuring macroeconomic stability and competitiveness, creating a more enabling regulatory framework, providing economic and social infrastructure and reducing its role in the productive and service sectors. Such an environment would provide the private sector with the impetus to save and invest in the productive sectors, and thereby contribute to output and employment but with careful regulation to ensure that it is environmentally sustainable in the long term.

In building a more resilient economic base, the PMCs could follow two broad approaches. The first is to diversify their economic base into tourism and services. Second, the PMCs need to obtain higher returns from their natural capital, i.e. from fisheries in all PMCs, and from forestry in some of the PMCs. Regarding the latter a fundamental question facing the PMCs is: how can these countries exploit their natural resources sustainably to maximize economic returns while preserving stocks for future generations? Efficient import substitution possibilities also need to be exploited. Recent trends in external trade show that the PMCs are moving in this direction. But much more remains to be done.

Foreign aid will and should continue to play an important role but the content needs to be changed and linked much more directly to overall development impact, greater improvement of public service delivery and growth. This report does not analyze aid-effectiveness in any detail. It shows nevertheless, that aid programs need to be better focused on getting coherent results, instead of being spread thinly among a multitude of small individually worthwhile activities. Further, the technical assistance component of aid programs is very high, and may well add to public consumption instead of investment by maintaining large public sector bureaucracies.

Working with the World

In the recent past, trends in Pacific Island trade indicate that:

- there have been major changes both in composition and direction of exports;
- the composition of imports has also changed; but
- vulnerability to external factors remains and will continue to do so.

Over the last decade, the structure of trade in the Pacific Islands has been changing. While the export of traditional commodities remains important, the Islands have expanded earnings from services, fish and forestry products. Manufactured exports rose from negligible to almost 8 percent in 1991-93 mainly due to the garment industry in Fiji. Islanders have also begun to import far more manufactured goods, machinery, beverages, and tobacco, while the share of food, chemicals, mineral fuels, oils and fats imported declined.

Notwithstanding attempts to diversify the export mix and to build links into new markets, the Islands remain vulnerable to external shocks. Trade penetration ratios are close to 80 percent of GDP, with imports accounting for more than half of GDP. With the exception of Fiji, the Islands run large merchandise and current account deficits, and correspondingly large capital inflows to finance these deficits. They are also heavily dependent on trade taxes for a large share of public revenue. Where even minor changes in the terms of trade can devastate external balances and economic growth, managing vulnerability and exploiting emerging opportunities become the governments' key economic challenges.

The recent changes in the global trading environment arising from the conclusion of the Uruguay Round of the GATT Agreement, NAFTA and trade deregulation in Australia and New Zealand will have some effect on the PMCs' trading environment. Benefits are likely to favor countries with open economies and those that have the capacity to adjust and take advantage of new market opportunities likely to arise from the projected real GDP growth rates of around 2.7 percent per year for the G-7 economies over the medium term. Two other favorable factors are the outlook for low real interest rates and inflation as well as the resurgence of higher private capital inflows. Some likely effects of changes in the

Figure 2: Composition of PMC Exports: 1982-84 & 1991-93

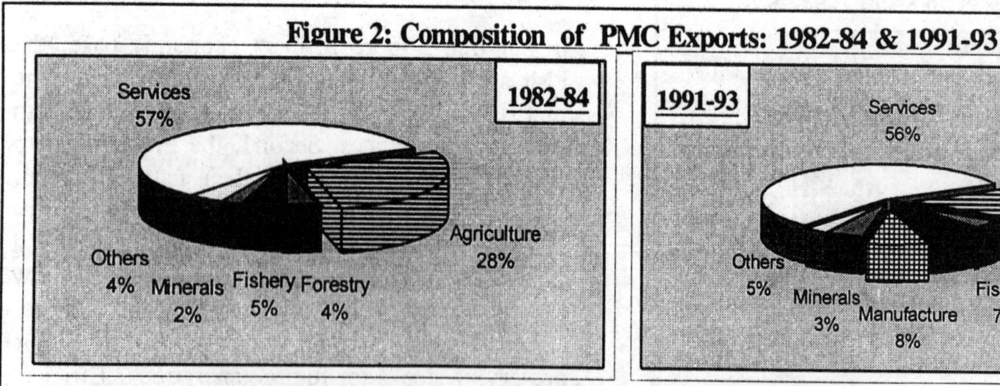

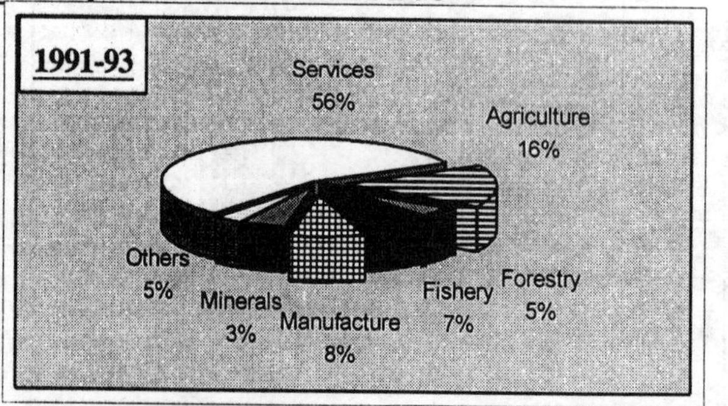

Total Goods & Services: US$748 million | **Total Goods & Services: US$1372 million**

global economic environment are that:

- overall growth and trade will increase dramatically;
- a more competitive trade environment will emerge; and
- trends toward regional integration will intensify.

To reduce their vulnerability to external shocks the Pacific Islands (along with all other countries) will need to increase the breadth and depth of their trading relations. To date, they have benefited from preferential trade agreements (such as SPARTECA) that have allowed their exports into major markets largely duty free. By reducing duties levied on their competitors, the new trade liberalization agreements will wipe out much of this competitive advantage. This explains why the growth in manufactured exports from Fiji is now threatened over the medium term.

Trade agreements such as SPARTECA that provide Island manufacturers the opportunity to enter new markets under the shelter of another nation's trade protection carry with them serious hidden costs. To meet the 50 percent local content requirement (reduced recently to 45 percent), for example, Island garment industries have been forced to buy capital goods and inputs from Australia and New Zealand rather than from more competitive Asian markets and have under-invested in new technology to maintain a high labor-cost share.

Building upon their small yet significant recent success in trade diversification, PMC governments need to focus more attention on *enhancing competitiveness* in the PMCs. This will require:

- the maintenance of a macroeconomic environment that meets the twin goals of price stability and competitive pricing of PMC resources;
- a reduction in the anti-export bias of trade policy, and tax regimes; and
- reducing barriers to domestic and foreign direct investment.

An Enabling Macroeconomic Environment. A low rate of inflation and the pricing of capital, labor and land so as to be internationally competitive are two of the main macroeconomic challenges. With small financial markets, even smaller domestically financed fiscal deficits can quickly spark inflationary upsurges, and discourage private investment and private saving. It points to the need for prudent fiscal management especially during periods of volatile external developments. Towards this end, a combination of exchange rate, public sector wage, and overall fiscal policies is the main set of instruments that can be used to ensure that domestic resources are competitively priced in global markets. If domestic resources are overvalued, then domestic investors will be encouraged to shift their capital abroad while overseas investors will be reluctant to make new commitments.

Reducing Anti-Export Bias. Several of the PMCs rely heavily on trade taxes to finance the recurrent costs of government. While providing a steady stream of revenue, high import duties raise the cost of doing business in the PMCs and discourage exports. In terms of providing protection to domestic producers, high import duties are counter-productive. Remoteness from major markets already provides the PMCs with a high degree of natural trade protection. While high tariffs convey a measure of protection to domestic producers, opportunities for import substitution are quickly exhausted because of small populations and low incomes. A progressive reduction of import duties over the medium term would lower enterprise costs and reduce the anti-export bias of PMC trade regimes. Lowering tariff rates would, by necessity, need to be accompanied by measures to develop new domestic revenue sources, suggesting the need for careful coordination of resource mobilization and trade reform measures.

Reducing Barriers. Competitiveness can be further enhanced by lowering costs to domestic and foreign businesses through reducing barriers affecting them. A healthy domestic private sector will be the first step towards attracting foreign investment. In addition to capital, foreign investment brings with it the technology and market access needed to penetrate new markets. GATT, the emergence of major regional trading blocs, and the opening up of protected markets signal growing competitiveness in the international environment for both foreign direct investment and trade. For the PMCs to attract foreign direct investment and expand trade, efforts will be required to:

- examine barriers to foreign direct investment;
- examine the framework for "niche market agreements" and the ability to assess costs, benefits, and risks; and
- strengthen trade and investment links with rapidly growing Asian economies.

Investment approval mechanisms, access to land, and restrictions on the hiring of expatriate workers are three of the most often cited impediments to foreign direct investment in the South Pacific. Establishing up-to-date foreign direct investment legislation, streamlining the FDI approval process, clarifying property rights and relaxing regulatory barriers to land use by foreigners, and easing requirements related to the hiring of expatriate workers are some of the measures that the PMC states could adopt to make the domestic economic environment more conducive to inward investment.

To offset adverse investment regulations and a perceived lack of competitiveness, PMC governments offer a wide range of fiscal incentives to lure private investors. But there is a lack of automaticity and transparency in the granting of investment incentives. In general, the investment incentives that are granted are distortionary, erode the tax base, and encourage rent-seeking behavior. A more appropriate strategy for PMC governments would be to move away from wide-ranging foreign investment incentives, and concentrate instead on improving the overall domestic enterprise environment.

Promoting trade, aid and investment links with all APEC countries including the rapidly growing Asian economies provides a means of diversifying market ties and finding new sources of growth. PMCs have certain resources that are in short supply in Asia—most notably calm, quiet Island locations, and a large share of the canning-grade tuna supply. Sparking the interest of all APEC entrepreneurs to invest in areas in which they already have technology, market links and expertise is an important challenge for the PMC leaders. Adjusting to trade standards and markets of the Pacific Rim countries and APEC presents a natural diversification strategy for the Pacific Island countries.

Tourism: Profiting from Paradise

In the unique natural setting of the Pacific Islands, tourism offers considerable potential for both revenue and jobs. While tourism grew 4.5 percent worldwide from 1988 to 1993, in the remote Pacific Islands, it grew 6.8 percent. Over the same period, the 8.7 percent growth in the East Asia and Pacific Region suggests that there is a far greater market waiting to be tapped.

Within the PMC group, Fiji alone offers frequent air services to Australia and New Zealand and direct access to long-haul markets. With beaches no longer pulling in new markets and repeat visitors in great numbers, however, promotion is shifting to terrestrial and marine attractions. Tonga and Western Samoa have strong cultural identities but limited and inconvenient flight connections. Among the Melanesian group, Vanuatu's tourism industry is limited by its airline and hotel capacity. The Solomon Islands are still at an early stage of tourism development. The Federated States of Micronesia, the Marshall Islands, and Kiribati are distinctly different from the five other Pacific Island Member Countries—far more remote from source markets, much smaller, and more widely scattered and not easily accessible.

The Pacific Islands' many cultural and natural assets are the foundation for a strong tourist trade. As more and more tourists have visited villages and become familiar with local cultures, governments have begun to recognize the importance of preserving and promoting local cultural assets. The Islands also possess unusual flora, fauna, and geophysical features—on land and under the sea. The key to developing Pacific Island tourism lies in the sensitive presentation of their cultural heritage and the careful management of the natural environment.

The Islands' geographical isolation and remoteness are their drawback as well as their blessing. Access to tourist markets is of necessity difficult and costly. A fundamental priority must therefore be to improve air access, flight frequency, and fare levels by rationalizing aircraft, routes, and services and developing an

Table 1: Drastic Variation Exists in the Access Fees Paid by Various Nations

Fishing Nation	Access Fees (percent value of catch)
USA	10 percent
Japan	5.0 percent
Taiwan	3.7 percent
Korea	2.2 percent
Average	4.4 percent

Source: World Bank staff estimates.

improved network of regional routes and inter-Island routes within countries. Improvements are also needed on links with larger neighboring destinations and source markets (particularly Australia and New Zealand) to supplement the present system of point-to-point links from each capital.

With global competition for development capital becoming intense, Pacific Island governments seeking investment in the tourist industry will need to reassure potential investors that the decision making process regarding investments will be consistent and timely; that government commitments (such as the provision of infrastructure or air services) will be honored; that there will not be unforeseen or excessive increases in government fees and charges; and that regulations will be applied consistently and without overlapping or duplication.

Fisheries: Harvesting the Bounty of the Sea

Fisheries are an important present and future resource in most PMC countries varying from about 7 percent of GDP in the Solomon Islands to higher shares in the Micronesian group. The Fisheries sector offers considerable potential for development both as a revenue earner from off-shore fisheries for some of the Islands and as a contributor to output and employment from coastal fisheries. In *offshore fisheries* PMC governments need to focus on three inter-related issues:

- strengthen the present system of resource management to ensure sustainability of the tuna resources for the benefit of future generations;
- increase rents received from access fees through collective action from the present level of about 4 percent of the output value; and
- manage public and private investment with the twin objectives of reducing the fiscal burden of existing investments, and preparing the groundwork for future private investment in the sector.

Active off-shore fisheries resource management comprises three components—a fisheries management system, a component for monitoring, control, and surveillance, and a fisheries judicial system for effective enforcement. A crucial requirement for this is that fishing access agreements must incorporate catch limits by species or other appropriate measures. The present system encourages overexploitation, which is not in the interests of the coastal states nor the distant water fishing nation fleets. There is also considerable variation under the present licensing arrangements—both in terms of the low average level of fees paid, and in payments across countries (see below). Limiting access effectively should also generate benefits in terms of helping to maintain the price of output in major markets.

Implementation of a multilateral approach to fee negotiation and licensing based on collaborative action has the potential to raise average access fees from the present level of 4 percent of output. In order to move in this direction Pacific Island countries need to work together first to define a long-term strategy to raise fees, and to develop the vital fisheries infrastructure (e.g., transshipment facilities and ports) which would complement the former. Negotiations under such a multilateral system should be carried out by professional negotiators.

Investment in modern off-shore fisheries is a highly capital-intensive activity requiring resources and private savings which most of the PMCs do not have. Consequently private investment will need to be foreign sourced. In order to manage investment more effectively, PMC governments first need to separate out any welfare objectives from economic ones when evaluating projects. Second, PMC governments should not be directly involved in commercial activities in the sector—this is an activity for the private sector. This implies that in the short to medium term, PMC governments involved in commercial activities must move out of such activities in order to reduce the existing fiscal burden. The strategy for this transition from public to private management should be to invite foreign participation, with the government a silent partner, requiring only payment of a fee to manage the enterprise. Over the medium term private operators should be provided an option to purchase the enterprise. Similarly new foreign investments in the sector should be allowed, but with an up-front annual fee payment to be made to government, independent of profit.

Coastal fisheries are an important source of food for all PMCs and therefore a source of foreign exchange savings. Present trends indicate a significant decline in coastal resources across all PMCs and a deterioration in the environmental quality of some coastal areas. Urgent action will be required to reverse this trend. The most important element of this strategy should be to shift the thrust of fisheries departments, particularly fisheries extension, away from fisheries development and redirect it to fisheries management. This will require institutional strengthening and re-training in many countries but the basic elements are already in place in most PMCs—customary systems of marine tenure exist in most PMCs. Given the limited resources of PMCs, it is advisable to use the customary systems complemented by modern methods and backed-up by modern systems to manage dwindling coastal resources. Such experiments have been demonstrated successfully in Vanuatu and other parts of the region.

Forestry

Throughout the Islands of the Pacific, tropical rainforests are rapidly disappearing. Widespread agricultural activities and commercial logging have resulted in deforestation and forest degradation. Timber harvesting rates are unsustainable and harvesting methods unnecessarily destructive. Regeneration rates range from slow to nil. In addition, inadequate logging agreements have enabled logging companies to reap windfall profits; moreover, governments and landowners lose revenues through transfer pricing, under-reporting of log exports and other malpractices.

Significant forest resources still exist in the Solomon Islands, Fiji, Vanuatu, and Western Samoa. If present practices are allowed to continue, however, the natural forests—and the myriad species they contain—may be gone in fifteen to twenty years. If forest resources are to be preserved and managed on a more sustainable basis, governments need to develop and enforce long-term, comprehensive national forestry policies based on sustainable management principles now. Action is urgently required in the following three key areas: protection and conservation of natural forests; improved management of natural forests; and a more equitable distribution of economic rents.

Protection and Conservation of Natural Forests

While governments in the region may recognize the social and economic importance of conserving their countries' unique gifts of flora and fauna for future generations, they have been slow to counteract the forces favoring rapid exploitation. Areas set aside for the protection of biodiversity in Fiji, Solomon Islands, Western Samoa and Vanuatu are quite inadequate. Effective systems of protected areas should be established immediately and in close consultation with communities and landowners to preserve biodiversity. These could include conservation areas, national parks, and ecological reserves.

Donor participation. Donors should explicitly include conservation of natural forests as a priority for grant aid support to the sector either directly or through assistance to local and international non government organizations, which are working with local landowners, to develop feasible and socially acceptable approaches to forest protection and conservation.

Management of Natural Forests

Although the forestry sector is a significant source of income to landowners and national governments in the region, the principles of natural forest management have not yet been adopted. Forestry operations typically "mine" the resource with little regard for regeneration. Whereas sustainable forestry may be difficult in natural tropical forests, there is ample scope for improving the way Pacific Island natural forests are currently managed:

- *Forest management plans.* Governments, owners, and managers should develop detailed plans for the management of natural forests for sustained timber production, with substantial areas set aside for conservation.
- *Sustainable yields.* To preserve natural forestry resources, total annual timber harvests must not exceed the best estimate of sustainable yield. The allocation of the total harvest, moreover, must be sustainable within each region.
- *Logging practice codes.* National Codes of Logging Practice, which seek to minimize the destructive impacts of logging should be developed, incorporated into logging contracts and enforced with realistic penalties.
- *Performance Bonds* and surveillance are internationally tested and effective means to ensure that logging companies comply with Codes of Logging Practice and with their contractual obligations and that economic/ecological benefits accrue to the country.

Equitable Distribution of Economic Rents

Governments and landowners in the Pacific are forsaking economic rents, to which they are entitled, to logging contractors. The chart in Figure 3 shows that resource owners consistently receive the smallest portion (10-15 percent) of log value, while loggers consistently receive 30-50 percent in the form of excess profits. Government taxes and levies vary from 30-35 percent in PNG and the Solomon Islands to 5-15 percent in Fiji and Vanuatu. Recent Bank research indicates that, based on current log prices and logging costs, the combined revenue collected by landowners and governments could be increased to 50 percent of f.o.b. log value while maintaining internationally competitive profit margins to loggers. In order to achieve this, it is recommended that governments should consider instituting stumpage and export taxes; increasing the royalties paid to landowners, merging field-based and export (output) taxes; and adopting independent inspection/surveillance of exports.

Pulling Together

Regional collaboration that combines the Islands' individually limited manpower, and financial and natural resources may in certain areas, allow for economies of scale, reduce vulnerability to external shocks, and thereby improve overall welfare. It could also lower the unit cost of essential infrastructure services. A regional approach to resource management and exploitation has the potential to significantly enhance the bargaining position of all the Island countries. If the PMCs can cooperate in key areas, they can begin to achieve the standards of living they value.

Yet in the past, regional efforts have had only mixed results, and costs in terms of limited staff time and administrative resources have been very high compared to the value added. It is therefore vital that the Pacific Island nations be highly selective in choosing areas requiring economic cooperation. The number of such efforts should therefore be small. Regional collaborations must also seek to benefit all participants, improving their welfare beyond what individual nations could have achieved on their own. National interests would therefore not outweigh and supersede regional interests. Finally, regional cooperative efforts must be designed to be flexible enough to adapt to changing circumstances and have the capacity to be self-policing and, if necessary, to terminate in the event of poor performance.

The Pacific Islands' regional cooperation efforts, while mindful of the general shortage of human resources and limited institutional capacity, should focus on four priority areas: (a) building trading relationships with larger, more dynamic trading blocs outside the region; (b) cooperative arrangements in transport; (c) a common approach to natural resource management; and (d) a regional approach to providing certain economic and social services.

- *Trade:* The benefits of trade within the PMCs are likely to be limited and largely offset by the administrative costs involved. Under these circumstances the PMCs may wish to adopt an outward orientation in this regard. This can be done through trade cooperation

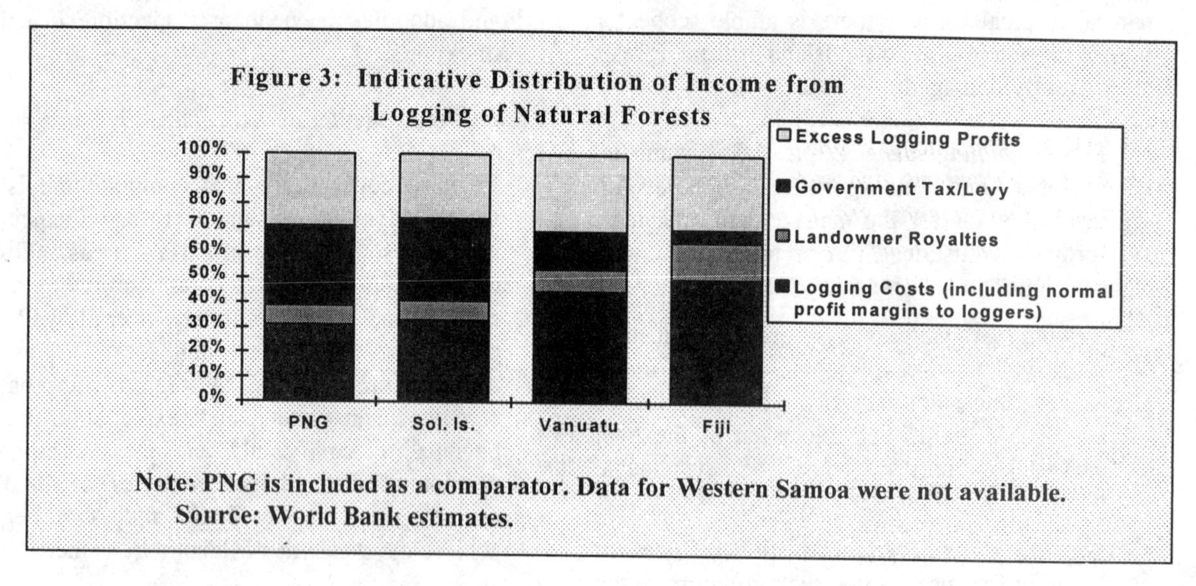

Figure 3: Indicative Distribution of Income from Logging of Natural Forests

Note: PNG is included as a comparator. Data for Western Samoa were not available.
Source: World Bank estimates.

and integration with larger more dynamic economies such as those of APEC. At the same time care needs to be exercised to avoid the high costs of inefficient administration and decision making.

- *Transportation.* There are many potential benefits from cooperation to promote better access to aviation and maritime transport. There is an urgent need to restructure the Forum Shipping Lines currently regulating ocean transport, for instance, and to separate commercial operators from services to the more remote Islands, which is a welfare function. Greater transparency in commercial goals and a clearer definition of appropriate demands for public support would increase the scope for ocean transport profitability. Moreover, standardization of ship design for the region could reduce initial capital costs for both repair and maintenance.

- *Natural resource management.* In both forestry and fisheries, the Islands could benefit substantially from regional collaboration. There is an urgent need to establish and implement a common code of conduct regulating logging operations in natural forests across the region. The need to improve the monitoring of logging and timber exports is equally urgent. In fisheries, collective initiatives could reduce costs significantly through economies of scale and improve monitoring, control, surveillance and conservation to help ensure that fishery stocks will be exploited in a sustainable manner. Negotiating access fees on a multilateral basis, moreover, will require regional collaboration on an unprecedented scale.

- *Economic and Social Services:* The two major areas where the Pacific Islands stand to gain are higher education and environmental management. In higher education there is an urgent need to resolve the current difficulties over the USP as this is a most valuable regional resource from which all countries have derived great benefit and can expect to do so into the future. Additionally, there is a need to re-orient regional training programs from the present emphasis on liberal arts and public administration towards business and technical programs in order to generate the human resources which will be required in the future. In the area of environmental management there is considerable potential for benefit from cooperation given the depth and similarity of environmental issues. Based on the frequency and rapidity of natural disasters in the region, a case can also be made for collaborating in the preparation for and response to such disasters. Finally, utilizing a regional agency such as SPREP, the PMCs can address the common nexus of coastal zone management issues and marine conservation needs of the region.

1. INTRODUCTION

Overview: *The Pacific Island Member Countries face a unique set of development challenges. Favorable physical environments and rich cultural traditions have endowed their populations with safe and secure lifestyles. But economic growth has been slow despite high levels of overall investment and foreign aid. The countries continue to depend on a narrow range of export commodities and remain vulnerable to external shocks. Recent changes in the global economic environment offer opportunities for economic diversification. At the same time these economies can sustainably exploit their natural resources to maximize revenues while preserving sufficient stocks for future generations.*

Scope and Content of the Report. The central objective of this report is to discuss how the Pacific Island Economies can enter the twenty-first century on a more resilient economic base. This report seeks to build upon the findings of the last two reports which have shown that past patterns of growth and development in the Pacific Island Member Countries (PMCs) do not appear to be sufficient to provide a progressive improvement in living standards in the future. The next century is sometimes referred to as the "Pacific Century" because of the major role the East Asian economies are likely to play. In view of such a scenario, the PMCs need to assess carefully emerging opportunities and challenges and decide on the kind of participation and development strategies that would be in their best interests in the future. Change is all the more essential because of PMCs' vulnerability to external influences as well as rising demands for modern goods and services within the PMCs.[1]

Table 1.1: Average Growth Performance, 1983 - 93
(in percent per annum)

	Pacific Islands	Caribbean a/	Africa & a/ Indian Ocean
Real GDP	2.1	3.2	5.4
Population	1.7	0.9	2.0
Per Capita Real GDP	0.4	2.3	3.4

a/ Selected island economies—see Table 1.2.
Source: World Bank.

In contrast to the last two reports which were country specific, this report is thematic in character and seeks to transcend inter-country differences. The key questions posed in this report are:

- How can the Pacific Islands—individually or collectively—build a more resilient economic structure in a rapidly changing external environment ?
- How can Pacific Island economies reduce their vulnerability to external events?
- How can the PMCs sustainably exploit their natural resources to maximize revenues while preserving sufficient stocks for future generations ?

Given the fragile resource base of the PMCs, the management of their natural resources has assumed considerable importance. Previous reports have also noted that there is still a tendency in the PMCs to look inward and remain isolated from the rest of the world. External factors do affect the PMCs in a significant manner and have been accentuated by recent

---

1 The eight Pacific Island Member Countries (PMCs) covered in this report are Fiji, Kiribati, Marshall Islands, Federated States of Micronesia, Solomon Islands, Tonga, Vanuatu and Western Samoa. The PICs form a wider group, and in addition to the PMCs, it includes Cook Islands, Niue, Tuvalu. Papua New Guinea, also a Pacific Island Member Country is covered in separate reports.

changes in external trading arrangements. Thus, the unifying theme of the report is about how the PMCs can diversify in response to these changes and optimize the use of their natural resources.

Background. The eight PMCs, spread across the Pacific Ocean in the form of hundreds of small islands and atolls, face a unique set of development challenges. Favorable physical environments and rich cultural traditions including the extended family system, customary land ownership and benefit sharing practices, have endowed their populations with a relatively safe and secure lifestyle. However, economic growth and diversification have been rather slow in the PMCs in the 1980s and in the early 1990s compared to other island economies (see Table 1.1). During the period 1983-88, real GDP per capita growth was negative in the PMCs, compared to robust growth in the other two island groups (see Figure 1.1). During 1989-93, however, the PMCs performed better than the Caribbean Island group as a whole, largely reflecting the recovery in Fiji, but their growth performance was below that in the Africa and Indian Ocean Group.

In 1992, GDP per capita averaged US$1,320 in the PMCs compared to US$3,280 in the Caribbean and US$1,390 in the African and Indian Ocean island economies. Per capita GNP varies considerably within the PMCs ranging from US$2,130 in Fiji to US$710 in Kiribati in 1993 (see Table 1.2). Population growth rates have been high. Solomon Islands and Vanuatu recorded the highest rates reflecting declining mortality and increasing fertility, but population growth rates have been much lower in Fiji. Rapid population growth per se is not a cause for concern if accompanied by commensurate levels of environmentally sustainable economic growth. But with low and erratic growth rates in most of the PMCs, high population growth rates would lead to declining or stagnant GDP per capita levels. Nevertheless, despite the many constraints and challenges faced by the PMCs arising from their small size, isolation and fragmentation, the countries have made considerable progress in their efforts to improve the quality of life of their people.

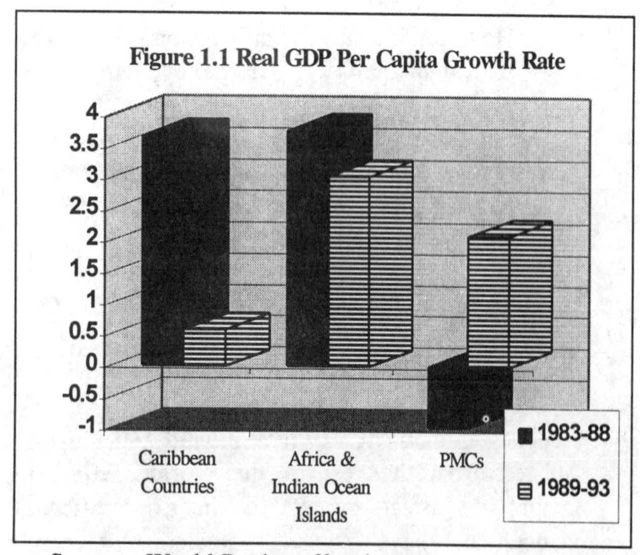

Source: World Bank staff estimates.

Average life expectancy in the PMCs is relatively high by world standards. In almost all the PMCs, people have an average life expectancy of over 60 years. This is comparable to the life expectancy in other island economies in Africa and the Indian Ocean, but is less than in the Caribbean, where the average life expectancy is 71 years.

Similarly, as a group, the PMCs show an infant mortality rate of 39 per thousand births which is lower than in the African and Indian Ocean island countries, where the average is 47. However, the infant mortality rate in the PMCs is much higher than that in the Caribbean countries estimated to be 23 per thousand births. Within the PMCs the infant mortality rates are lower in Tonga (21), Fiji (23), and Western Samoa (25).

Overall literacy rates in the Pacific are generally higher than the average in developing countries. Most Pacific countries have made great progress in extending access to primary education in the last decade and primary enrollment rates are comparable with those of other island economies. Except for the Solomon Islands, primary education is virtually universal in all the other PMCs. However, primary school dropout rates are high in the PMCs compared to other developing countries.

As for health status, there have been widespread gains over the last two decades with increased life expectancy and decreased infant mortality in most

PMCs. Overall, infant mortality and child health conditions have improved, though conditions vary across countries. Solomon Islands and Vanuatu provide examples where diseases of underdevelopment still account for most sickness and death. In the other PMCs, the main causes of death are non-communicable diseases related to poor diet, and the ills of urbanization. In several PMCs, pregnancy and motherhood also continue to pose a significant risk to the health of women. In fact, the Pacific regional average for pregnancy and motherhood-related deaths is considered to be significantly higher than the global average.

The archipelagic nature of the PMCs have endowed them with a more extensive command over ocean resources (see Table 1.2). For example, the average sea to land area in the PMCs is 13 times that of the Caribbean countries. However, their spread over larger sea areas has also led to higher unit costs of transportation and hence a constraint even to supply their small domestic markets. As for external markets, the PMCs are constrained by the "tyranny of distance". They do not have the advantage of proximity to the large high income American markets, enjoyed by the Caribbean countries.

Furthermore, the PMCs which depend on a few commodities are subject to terms of trade shocks and remain highly vulnerable. First, the terms of trade became unfavorable in the 1980s; prices for PMC commodities (e.g., coconut, copra) declined in the 1980s. Second, in the recent past, there has been increasing activity in a narrow set of natural resource-based activities, i.e., in fisheries and forestry. Accordingly, the discussion in this report will be broadly structured as follows:

- Recent trends in Pacific Island trade and likely effects of changes in the global economic environment;
- Trade and management of resource-based activities; and
- Options for regional cooperation.

Table 1.2: Comparative Indicators

	Population ('000) 1993	Population Growth Rate (1983-93) (% p.a.)	Land Area (km^2)	Sea Area ('000km^2)	GDP 1993 (US$mill)	GNP Per Capita 1993 (US $)	Life Expectancy at Birth (years)a/	Infant Mortality Rate ('000 births)
Pacific:								
Fiji	762	1.31	18272	1146	1647	2130	72	23
FSM	105	2.71	705	2500	194	1850 b/	64	52
Kiribati	76	2.01	810	3550	32	710	58	60
Marshall Islands	51	3.99	181	1942	85	1670 b/	61	63
Solomon Islands	354	3.00	27990	1500	245	740	61	44
Tonga	98	-0.18	720	543	145	1530	68	21
Vanuatu	161	2.71	12000	680	186	1230	63	45
Western Samoa	167	0.40	2934	130	122	950	65	25
Caribbean:								
Antigua & Barbuda	67	0.68	440	110	457	6390	74	20
Barbados	260	0.32	430	167	1631	6240	75	10
Belize	205	2.62	22800	n.a	524	2440	69	41
Dominica	72	-0.26	750	15	189	2680	72	18
Grenada	91	0.02	340	27	214	2410	71	29
St. Kitts & Nevis	41	-0.78	360	11	177	4470	68	34
St. Lucia	158	1.85	610	16	496	3040	70	19
St. Vincent & Grenadines	110	0.88	340	33	191	2130	71	20
Africa & Indian Ocean:								
Cape Verde	398	2.60	4030	790	325	870	68	40
Comoros	528	3.67	2230	249	276	520	56	89
Maldives	236	3.31	300	959	132	820	62	55
Mauritius	1111	1.01	850	1171	3280	2980	70	18
Sao Tome & Principe	125	2.24	960	128	44	350	68	65
Seychelles	70	0.79	270	1349	443	6370	71	16

a/ 1992 or most recent estimate; b/ GDP per capita.
Source: World Bank, IMF Staff Reports and Recent Economic Development Reports.

The External Trading Environment. Major changes have taken place in the composition and direction of trade in the PMCs, as shown in Chapter 2. Although merchandise exports are somewhat more diversified than a decade ago, the PMCs still remain vulnerable to external shocks. Thus, the key issues facing the PMCs will be that of managing this vulnerability and exploiting emerging opportunities. Export destinations have also changed considerably in the 1980s. Japan and other Asian countries have emerged as export destinations for Fiji, Solomon Islands, Tonga, Vanuatu and FSM—indicating a shift away from traditional ties to more market-based arrangements.

The new global trading environment presents both challenges and opportunities for the PMCs. The benefits arising from preferential access to protected markets—sugar to Europe and the US, copra to Europe and textiles to the Pacific—will diminish over time. At the same time, the overall boost to global growth and trade afforded by a reduction in trade barriers will open up new sources of demand for PMCs' traditional export commodities. Analysts predict that prices of primary commodities may rise in the medium term. This by itself will have a positive effect on export earnings in the PMCs. Likewise an increase in private capital flows may benefit the PMCs by expanding the export capacity in sectors such as tourism and fisheries. As regards imports, the PMCs are likely to be adversely affected by rising food, petroleum and manufactured goods prices. With most countries already experiencing large trade deficits, high import prices may lead to widening balance of payments deficits, pointing to the need for flexible macroeconomic management in the face of changing market conditions.

The above issues will be discussed in Chapter 2, which explores suggestions for developing a trade policy framework to encourage diversification. Considering the limited degrees of freedom imposed by the PMCs' narrow production base, Chapter 3 will focus on the importance of economic diversification into tourism–a sector in which PMCs have made significant strides in recent years, with a growth in visitor arrivals significantly exceeding worldwide growth. Today, Fiji alone attracts twice as many visitors as French Polynesia—a favorite destination for many decades.

Returns from Natural Resources. One opportunity for the PMCs is to expand natural resource based activities and improve its management. In off-shore fisheries, resources are still biologically underexploited. The challenge here is to obtain a fair return from this resource in the form of rents from foreign fishing vessels in the territorial waters of the PMCs. At the same time, to prevent a rapid depletion of natural resources, there is a need to ensure these resources are sustainably developed. Furthermore, the PMCs need to receive adequate economic rents for their natural capital. In the case of coastal fisheries, there is evidence of over-exploitation of certain fishery stocks, particularly in the vicinity of urban centers—pointing to the need for better management of this sector.

As regards forestry, propelled by currently high timber prices, logging operations in some PMCs (e.g., Solomon Islands) are until recently, proceeding well beyond sustainable levels. The collaboration between foreign investors and traditional land owners with forest reserves is difficult to control, but indirect methods, particularly market-based ones (export taxes, stumpage fees, forest surveillance), are needed to manage this natural resource. Thus, Chapters 4 and 5 discuss the possibilities for PMCs to link up with global markets without endangering their fragile resource base in the longer term.

The discussion will illustrate that:

- obtaining a larger share from natural resources is a "win-win strategy";
- it helps external balance and domestic revenues; and that
- resources can be exploited in a more sustainable manner.

Regional cooperation provides one means of fostering global links through achieving greater economies of scope and scale. Factors such as the geographic remoteness, extreme dispersion, small populations and land areas, have combined to limit the productive base of the PMCs. Furthermore these same factors are responsible for the diseconomies of scale, leading to high costs in production, particularly with respect to unit costs of infrastructure, which further constrain competitiveness and efficient production. Thus, integration through regional collaboration, based on combining the manpower, financial and natural resources of the region, has the potential to improve welfare by allowing economies of scale to be exploited, thereby reducing the vulnerability of the PMCs. The report argues that cooperation by Pacific Island countries does not necessarily create net benefits to PMCs because gains from economies of scale, trade access, growth or market power are easily offset by administrative costs and diversion of effort. The chapter discusses four areas of regional integration: (a) co-operation in trade and services within the APEC framework; (b) aviation and ocean transport; (c) natural resource management; and (d) co-operation in economic and social services, particularly in higher education and environmental management.

The substantive discussion in this report will begin with the story of growth and external trade in the PMCs, in Chapter 2. This aims to provide the backdrop for the subsequent discussion on building upon the PMCs' small but significant export diversification, focusing greater attention on tourism and negotiating better terms for natural resources.

2. GROWTH AND TRADE IN THE PACIFIC ISLAND ECONOMIES

Overview. *Economic growth in the PMCs during the last decade has been very volatile, reflecting, in part, their dependence on a narrow range of primary export commodities which are subject to exogenous shocks as well as natural disasters and political developments. Trends in economic growth closely reflect those of external trade. Despite significant diversification in the 1980s, the PMCs remain vulnerable to external shocks. This vulnerability continues to have adverse effects on their fiscal balances—mainly via trade taxes and on the balance of payments situation through export earnings. With a view to setting the stage for subsequent chapters, the discussion highlights issues such as recent changes both in the composition and in the direction of trade, vulnerability to external factors, and how to manage this vulnerability and exploit emerging opportunities. Recent changes in the global environment point to the need for further economic diversification and strengthening links with non- traditional markets.*

Growth, Investment and Shocks

The PMCs as a group recorded an average annual output growth rate of 2.1 percent during the period 1983-93. Real GDP growth per capita was much lower and averaged 0.4 percent per year in the period 1983-93. If Fiji, which accounts for two thirds of the groups' output, is excluded, per capita GDP growth fluctuated around a low negative rate of -0.2 percent annually in the same time period.

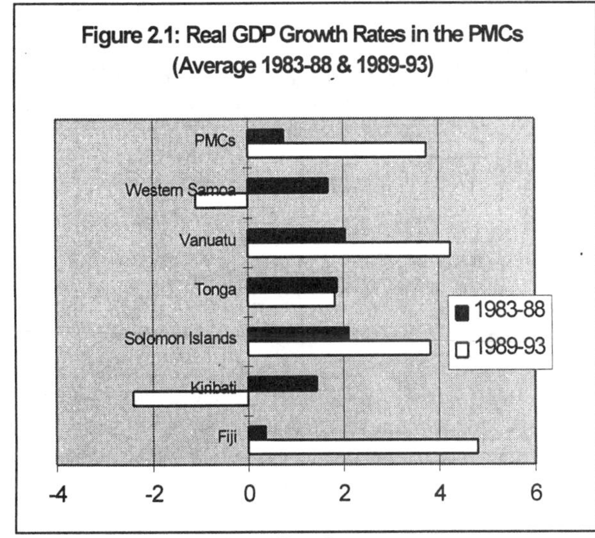

Source: World Bank staff estimates.

However, despite low average growth performance over the last decade, there was substantial improvement in the early 1990s. The general trend indicates that PMC average output growth improved from 0.8 percent in the period 1983-88 to 3.8 percent in 1989-93. Also, there was a remarkable improvement in the per capita GDP growth rate which increased from -0.1 percent annually to about 2 percent. However, if Fiji is excluded, the increase in growth rate is smaller.

For the individual PMCs, growth performance was mixed: (see Figure 2.1) with an improvement in Fiji, the Solomon Islands, and Vanuatu, stagnation in Tonga, and declines in Kiribati and Western Samoa.

However, despite favorable levels of natural and human resources, high levels of investment and aid, and reasonably prudent economic management, growth patterns among the PMCs are characterized by low and extremely volatile growth rates. The pattern has been a series of growth spurts followed by plunges that effectively cancel each other out. But this is not surprising given the PMCs' extreme vulnerability to external shocks, i.e., both natural disasters and the dependence on production of a narrow range of commodities which are subject to large price and quantity variations. Thus, economic growth and external trade in the PMCs are very closely related.

Table 2.1: Average GDP Growth Rates and Investment Rates, 1983-1993 b/

	Real GDP Growth Rate (Average % p.a.)	Standard Deviation	Gross Investment/GDP (Average % p.a.)	Private Investment/GDP (Average % p.a.)	Public Investment/GDP (Average % p.a.)
Fiji	2.4	6.0	18.1	9.2	8.9
FSM a/	0.8	3.6	-	-	-
Kiribati	0.8	5.0	31.0	12.0	19.0
Marshall Islands a/	0.8	2.0	-	-	-
Solomon Islands	3.2	6.0	30.7	15.1	15.6
Tonga	2.1	2.9	30.0	10.4	19.6
Vanuatu	2.8	3.0	32.4	20.4	12.0
Western Samoa	1.0	3.3	32.1	5.6	26.5
Average PMCs	2.1	4.4	28.5	11.5	17.0

a/ 1988/89-92/93.
b/ Data for investment ratios are the averages from 1980-92.
Source: World Bank Reports; IMF Recent Economic Development Reports.

This pattern of considerable fluctuation around a very low base growth rate is found for each of the six PMCs considered here. As shown in Table 2.1, five of the six island countries had average growth rates less than 3 percent; only Solomon Islands had a higher growth rate (3.2 percent) and, even in this case, per capita growth averaged only around 0.4 percent. While the timing of growth spurts and declines is different across the individual countries, the long-run picture of stagnation is remarkably similar.

Investment. A notable feature of the Pacific Islands development experience has been the coexistence of low growth with high investment. During 1980-92, the average gross investment rate was 28.5 percent (see Table 2.1), while average growth, as noted above, was about 2 percent. Indeed, in terms of investment rates, the region is similar to the high-performing East Asian countries, but, unlike these countries, investment efficiency appears to be very low. The only exception to this pattern is Fiji, where gross investment rates declined by half during the 1980s and are now around 13 percent; of course, even in Fiji, the average growth rate has been low.

Public investment tends to dominate in the PMCs. Average public investment rates are around 17 percent while average private investment rates are around 11.5 percent. However, individual PMCs vary greatly in the relative importance of public versus private investment. In Western Samoa, Kiribati and Tonga, public investment has tended to be much higher than private investment whereas in Fiji and Solomon Islands, the two have been roughly equal. In Vanuatu, on the other hand, until very recently, private investment has tended to dominate. This pattern of public versus private investment shows an interesting relationship to the pattern of growth: where public investment has tended to dominate, growth has been lower. For example, Western Samoa and Kiribati have had the lowest average growth rates among the PMCs, whereas Solomon Islands and Vanuatu have had among the highest.

Productivity Impact of Public Expenditures. The composition and effectiveness of public sector expenditures has a direct influence on growth. Composition refers to the distribution between government investment and consumption as well as to the level and economic return of government investment among different sectors. The data show public consumption in the PMCs to be high. The average public consumption rate during the period 1980-92 was 27 percent of GDP. Disaggregation by country shows considerable variance: Fiji, Tonga and Western Samoa have much lower rates than Vanuatu, the Solomon Islands and Kiribati. With a public consumption rate of over 50 percent of GDP, Kiribati is the slowest growing country in the region, which suggests a negative relationship between public consumption and growth.

Role of Aid. Aid has been a dominant feature in the PMC economies during the past two decades. On average, official development assistance amounted to almost 27 percent of

GDP during 1980-92. This average, however, conceals much variation. At one extreme, aid amounted to only around 3.3 percent of GDP for Fiji while, at the other extreme, it amounted to 56 percent for Kiribati. For the remaining four PMCs, the aid ratio averaged between 21 percent and 27 percent of GDP. Thus, except for Fiji, aid was a major source of development financing with a substantial capacity to influence economic growth. The ability of aid to influence depends on how it is provided and how it is used. For most PMCs, the great bulk of aid has been in "services" i.e. technical assistance, or supplies "in kind" on grant terms, rather than loans. Only in Solomon Islands and Western Samoa does the ratio of loans in total aid exceed 15 percent. Thus, there is little reason to consider the external debt service burden as a factor determining growth performance.

A dominant characteristic of aid in the PMCs is the high proportion of technical assistance; around 45 percent of all grant aid has been in the form of technical assistance (see Table 2.2). It is not clear what relationship this might have to growth performance. On the one hand, it is thought that the bulk of the funds provided as technical assistance replaces current public expenditure such as in schools, hospitals and some ministries and that it accrues as income to expatriates rather than as tangible investments to the aid-receiving country. Technical assistance also takes the form of PMC nationals being trained abroad in the donor country or of expatriates providing training and advice in the recipient country or implementing investment programs. Thus, technical assistance does provide expertise, equipment and training of local professionals. It also helps meet shortages in specific areas, a role that could theoretically improve productivity.

Table 2.2: Sectoral Allocation of Development Assistance (Avg. 1986-92)

(%)

Country	FIJ	KIR	TON	SOL	VAN	WSM
Social infra.	18.1	24.4	11.8	14.2	11.4	7.9
Econ infra.	9.9	8.9	17.8	14.1	15.5	34.6
Production	15.1	7.6	12.3	23.6	11.4	9.3
o/w Agric.	(9.1)	(4.1)	(4.9)	(18.6)	(6.7)	(9.1)
Prog. type	5.1	2.4	8.1	2.7	2.9	3.4
Tech. Asst.	50.9	55.1	43.7	44.4	55.1	36.7
Other	0.9	1.6	6.3	1.0	3.7	8.1
Memo item:						
Total (US$m)	47.8	19.0	21.8	45.7	42.5	39.1

Source: OECD/DAC.

Investment and Growth. The role of investment in explaining growth was analyzed with the aid of econometric methods.[1] The results suggest that further increases in public investment of the type and efficiency experienced in the past, may not lead to additional growth in the typical PMC economy. This result probably reflects the fact that, in the aggregate, public investment in the PMCs probably has been in low-return areas such as public buildings and much may have been managed ineffectively and have led to low returns. The investments of public enterprises engaged in loss-making commercial activities have probably also contributed much to this outcome. However, some components of public investment may have a positive relationship with growth. In particular, investments in such physical and social infrastructure as access roads, electricity supply, school buildings and health clinics are likely to have improved the prospects for growth. Such a positive relationship has been widely observed in other countries. But for present purposes, there was insufficient data to permit analysis of the different effects of the specific components of public investment.

Public consumption is also found to have a statistically significant negative impact on growth in the PMCs. Here again, there is a need to differentiate between wasteful current expenditures on activities that could be performed more effectively by the public or private sector and vital expenditures on basic services including health and education. Quality of life and the quality of the labor force needed for sustainable economic growth

1 World Bank "Determinants of Growth in Pacific Island Member Countries," Working Paper. These results, however, need to be interpreted with caution given the weakness of economic data in the Pacific. Several countries lack the capacity to conduct field surveys to gather data for computation of national income estimates and to organize and compile existing data. Nevertheless, the above analysis provides preliminary results, which merit further study.

crucially depends on recurrent cost support for health and education. Such expenditures, for example, will include salaries for health workers and provision of essential pharmaceuticals or teacher salaries, school books and teaching materials. Again, the data did not permit a disaggregated analysis.

The results of the statistical analysis suggest a positive relationship between private investment and growth during the 1980s indicating the often quick yielding nature of private investment, as noted above. Indeed this is the only positive policy variable supported by the empirical analysis, and thus confirming the importance of the role of the private sector in economic growth emphasized in previous reports.

However, for several PMCs, the private investment rate has tended to decline in recent years. The decline was sharpest in Fiji and Kiribati and less pronounced in Solomon Islands and Western Samoa. No strong trend is detectable in Tonga and Vanuatu. The pattern of general decline in private investment rates is, of course, consistent with the low growth rate observed among the PMCs over the same period.

The Role of the State. A broad conclusion that can be drawn from the above discussion concerns the respective roles of government and the private sector. Experience of some of the East Asian economies and even small island economies in the Caribbean and Asian regions have demonstrated how a development partnership between the state and the private sector can work to produce heartening results. Typically, in such a partnership the state focuses on ensuring macroeconomic stability and competitiveness, creating a more encouraging regulatory environment for the private sector, providing infrastructure support, (both economic and social), and reducing its role in the production and service sectors to create more "space" for the private sector. In other words, the state is market friendly and complements the private sector rather than supplanting it. Such an environment provides the private sector with a level of confidence and a framework to save and invest in the productive sectors and thereby contribute to output and employment.

Effects of Disasters and Shocks. PMCs' economies are subject to three types of shocks: natural disasters like cyclones, volcanic eruptions and tidal waves; economic shocks like sharp adverse movements in terms of trade; and other shocks which may be political or economic in nature. The PMCs have experienced shocks of all three varieties during the last decade, and short-term performance was influenced by these factors to a great degree (see Figure 2.2).

Cyclones occur with notable frequency and ferocity in the PMCs. During the thirteen year period from 1980 to 1992, major cyclones hit every one of the islands except Kiribati at least once. Fiji, Solomon Islands, Vanuatu and Western Samoa were hit at least four times in this period. Often, the damage caused by cyclones results in negative growth for the economy, either in the same year or in the next. The most recent example of this is Western Samoa which experienced negative growth rates three years in a row during 1990-92 on account of cyclone activity in the years 1990 and 1991. Much of the damage is caused to exports as shown by the following examples of negative export growth rates in the year of a cyclone: Fiji (1980): -31 percent; Vanuatu (1985): -42 percent; Western Samoa (1990): -25 percent; and Western Samoa (1991): -39 percent. The evidence clearly shows that cyclones have the capacity to inflict great damage to the productive base of the PMCs and this should be taken into account in any assessment of the growth experience of the PMCs.

Figure 2.2: Real GDP Growth Rates 1983-1993

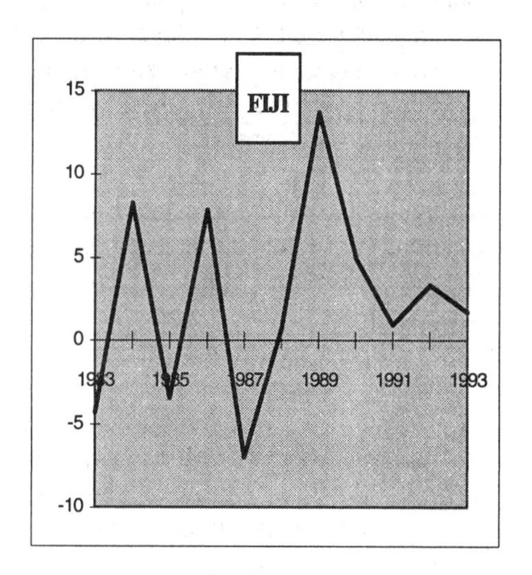

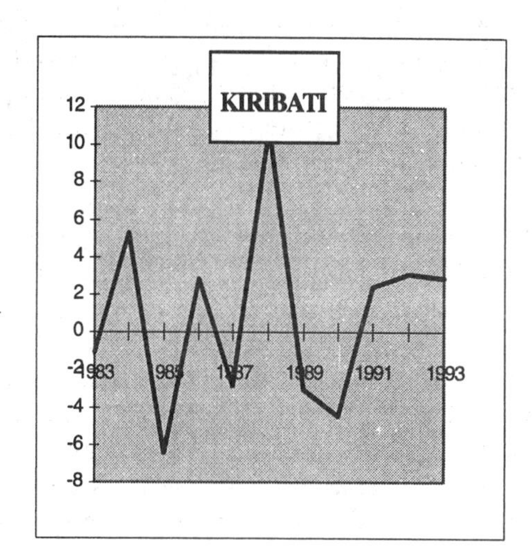

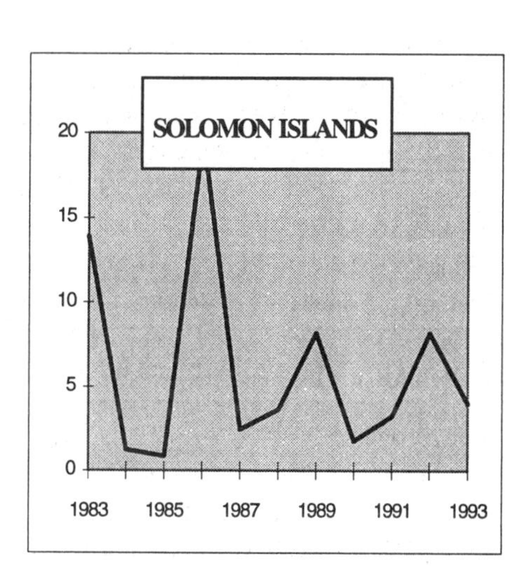

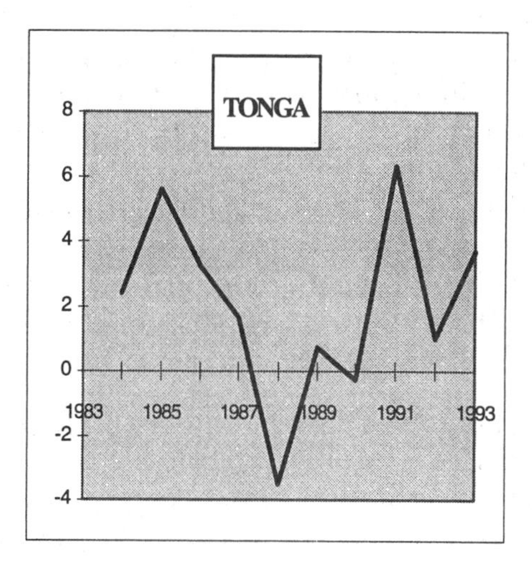

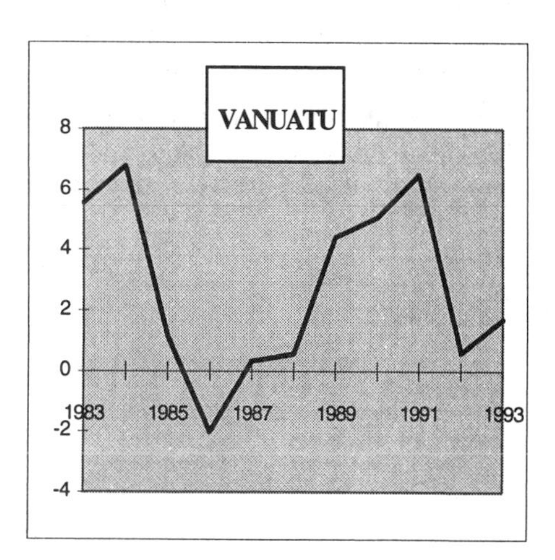

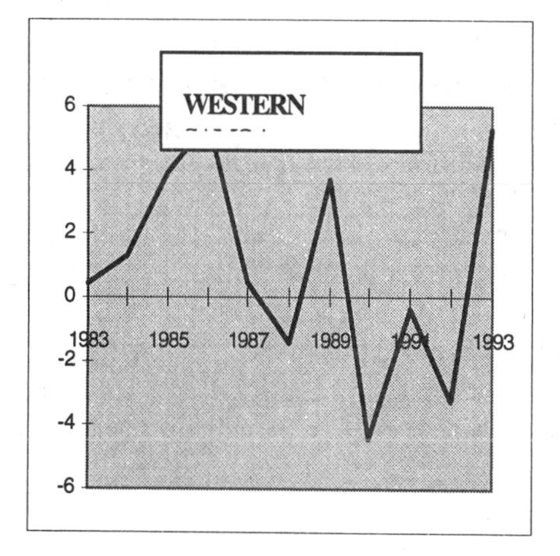

Source: World Bank staff estimates.

Terms of trade shocks are another major concern for the PMCs. Since most PMCs are heavily reliant on a few primary exports, on the one hand, and on imports of food and fuel, on the other, adverse movements in the prices of these goods can have a major impact on growth. Volatile terms of trade can have an indirect effect on growth also. A pattern of large swings in export prices generates considerable uncertainty with regard to earnings, which in turn discourages long-term investment and keeps growth lower than it would otherwise have been.

The data show that, on average, terms of trade deteriorated slightly for the PMCs during 1980-92 (see Figure 2.3). This is consistent with the observed pattern of low average growth. What is more relevant, however, is the high volatility that is shown by the data. The coefficient of variation for changes in terms of trade across all six PMCs is over 5. This compares with coefficients of less than 1 for such macroeconomic variables as investment, consumption, inflation and aid flows. The only variables that have similar volatility in the PMC context are GDP growth rates and export growth rates. This pattern suggests a strong link, working through exports, between external shocks, terms of trade changes and overall growth.

An analysis was carried out on external shocks to the economies of Fiji, Western Samoa and Solomon Islands during 1983-93 resulting from changes in the terms of trade and global demand. The results indicate that terms-of-trade shocks both positive and negative can be very large, are difficult to anticipate, and may linger for several years. Furthermore, the evidence suggests that it has been difficult to coordinate export promotion, import substitution and economic compression policies in response to such shocks. The manner in which the PMCs responded to adverse external conditions was mainly through increasing recourse to financing from both ODA and private remittances.

Certain policy measures were also pursued to enhance competitiveness. During the 1985-1993 period, the PMCs responded to declining terms of trade by allowing a depreciation of the real exchange rate and by diversifying exports (see Figure 2.4). In all of the PMCs, except Tonga and FSM, the real exchange rate declined during 1985-1993, as policymakers struggled to restrain imports and enhance the competitiveness of exports. In Fiji, Tonga and Solomon Islands, there was a conscious shift in exports away from low value traditional products towards higher value non-traditional products (e.g. garments, squash and tropical hardwoods). This shift in export mix led to an improvement in the terms-of-trade for these nations.

The strong links between external conditions and growth, and relatively weak links between

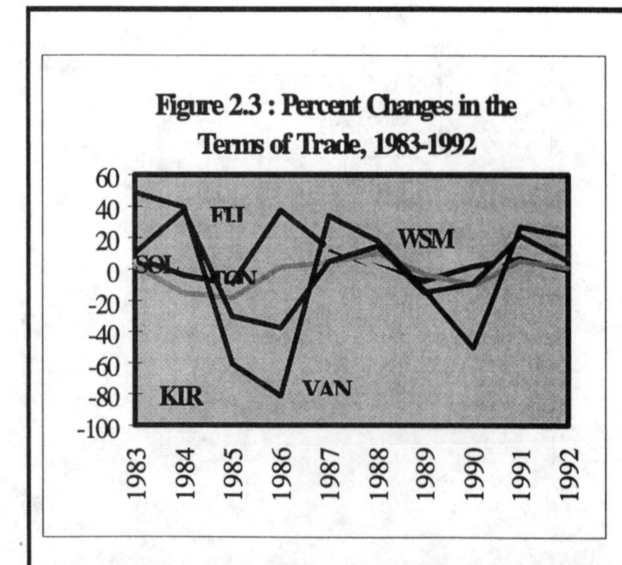

Figure 2.3 : Percent Changes in the Terms of Trade, 1983-1992

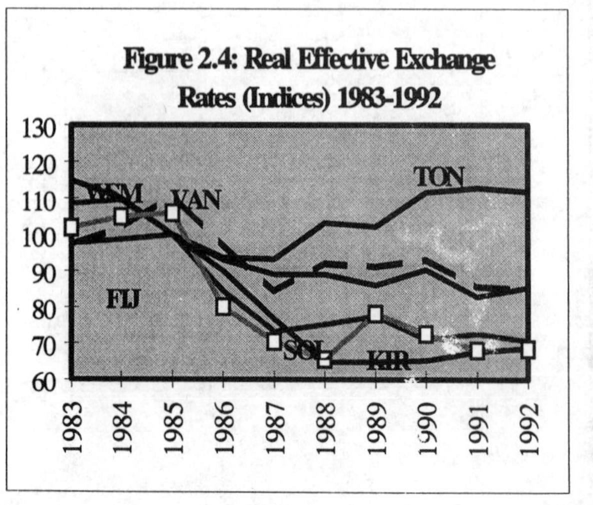

Figure 2.4: Real Effective Exchange Rates (Indices) 1983-1992

Source: World Bank and IMF reports.

investment, public spending and economic output pose special challenges for PMC policymakers. The PMCs remain vulnerable to external shocks and this vulnerability continues to have adverse effects on their fiscal balance through trade taxes and on the balance of payments via lower export earnings. In most of the PMCs, government expenditure is typically between 40 and 70 percent of GDP and well in excess of domestic tax and non tax revenue. Fiscal policy is the main instrument of macroeconomic management, owing to limitations on monetary policy in small open economies with relatively high levels of external grants and worker remittances. Thus, effective use of fiscal policy instruments to widen the revenue base and to change the composition of expenditures, can contribute significantly not only in cushioning the effects of external shocks, but also promoting growth and development to build a more resilient economic base. Given that domestic economic conditions are so closely linked to trade outcomes, how can the PMCs best exploit global market opportunities? A closer review of changing trade conditions can help answer that question.

Pacific Island Trading Conditions

The PMCs are very open, or trade- dependent economies. Trade penetration ratios average close to 80 percent of GDP (see Table 2.3) with the import content of most activities also very high, often in excess of 50 percent. Exports have in the past been confined to a narrow range of primary commodities and earnings from these exports usually equal to only 5-15 percent of imports. Most imports are for essential commodities with machinery, capital goods and petroleum imports accounting for 50 to 60 percent of total imports. Food imports are particularly important in Kiribati, Marshall Islands and Vanuatu. Other consumer goods account for less than a quarter of import requirements.

Hence, trade is characterized by large merchandise trade deficits ranging from 5 percent of GDP in the Solomon Islands to as much as 81 percent of GDP in Western Samoa. Invisible earnings are important in all these countries: tourism in Fiji, Vanuatu, Tonga, and Western Samoa, investment income for Kiribati; and remittances from nationals working abroad in the case of Kiribati, Tonga, Vanuatu, and Western Samoa. Services,

Table 2.3: Selected Indicators of External Trade, 1993

	Imports f.o.b	Exports f.o.b.	Trade Deficit	Net Service Flows	Current Account Deficit a/	Trade Penetration Ratio b/	Terms of Trade	Real Effective Exchange Rate c/
	million $	million $	% of GDP	million $	% of GDP	% of GDP	1984=100	1985=100
Fiji	-653.0	422.0	-14.0	182.0	-3.6	65.3	94.7	71.3
Solomon Islands	-144.5 d/	131.7	-5.2	-43.4	-21.1	112.7	73.9	65.0
Tonga	-50.7	12.0	-26.7	-12.3	-11.9	42.9	108.2	128.7
Western Samoa	-102.0 d/	6.5	-81.3	12.8	-44.0	92.4	53.3	86.2
Vanuatu	-72.7	22.7	-26.9	3.5	25.0	51.3	n.a.	95.6
Kiribati	-27.8	3.0	-77.3	6.3	-37.4	96.0	37.8 e/	96.7 e/
Marshall Islands	-75.5 d/	9.5	-77.3	-4.3	-84.0	99.5	n.a.	96.1
FSM	-148.1	25.6	-63.0	16.4	-67.0	89.4	n.a.	101.9

a/ Current account deficit excluding official transfers; b/ Ratio of total merchandise trade to GDP; c/ IMF definition. A reduction refers to a real depreciation; d/ c.i.f.; e/ Refers to 1992 data.
Source: : World Bank, Country Economic Memoranda, 1993, IMF Staff Reports and Recent Economic Development Reports, NCDS Statistical Data Base of the South Pacific Nations, and National Reports of the Central Bank or Monetary Authority.

Figure 2.5: Composition of PMC Exports: 1982-84 & 1991-93

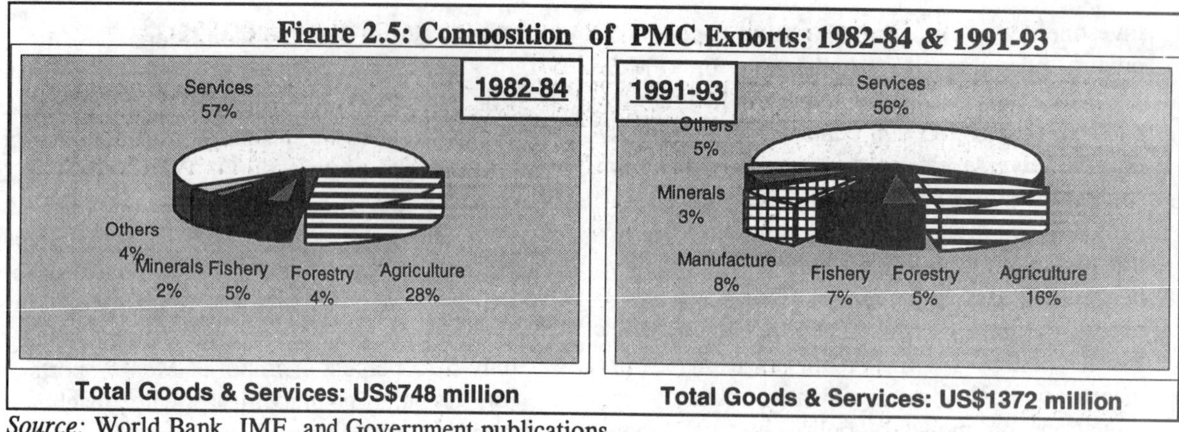

Source: World Bank, IMF, and Government publications.

therefore, make a positive contribution to the current account, except in the Solomon Islands, Marshall Islands and the Federated States of Micronesia. Current account deficits are small (4 percent of GDP) in Fiji, reflecting the importance of tourism earnings in that country, but are very large (12 to 84 percent of GDP) in the other PMCs. In these countries, aid and worker remittances play an important role in financing import requirements.

In the recent past, trends in Pacific Island trade indicate, that:

- there have been major changes both in composition and direction of exports;
- the composition of imports has also changed; and that
- vulnerability to external factors will continue to remain.

Trends in Exports. The structure of trade has been changing in the last decade. While primary commodities are still very important, growth over recent years has been strong in value-added products or manufactures (mainly in Fiji). Between 1982-84 and 1991-93, the share of agricultural commodities in total exports fell from 28 percent to 16 percent (see Figure 2.5). A decade ago, exports of manufactures were insignificant but by 1991-93, manufactured goods accounted for 8 percent of total exports, dominated mainly by Fiji. The other PMCs still rely heavily on primary product exports, although considerable diversification has taken place within their export mix. These changes in the export mix illustrate the PMCs' ability to respond to unfavorable primary commodity prices by diversifying into higher value-added products and manufactures and finding "niche markets", despite a formidable set of constraints typical of small island states. However, as noted in the last regional economic report, niche-type activities are known to shift frequently, and technological progress or changes in consumer preferences could lead to a rapid disappearance of niche markets. Thus, reliance on such industries as long-term sources of employment and growth has to be treated with caution.

Figure 2.6 Composition of PMC Imports: 1982-84 & 1991-93

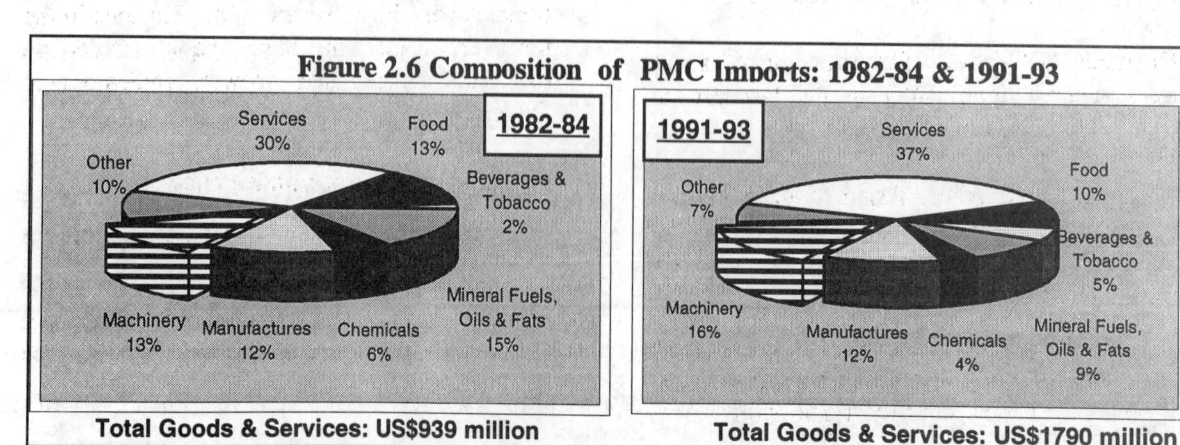

Source: World Bank, IMF, and Government publications.

Table 2.4: Destination of Export Trade in Percentage, 1982-84 and 1991-93

(1982-84)

	US [b]	EU	Australia & New Zealand	Japan	Other Asia	Other
Fiji [a]	11 (10)	26 (30)	24 (18)	6 (3)	9 (2)	24 (37)
Solomon Islands	1 (0)	24 (26)	3 (3)	34 (33)	28 (14)	11 (24)
Tonga	17 (1)	5 (14)	18 (77)	55 (0)	2 n.a.	3 (8)
Western Samoa	23 (45)	0 (15)	67 (35)	0 (1)	0 (0)	10 (4)
Vanuatu	0 (0)	50 (74)	13 (1)	19 (13)	6 (6)	13 (6)
Micronesia [c]	18 (28)	n.a. n.a.	n.a. n.a.	78 (48)	n.a. n.a.	4 (24)
Kiribati [d]	13 (45)	20 (40)	1 (1)	0 (6)	49 (0)	17 (8)

a/ 1984 and 1991; b/ Including the United States and American Samoa ; c/ 1987 and 1992 ; d/ 1983 and 1991.
Source: World Bank, Country Economic Memoranda, 1993, IMF Staff Reports, NCDS Statistical Data Base of the South Pacific Nations.

Even within the traditional product categories, the PMCs have demonstrated an ability to nurture successful new export industries. This includes garments in Fiji; squash in Tonga; logging in the Solomon Islands, veal in Vanuatu, seaweed in Kiribati, and sashimi in the Federated States of Micronesia.

Trends in Imports. Composition of imports has also changed over the last decade with the shares of machinery, and beverages and tobacco, and of services increasing significantly, while the share of food, chemicals, mineral fuels, oils and fats declined for the PMCs as a group (see Figure 2.6).

Direction of Trade. The direction of exports has changed significantly in the last decade (see Table 2.4). For example:

- Japan and other Asian countries have emerged as major export destinations for Fiji, Solomon Islands, Tonga, Vanuatu and Federated States of Micronesia;
- In terms of merchandise trade flows, there is considerably less reliance on Europe, as Pacific Island country trade shifts away from "administrative" and "traditional" ties to more market-based arrangements. The Solomon Islands is the only PMC increasing trade with Europe in non-traditional products (based on one successful joint venture with Japan to supply canned Tuna to U.K); and
- Intra-regional trade has diminished in importance, except for Fiji, where its significance has increased.

Vulnerability. Despite attempts to diversify the export mix and to build links into new source markets, vulnerability to external shocks remains very high. Hence minor changes in the terms of trade can have major effects on external balances and growth. Indicators of vulnerability include:

- large merchandise trade deficits;
- large current account deficits, except in Fiji;
- high trade penetration ratios, ranging from 50 to 100 percent of GDP in 1991-93 (see Table 2.3);

- high export concentration ratios (see Table 2.5) where the average three-product export concentration ratio for the PMCs is 80 percent, compared to 64 percent for Sub-Saharan Africa and 26 percent for Australia. This further underscores the continuing vulnerability of PMCs to global developments;

Table 2.5: Export Concentration and Trade Taxes

	Three Product Export Concentration Ratio (%)		Trade Tax Contribution to Domestic Revenue (%)	
	82-84	91-93	82-84	91-93
Fiji	77	70	26	30
Kiribati	99	89	22	24
Marshall Islands	98	97	25	27
Solomon Islands	71	76	50	65
Tonga	55	72	54	52
Vanuatu	93	75	60	53
W Samoa	64	67	44	58
FSM	93	94	9	7
Sub Sah African	79	64	-	-
Australia	-	26	5	2
New Zealand	-	36	5	2
Barbados	-	-	17	11
Madagascar	-	-	17	11

Source: Bank Staff Estimates.

- the importance of trade taxes to total revenue varies considerably among the PMCs, accounting for a large share in the Solomon Islands, Tonga, Vanuatu and Western Samoa; a moderate share in Fiji, Kiribati and Marshall Islands; and a small share in the Federated states of Micronesia (see Table 2.5). Hence domestic revenue will also be heavily affected by external performance.

The Changing Global Economic Scene

The External Trading Environment. The far-reaching changes arising from the conclusion of the Uruguay Round of the GATT Agreement, NAFTA and trade deregulation in Australia and New Zealand will significantly affect the external trading environment of the PMCs. These changes will affect economic performance in the PMCs owing to their dependence on a few commodities such as sugar, coconut, cocoa, fish products, garments, and service sectors including tourism. Benefits are most likely to favor countries with open economies and those that have the capacity to adjust and take advantage of new market opportunities likely to arise from the projected real GDP growth rates of around 2.7 percent per year for the G-7 economies over the medium term. Faster growth means more international trade—projected to grow at around 6 percent per year. Two other favorable factors are the outlook for low real interest rates and inflation as well as the resurgence of higher private capital inflows. More importantly, the Uruguay Round Agreement is expected to accelerate world trade and thereby help expand developing country production and exports.

The global trading environment is changing in several ways that will be of importance to the PMCs. Some likely effects of changes in the global economic environment are:

- with global trade liberalization, marked by the conclusion of the GATT Uruguay Round Accord, it is estimated that overall growth and trade will increase dramatically;

- a more competitive trade environment is likely to emerge;

- trends toward regional integration and emergence of regional growth centers in East Asia, Europe, and North America; and

- moves towards free trade in OECD states, such as Australia and New Zealand, to overcome sluggish growth and enhance external performance.

The economic fortunes of the PMCs are closely linked to developments in the world economy. Viewed in its broadest terms, PMC trade encompasses the exchange of merchandise, aid flows, migration and tourism. And with their small domestic markets, trade is by definition a major source of economic growth and development. However, despite remoteness, wide geographic span and sparse populations, the PMCs have astutely capitalized on global opportunities. The changes in the composition and direction of PMC trade is evidence of the region's ability to take advantage of new global market opportunities.

But a high degree of trade dependence implies that the PMCs are vulnerable to changes in world market conditions. They are "price-takers" on world markets, and hence even minor changes in global trading conditions can have significant effects on domestic economic performance. The vagaries of nature and shifts in aid policy compound the vulnerability. Managing vulnerability while taking advantage of global market opportunities is one of the key challenges for Pacific Island policymakers. One of the ways in which vulnerability can be managed is to increase the breadth and depth of the trade and investment linkages between the Pacific Island states and the global markets. Opportunities to improve trade performance abound. The challenge for the PMCs will be to ensure that these opportunities are identified and exploited in a truly competitive fashion.

The Changing Trade Environment

Preferential Arrangements

The PMCs have benefited from preferential trade agreements which convey duty-free or low-duty rate access for their exports into the markets of the major industrial countries. Trade liberalization while creating significant new opportunities is contributing, however, to the erosion of these benefits.

All of the PMCs receive "generalized system of preference" (GSP) treatment which accords them the lowest duties on offer for products exported to OECD nations. FSM and the Marshall Islands have special trade access agreements with the US granting them, for example, duty-free access for tuna canned in water up to a limit of 10 percent of total US demand. Fiji, Kiribati, Solomon Islands, Tonga, Tuvalu, Papua New Guinea, Vanuatu and Solomon Islands are signatories to the Lome convention which, in addition to development assistance, provides them with duty-free access for most products to European Union markets. Under the Lome Agreement, the aforementioned PMCs are also eligible for compensatory financing in response to a secular decline in international trading conditions. In addition, as a founding signatory to the Commonwealth Sugar Agreement, Fiji is provided a quota of 200,000 tons of sugar for export to the European Union. The European Union and the United States have also granted Fiji a quota for garment exports.

Within the Southern Pacific, PMCs are provided duty-free access to the markets of Australia and New Zealand (see Table 2.6). Preferential market access into Australia and New Zealand has been particularly important to the development of garment exports and footwear from Fiji, and automotive wiring harnesses from Western Samoa. As Australia and New Zealand reduce trade protection, competition will intensify in these markets.

Since 1989, Australia and New Zealand have undertaken coordinated, wide-ranging trade liberalization programs. Under these programs, a free trade zone has been established between Australia and New Zealand and specific timetables were set for the phase-down of tariffs in garments, footwear and motor vehicles (see Table 2.7). Textile trade between Australia and New Zealand was liberalized under the Closer Economic Relations (CER) Treaty of 1989 and New Zealand abolished quotas on textile imports in 1992. Since the CER treaty, trade has increased significantly between Australia and New Zealand. In the textiles area, for example, New Zealand's share of the Australian market increased from 4 to 11 percent. As import tariffs in Australia and New Zealand decline, the tariff preference that Fiji's garment and footwear exporters enjoy will fall by an average of 33 percent between 1994-2000.

Fiji's export-oriented garment industry has been built around low-value-added cut, make and trim (CMT) assembly operations. It is in these types of operations that low-wage Asian producers, many of whom have access to nationally produced raw materials, are likely to have a comparative cost advantage as Australian and New Zealand tariffs fall. Fiji and other PMC garment producers can maintain their foothold in the Southern Pacific markets by diversifying production into "specialty garments" (e.g. diving wear), by promoting the region's ability to provide small

Table 2.6: SPARTECA and Trade Expansion: PMC Trade with Australia and New Zealand
(1987-1993)

Australia's Total Imports, 1987-93 (A$'000) (New Zealand's Total Imports, 1987-93 (NZ$'000))								
COUNTRY	1987	1988	1989	1990	1991	1992	1993	1987/93 % change
Fiji	40,161 (19,488)	62,901 (38,009)	96,229 (83,103)	93,745 (114,517)	89,070 (72,888)	114,998 (53,631)	158,151 (42,417)	294 (118)
Solomon Islands	1,908 (928)	2,737 (633)	5,350 (609)	6,194 (856)	1,533 (939)	2,508 (1,257)	2,628 (792)	38 (-15)
Tonga	2,261 (4,241)	2,191 (3,323)	3,164 (2,699)	2,339 (3,043)	1,708 (2,259)	1,979 (1,625)	1,879 (1,218)	-17 (-25)
Western Samoa	2,323 (9,810)	3,189 (7,431)	1,485 (9,425)	1,834 (6,347)	3,542 (8,064)	34,449 (6,409)	69,667 (7,414)	2,899 (-25)
Vanuatu	683 (79)	920 (68)	1,477 (90)	2,413 (61)	1,193 (52)	1,474 (120)	1,728 (107)	153 (40)
Marshall Islands	0 (0)	0 (0)	0 (0)	0 (0)	45 (5)	127 (30)	1 (40)	n.a. (n.a.)
FSM	0 (0)	0 (0)	0 (0)	0 (0)	15 (6)	35 (0)	18 (0)	n.a. (n.a.)
TOTAL	47,336 (35,546)	71,938 (49,464)	107,705 (95,926)	106,525 (124,824)	97,106 (181,319)	155,570 (218,642)	234,072 (51,988)	394 (46)

Source: Government of Australia, Department of Foreign Affairs and Trade; Government of New Zealand, Department of Statistics.

lots and "just-in-time" service to Australia and New Zealand, and by upgrading design, assembly and packaging technology to be able to provide a more complete range of services.

Preferential trade agreements, such as SPARTECA, provide PMC manufacturers with an opportunity to enter new markets under the shelter of another nation's trade protection. But there are also serious, hidden costs associated with languishing under another country's trade protection. For example, to meet the 50 percent local content requirements, regional garment industries have sourced capital goods and raw materials in Australia and New Zealand rather than from more competitive Asian markets. They have also under-invested in new technology to maintain a high labor cost share so as to meet the 50 percent local content requirement.[2] Such factors tend to lock-in a high-cost structure in the industry, and reduce incentives to modernize and become globally competitive, as will be necessary when garment tariffs in Australia and New Zealand decline.

As shown in Table 2.4, the USA has become an important export market for Fiji (garments and sugar) and for Western Samoa and FSM, from which fresh and canned fish are the most important exports. The USA is also a major market for services (principally tourism) in Fiji, FSM, and Marshall Islands. The export of canned fish to the USA could suffer from trade diversion effects associated with NAFTA, but only if Mexico significantly expands canning capacity and reduces its production costs.

---

2 New Zealand has cut the rate 45 percent and some relaxation of SPARTECA rules by Australia is considered to have an equivalent effect.

Table 2.7: Schedule of Tariff Reductions in Australia and New Zealand
(%)

AUSTRALIA			
General Tariff Schedule	**1992**	**1994**	**1996**
High Rates	15	10	5
Medium Rates	10	8	5
Low Rates	8	8	5
Specific Items (General Rates & Ldc Rates)	**1994**	**1996**	**2000**
Apparel and finished textiles *general*	43	37	25
LDC	38	32	20
Cotton sheeting and woven fabrics *general*	31	25	15
LDC	26	17	10
Other fabrics *general*	27	23	15
LDC	22	18	10
Footwear *general*	33	27	15
LDC	28	22	10
Automotives *general*	30	25	15
NEW ZEALAND			
General Tariff Schedule	**1992**	**1994**	**1996**
High Rates	25.5	22.0	14
	23.5	20.0	14
Medium Rates	18.0	16.0	12
	15.0	13.0	10.0
Low Rates	12.0	10.0	8.0
	9.0	8.0	6.0
Bottom Rates	5.0	5.0	5.0
Specific Items:	**1994**	**1996**	**2000**
Motor Vehicles	35.0	30.0	25.0
Clothing	40.0	35.0	30.0
Footwear (adult)	45.0	39.0	30.0

Source: Government of Australia, Trade and Investment Promotion Service, "Australia's Trade Arrangements for Developing Countries", 1994. New Zealand Treasury, Budget, 1992 and I. Duncan et. al., "Dismantling the Barriers: Tariff Policy in New Zealand" (Wellington: NZIER, 1992).

Significant changes in fisheries trade between Mexico, the USA and Canada are not anticipated. Unlike the island economies in the Caribbean that are highly dependent on preferential access for manufactured goods to the USA, the main PMC export to the US market, fresh fish, enters at already low tariff rates. For the PMCs, the trade diversion effects from NAFTA will tend to be offset by the trade creation effects; in other words, higher incomes generated in North America will create more demand for PMC goods and services, offsetting the potential fall in demand resulting from increased Mexican exports to the US market.

Implications of GATT. Of the PMCs, only Fiji is a full contracting party to GATT, having joined in November 1993. PNG, Solomon

Islands, Kiribati, and Tonga are de facto members. Fiji participated in the Uruguay Round negotiations and has applied for membership in the World Trade Organization (WTO). In its Uruguay Round Submission, Fiji has agreed to reduce and bind tariffs for 52 categories of goods, and has scheduled reductions of tariffs for milk and rice. Although the other PMCs did not participate directly in the Uruguay Round negotiations, they will be affected by the outcomes.

Practically all of the PMCs' present and potential exports will suffer from some measure of preference erosion as a result of GATT-agreed tariff reduction. For certain African nations, the loss of trade preferences could cause a sharp fall in exports. But how important will this actually be to short and medium-term trade performance in the Pacific Island states? The answer to this is probably very little in the short run, but potentially much more so over 5 to 10 years unless PMC economies adjust to a more competitive global marketplace.

The great majority of tropical commodities that the PMC nations export will be largely unaffected by preference erosion, because tariffs are very low to begin with and because preference holders dominate these markets. The effects could be greater still for temperate products, where tariff barriers are quite high and where low-cost sources of supply already hold a significant share of the market. Refined sugar and canned-tuna for export to the European market are cases where trade preferences are high and could potentially be eroded by tariff reduction, although the EU has not included reforms that would significantly erode PMC trade preferences in its Uruguay Round offers.

Sugar. Fiji exports approximately 390,000 tonnes of sugar of which about 74 percent of the sales value is obtained at preferential prices, at almost double market prices. The most significant of these markets is the EU which, under the Sugar Protocol to the Lome Convention, agrees to purchase up to 200,000 tonnes of sugar per annum from Fiji at EU support prices. As of July 1994, EU intervention prices were 2.5 times higher than world market prices. Fiji also has a quota of 0.9 percent of US sugar imports, or 11,000 tonnes in 1994, which was priced (in mid-1994) at 90 percent above world market levels. The Government has also entered into a contract to supply Malaysia with 110,000 tonnes of refined sugar, at approximately world market prices.

The high sugar prices that Fiji receives as a result of trade preferences appear to have encouraged the industry to lose competitiveness and become a high-cost source of supply. Production has shifted onto marginal lands; yields have stagnated; factories operate well below capacity; cane-burning is commonly practised; and milling yield remains far below that achieved by neighboring producers.[3] The world's most efficient producers, such as Australia, can profitably export sugar at world market prices, which have ranged from US 9-12 cents/lb in recent years. The Fijian sugar sector received US 20 cents/lb in 1992.

Under GATT, the USA and the EU have agreed to convert sugar import quotas to tariffs. The US has established a tariff of 17 cents per pound which will be reduced by 15 percent (to 14.45 cents per pound) by the year 2000. Similarly, the EU has agreed to replace its variable import levy for white sugar by a fixed tariff rate and reduce this by 3.3 percent per year until it reaches the 20 percent total reduction required. The EU has also agreed that subsidized sugar exports from EU producers will be reduced by 340,000 tons from the average quantity of 1,277,000 tons in 1986-90.

Even after GATT, internal sugar prices in the EU and the USA are forecast to remain well in excess of world market price levels.[4] The high tariffs levied on sugar imports into the US and EU will keep internal prices high. In addition, Fiji may gain a portion of the approximately 400,000 tons which are imported by Portugal now that it is has become a member of the

---

[3] This is discussed in more detail in M. Singh, "Sugar: the Challenge", The Pacific Island's Review, July 1994, and in D.Mitchell, "Fiji Sugar Sector Study", World Bank, 1994.

[4] See D. Mitchell, "Fiji Sugar Sector Study", World Bank, August 1994.

European Union. The EU has also argued that the Lome Sugar Protocol supersedes GATT commitments.

Sugar is one of the world's most protected agricultural commodities. As such, this makes it vulnerable to various "liberalizing initiatives". In Europe, the combination of interests that gave rise to the agreement to provide Fiji, and other ACP states, with preferential market access no longer exists. The Commonwealth Sugar Agreement was entered into at a time when Europe was a significant sugar importer, when British industry (principally Tate & Lyle) owned large plantation holdings and was concerned with safeguarding its access to European consumers. The situation is vastly different now. Despite the Lome-imports, Europe is now the world's largest sugar exporter. Britain's sugar plantation holdings are no longer of any importance. And finally, implementation of the sugar protocol has become very expensive, costing the European Union approximately ECU 600 million in 1993. Even amongst other ACP states, this level of fiscal support is considered excessive compared with other forms of Lome assistance.

Moreover, the current Lome Convention will expire in February 2000. While some form of preferential arrangement may replace the existing arrangement, current benefits are likely to be reviewed. This points to the need for Fiji to become more efficient and competitive in sugar production to build up resilience to any possible preference erosion from such a review.

Fisheries. The tariff preference granted to PMC canned tuna in the EU markets is 24 percent over the MFN rates. The EU has declined to reduce its variable levy for canned tuna, although it has agreed to an 18 percent aggregate reduction in import tariffs for processed fish products. The cannery operations in Fiji, Solomon Islands and in PNG (in 1995) rely primarily on the EU market and, without preferential tariffs, would find it difficult to compete with the much larger canning operations (partly state-owned) in Thailand, the Philippines and the USA. Even with tariff protection in the EU market, the PMC tuna canning operations have recorded a dismal financial performance. Asian exporters have lobbied the EU to significantly reduce its MFN tariffs. Should this occur, PMC canning operations would have to adjust to a 20 to 25 percent fall in export prices.

There has also been concern that the reduction in OECD agricultural subsidies could lead to higher global food prices. If temperate product prices of foodstuffs rise by 5 to 10 percent as a result of GATT reforms, this would increase PMC import requirements by between 2 and 4 percent but at the same time there might be some stimulus for domestic food production. This would require, on average, an additional 2 percent of national income to meet higher food import costs. Existing evidence does not point to a significant rise in global food prices as a result of GATT. At most, a short-term slowdown in the long-term decline in global food prices is outweighed. The GATT recognized that least developed nations, and developing nation food importers may be adversely affected by these provisions. A special decision of the Uruguay Accord defined objectives related to food aid, food grants and aid for agricultural development. In addition, the possibility of World Bank and IMF providing short-term financing for commercial imports was also raised.

There will be both positive and negative effects on the PMCs as a result of the GATT accord. The GATT will expand global trade and with it demand for PMC products. At the same time, tariff preferences will erode for tree crop products and may, in the future, erode for sugar and canned tuna.

Extension of Accord Into Services and Intellectual Property Rights. The Uruguay Accord has also extended the principle of national and MFN (most favored nation) treatment to trade related services. The framework agreement services seeks out the principle of establishing clear, transparent and objective criteria for licensing service providers, eliminating restrictive barriers to cross border trade in services and eliminating restraint on temporary employment of skilled expatriates. Similarly trade and intellectual property rights were also included in the GATT discipline.

Extending GATT discipline into these areas is essentially designed to reduce trade friction and uncertainty arising from the varying national treatment of these issues. The PMCs have much to gain, and very little to lose. In the PMCs, services account for more than half of all foreign exchange earnings and encompass a wide range of activities, including tourism, offshore banking, merchant marine services, and overseas employment by temporary migrants. The PMCs can gain to the extent that addressing barriers to foreign direct investment in services and safeguarding intellectual property rights will boost investor confidence. This is likely to increase investment flows and also ease access for skilled PMC citizens to developed country markets.[5]

Given the year-to-year volatility in PMC terms-of-trade, a 1 to 2 percent shift in export earnings due to GATT might well be imperceptible. Furthermore, narrow markets imply that PMC export prices can differ significantly, both in magnitude and direction-of-change, from global market prices.[6] Accordingly, the degree to which GATT-induced effects will actually impact upon the PMCs is closely linked to the efficiency of price-transmission between global and national markets.

That the "net" effects of the GATT Uruguay Accord are predicted to be relatively modest is a common finding. The results of a comprehensive attempt to model the effects of GATT on the trade performance of Caribbean states were examined. For these nations, the net effects of the GATT Uruguay Round also tend to be within 0 to 2 percent of export earnings.

While the forecast quantitative effects of GATT are small, this does not imply that the global economy is not changing in a fundamental fashion. Trade reform on a global scale triggers further reforms in initial trading nations. The trade liberalization efforts in Australia and New Zealand, and the emergence of regional free-trade zones, are signs of further moves to a more competitive international economy.

The PMCs will need to adjust to the changing global environment. There will be short-term adjustment costs, but against this the prospects for significant long-term gains.

A more important consideration, however, is that competitiveness has become the single most important determinant of a nation's ability to capitalize on a growing global trading environment. How to exploit emerging opportunities in a changing and increasingly competitive global marketplace is a key issue facing Pacific Island policymakers.

Recommendations

A three pronged strategy is required to *enhance competitiveness* in the PMCs. This will require:

- the maintenance of a macroeconomic environment that meets the twin goals of price stability and competitive pricing of PMC resources;
- a reduction in the anti-export bias of trade policy, and tax regimes; and
- reducing barriers to domestic and foreign direct investment.

An Enabling Macroeconomic Environment. A low rate of inflation and the pricing of capital, labor and land so as to be internationally competitive are two of the main macroeconomic challenges. With fragile financial markets, even small domestically financed fiscal deficits can quickly spark inflationary upsurges, as has occurred with some frequency in Solomon Islands, Western Samoa and Vanuatu during 1990-94. High rates of inflation will tend to discourage private

---

5 Australia has been one of the main recipients of PMC migrants. In recent years restrictions on net immigration have been tightened. A loss of access to Australian labor markets would have serious repercussions for those PMC economies (Tonga, Western Samoa, Kiribati, Fiji) which are highly dependent on remittances and overseas employment.

6 The difference between export prices in the Solomon Islands and the world market were analyzed. The results illustrate the relatively "weak" transmission of global prices to PMC markets. This can be explained by a combination of factors including narrow markets, non-competitive trading systems, "small-lot" pricing, and year-to-year fluctuation in PMC export quality, relative to world market norms.

investment and private saving, and point to the need for prudent fiscal management especially during periods of volatile external developments. Towards this end, exchange rate, public sector wage, and fiscal policies are the main instruments that can be used to ensure that domestic resources are competitively priced in global markets. If domestic resources are overvalued, then domestic investors will be encouraged to shift their capital abroad while overseas investors will be reluctant to make new commitments.

The new portfolio of export oriented industries in the PMCs—tourism, garments, high value agricultural commodities, niche market fisheries products—tend to be highly responsive to improved price prospects, in contrast to the lower short-run response in the traditional exports (e.g. tree crops). This underscores the need to develop and sustain a strategy of enhancing macroeconomic competitiveness as an integral part of any effort to improve trade and global market integration.

Reducing Anti-Export Bias. Several of the PMCs rely heavily on trade taxes to finance the recurrent costs of Government. Solomon Islands, Tonga, Western Samoa and Vanuatu derive more than half of their domestic revenues from trade taxes. Fiji, Kiribati and Marshall Islands derive between a quarter and a third of their domestic revenues from trade taxes. In half of the cases, trade taxes have become a more important source of domestic revenue over the decade 1983-1993. The PMCs are considerably more reliant on trade taxes for Government revenue than are the Northern Pacific nations or other small-island countries such as Barbados.

While providing a steady stream of revenue, high import duties raise the cost of doing business in the PMCs and discourage exports. In terms of providing protection to domestic producers, high import duties are counter-productive. Remoteness from major markets already provides the PMCs with a high degree of natural trade protection.

PMC Governments have consciously attempted to reduce the coverage of import licensing and to lower tariffs in order to reduce enterprise costs. This is reflected in a decline in the effective average import duty rates between 1984-1993. While heading in the right direction, effective average import duty rates are still in the 10 to 40 percent range, significantly higher than in Australia or New Zealand, and on the high end of the range found in other small island economies.

High import duties for final goods, combined with generally low duty rates for raw materials, can result in very high effective rates of protection. These range from 7 percent in the low-tariff Marshall Islands to an estimated 63 percent in Tonga, with most values clustered around the 30 to 40 percent range. While indicative ERPs are not as high in the Pacific Island States as in some Caribbean nations, they are still high enough to discourage exports. And while high tariffs convey a measure of protection to domestic producers, opportunities for import substitution are quickly exhausted because of small populations and low incomes. A progressive reduction of import duties over the medium term would lower enterprise costs and reduce the anti-export bias of PMC trade regimes. However, lowering tariff rates would, by necessity, need to be accompanied by measures to develop new domestic revenue sources such as a value added tax or a consumption tax. This highlights the need for careful coordination of resource mobilization and trade reform measures.

Reducing Barriers. Competitiveness can be further enhanced by lowering the cost of doing business through reducing barriers to private investments, both domestic and foreign. Although private entrepreneurship is still in its infancy in the PMCs, recent examples have shown that it can contribute significantly to growth and employment provided it is competitive. Moreover, a healthy domestic private sector will be the key to attracting foreign investment via joint ventures. In addition to capital, foreign investment brings with it the technology and market access needed to penetrate new markets. GATT, the emergence of major regional trading blocs, and the opening-up of protected markets in the Northern Pacific, signal growing competitiveness in the international environment for both foreign direct investment and trade. For the PMCs to develop domestic private investments and attract foreign direct investment and expand trade, efforts will be required to:

- examine barriers to domestic and foreign investment;
- examine the framework for "niche market agreement" and the ability to assess costs, benefits, and risks; and
- strengthen trade and investment links with rapidly growing Asian economies.

Foreign Direct Investment Requirements. Investment approval mechanisms, access to land, and restrictions on the hiring of expatriate workers are three of the most often cited impediments to foreign direct investment in the South Pacific (see Table 2.8). Many of the PMCs do not have up-to-date foreign direct investment legislation. Investment applications tend to be time-consuming and require clearance from several layers of government bureaucracy including, in some instances, the senior most ranks of Government. Once an investment is approved, lengthy deliberations are often required to obtain a suitable investment site.

With the exception of Fiji where about 10 percent of the land is freehold, land cannot be purchased by foreign investors. In several PMCs, property rights in land are poorly defined, while in others land lease periods are insufficient for long-gestating investment projects.

All PMCs limit issuance of expatriate work permits to selected skill categories. Periodic revocation of stay permits is still practised in some PMCs and signals wavering government support for foreign investment as a whole. Application procedures for expatriate work permits tend to be both time-consuming and costly.

Establishing up-to-date foreign direct investment legislation, streamlining the FDI investment approval process, clarifying property rights and relaxing regulatory barriers on foreign land use, and easing requirements related to the hiring of expatriate workers are some of the measures that the PMC states could adopt to make the domestic economic environment more conducive to inward investment.

Rationalizing Fiscal Incentives. To offset adverse investment regulations and a perceived lack of competitiveness, PMC Governments offer a wide range of fiscal incentives to lure private investors. The different foreign direct investment incentives are listed in Table 2.9. In all PMCs, there is a lack of automaticity and transparency in the granting of investment incentives. In general, the investment incentives that are granted are distortionary, erode the tax base, and encourage rent-seeking behavior. There is little evidence, furthermore, that such incentives actually attract foreign investment. And in some instances, the incentives are actually a form of disguised subsidy to a small category of enterprises that generate little domestic value-added. A more appropriate strategy for PMC governments would be to move away from wide-ranging foreign investment incentives, and concentrate instead on improving the overall domestic enterprise environment.

Strengthening Trade And Investment Links With APEC. Promoting trade, aid and investment links with all APEC countries including the rapidly growing Asian economies provides a means of diversifying market ties and finding new sources of growth. PMCs have certain resources that are in short supply most notably calm, quiet island locations, close to a third of the world's total fish supply. Close cooperation through trade and investment characterizes the strategy of integrated Asia-region development that has led to the emergence of multi-country growth-triangles in East Asia,[7] while links with some APEC countries are well developed. Sparking the interest of Asian entrepreneurs to invest in areas in which they already have technology,

---

[7] See T. Nagasaka, "Globalization of Japanese Corporations and Their Changing Role in Asia-Pacific Development" in I. Yamazawa and F. Lo (eds), *Evolution of Asia-Pacific Economies: International Trade and Direct Investment*, Asian And Pacific Development Centre, 1993, and World Bank, East Asian Leadership in Liberalization, 1994 for a discussion of the close links between Asian FDI and trade, and the emergence of multi-country growth centers.

market links and expertise is an important challenge for the PMCs leaders.

Japan is the single largest Asian investor in the PMCs. Between 1981 and 1992, there were 90 instances of Japanese foreign investments in Fiji, 28 in Vanuatu, 27 in the Marshall Islands, 10 in Western Samoa, and 6 each in the Cook Islands and Solomon Islands. The total amount invested was about US$350 million of which 43 percent was in Fiji, 27 percent in Vanuatu and 30 percent divided among the other countries. While Japanese FDI has been the largest single source of foreign investment into the Pacific Island region and has assumed a prominent position in the local fisheries industry and tourism, it has been very small (less than one percent of outward investment) in the overall scheme of Japanese overseas investment.

While improved flows of information and political contact are vital to stimulating investor interest, it is equally important that an investment environment is moulded that is conducive to sustained growth and development.

Perceptions may not always match reality. Even so, adverse perceptions discourage investors from expanding operations in the region, and underscore the importance of improving the overall business environment. Measures to strengthen economic infrastructure, bolster human resource development, establish stable regulatory regimes, protect law-and-order, and improve shipping and aviation links between major markets and the PMCs are a high priority. Such measures will improve not only the PMCs ability to attract inward investment, but also to mobilize effectively and harness local private initiative.

Improving the private sector investment environment is necessary to stimulate trade-expanding private initiatives, but it is not sufficient to guarantee that this investment will result in strong sustained growth. As noted above, the PMCs in the 1980s have been plagued by weak links between investment and growth. One of the keys to improving the effectiveness of trade-expanding investment is to ensure that clear and coherent strategies are adopted in support of those sectors with the most productive potential namely tourism, fisheries and forestry. The challenge is to define appropriate strategies for increasing the PMCs' capacity and competitiveness in providing recreational services, fish and forestry products while ensuring that the resource-base, from which these goods and services are drawn, is sensibly managed for present and future generations.

Table 2.8: Foreign Direct Investment Regime

	Approval Mechanism	Access to Land	Expatriate Workers
Fiji	Fiji Trade and Investment Board acts as a one-stop shop for all necessary approvals for new projects.	Limited freehold land available. Land must be leased from native landowners or the Native Land Trust Board.	Foreign investors are not expected to employ expatriates when suitably trained local employees are available. Delays are experienced in obtaining work permits for short-term technicians.
Solomon Islands	Approval needed from Foreign Investment Board (FIB) on advice of Foreign Investment Division of Ministry of Commerce and Primary Industries. Approvals of other Ministries are arranged by the FIB, and approvals tend to require about one month.	Registered land may be leased; land registration is limited to 12 percent of the nations total land and land conflicts arise.	Expatriates permitted only if trained nationals are unavailable. Periodic checks and withdrawal of stay permits used to enforce this policy.
Tonga	Proposals reviewed by Standing Advisory Committee on Industrial Licensing of Ministry of Labor, Commerce and Industries.	Land may only be leased by foreigners.	No formal restrictions, although Government prefers the hiring of national workers.
Western Samoa	Proposals must be submitted to the Department of Trade, Commerce and Industry, reviewed by the Enterprises Incentives Board and approved by Cabinet.	Land may be leased. Limited freehold land is also available.	Expatriate permits granted only if skills are unavailable locally. Permits are reviewed every 6 months.
Vanuatu	Ministry of Finance approval is required of new investors.	Land may be leased for up to 75 years. Government will assist in land negotiations. Undeveloped land must be improved within 5 years.	Permits granted only if there are no qualified national employees. Periodic checks used to ensure that overseas workers are complying with permits.
Kiribati	Approval of the Foreign Investment Commission is required. Projects above US$195,000 require Cabinet approval.	Land may not be owned by foreigners.	Expatriates allowed where qualified national employees are unavailable.
Marshall Islands	Cabinet must approve each foreign investment application.	50 year land leases are possible, although limited land registration, multiple owners and land rights based on usage predominate.	Expatriates allowed only where qualified national employees are unavailable. Permits for semi-skilled expatriates are limited.
Federated States of Micronesia	Foreign Investment Permits are Issued by the Department of Resources and Development with the concurrence of the State Authorities.	Land may only be leased and, in two states, the maximum length of leasehold is 25 years.	Expatriates account for a fifth of the labor force and permits are readily available.

Source: Price Waterhouse, Review of the Foreign Investment Climate in South Pacific Forum Countries, South Pacific Forum, Suva, 1994. World Bank, Country Economic Memoranda, 1993, IMF Staff Reports and Recent Economic Development Reports.

Table 2.9: Foreign Direct Investment Incentives

Fiji	i) Tax Free Zone/Tax Free Factory scheme under which investors have a 13 year corporate tax holiday, import and excise duty exemptions for capital goods and raw materials, and exemption on excise duty for products manufactured within the zone. ii) Tourism investment allowance and 55 percent accelerated depreciation allowance; iii) mining promotion measures providing tax exemption of income, expenditure deduction and accelerated depreciation; and iv) loss carry forward allowances.
Solomon Islands	Solomon Islands Investment Board may structure an individual incentives package for a foreign investor which may include: i) up to 10 years tax holiday; ii) up to 15 years exemption from withholding tax; iii) up to 10 years exemption on withholding tax for non-residents; iv) loss carry forward; v) accelerated capital write off for tourism projects; vi) double tax-deduction for training; vii) 150 percent deduction for inter-provincial transport of raw materials and export promotion expenditures.
Tonga	Incentive packages are structured for each investment and may include: i) income tax holiday of 5 years, and a possible 5 year extension; ii) additional tax holidays granted for expansion; iii) assets may be depreciated after the tax holiday; iv) capital goods may be imported duty-free for two years; v) raw materials for export industries are exempt from customs duties; vi) a 50 percent concessional rate of port and service tax is provided; vii) time-bound protection from competition; viii) industrial estate space provided; ix) priority access to phone and water connections.
Western Samoa	Incentives Governed by Incentive Legislation, Enterprise Incentives and Export Promotion Act of 1992/93 include: i) tax and dividend-tax holiday up to 5 years; ii) import duty exemption for capital goods and raw materials of 5 years; iii) export enterprises are eligible for a 15 year tax holiday, relief on all customs duties, and a subsequent tax rate of 25 percent on corporate income; iv) an export finance facility provides pre- and post-shipment credit at concessionary rates; v) industrial free zone site space with duty-free trade.
Kiribati	Case-by-case incentives include: i) 10 percent preferential tax rate for five years for pioneering firms; ii) accelerated depreciation allowance and three year loss carry-forward; iii) loan interest deduction; iv) first-time import duty exemptions for capital goods; v) government equity investment or joint-venturing; vi) public infrastructure investment undertaken to assist specific projects.
Vanuatu	Incentives are provided on a project-by-project basis. Tax haven status of Vanuatu allows freedom from corporate tax, income tax, estate duties, withholding tax, sales tax, and non-capital gains tax. Total or partial exemption from import duties for capital goods and raw materials may be offered to investors in fisheries or tourism.
Marshall Islands	Cabinet may provide tailor-made investment incentives on each project. Standard incentives include an income tax exemption offered for up to 5 years for firms in priority sectors and duty-free imports offered to export-oriented firms.
Federated States of Micronesia	Cabinet may provide tailor-made investment incentives which have included exemption from gross revenue tax and custom's duties. US firms may obtain grants for preparing feasibility studies, special loans from the Small Business Administration, and Economic Development Administration grants for expanding facilities that promote commercial development.

Source: Price Waterhouse, Review of the Foreign Investment Climate in South Pacific Forum Countries, South Pacific Forum, Suva, 1994. World Bank, Country Economic Memoranda, 1993, IMF Staff. Recent Economic Developments and Reports.

3. TOURISM

Overview: Tourism offers considerable potential in terms of output and employment growth. There is now an increasing recognition in the PMCs of the economic importance of tourism, more so considering the strides made during the past few years. The PMCs have performed well over the past 5 years with a visitor growth rate exceeding world wide growth but at the same time it fell far short of the visitor growth rate of 8.7 percent for the East Asia and Pacific Region. The failure of the PMCs to move in tandem with the East Asia-Pacific Region as a whole reflects the constraints to tourism development arising from geographical isolation, the dispersed nature of the PMCs, and their limited resources. But the key to developing PMCs' tourism product lies in the sensitive presentation of their cultural heritage and the careful management of the natural environment. The main issues are those of improving access to land, developing the tourism product and of the government playing a supportive role to private sector initiative in tourism development.

Background and Introduction

Introduction

During the 1980s, tourism surpassed primary commodities as a source of export earnings and economic growth. The allure of the Pacific Islands has been translated into a set of competitive, recreational services that provide a significant share of incomes, export earnings and employment (see Table 3.1). The potential for future expansion of tourism is substantial—a significant share of the PMCs' rich heritage of cultural and natural assets has yet to be made easily accessible to visitors—and the Asia-Pacific region as a whole is witnessing rapid growth in tourism. The challenge is to harness the untapped supply-potential of the PMCs to meet the fast growth in different segments of visitor demand.

But this challenge is not the same for all countries; nor, given differences in endowments, should the strategies be the same. As a group, the PMCs range from Fiji, with a long-established industry and a well-known tourism product, to newly developing visitor locations such as FSM, which attract growing interest in specialty niche markets. What all of the PMCs share, however, is the potential for tourism to make a far more significant contribution to economic growth and development.

The economic significance of tourism is illustrated by Fiji, which has the most mature tourism industry of all the PMCs. Tourism is Fiji's leading foreign exchange earner which contributed F$363.6 million in 1993. Since 1990 foreign exchange earnings from tourism have increased by F$69 million which has more than offset the F$53 million decline in earnings from gold, timber and fish over the same period.

Of the other PMCs, tourism is of greatest

Table 3.1 : Tourism in PMC Economies, 1993

	Per Capita GNP	Population ('000)	Visitors ('000)	Tourism Earnings (% of GDP)	Direct Employment in Tourism
Fiji	2,130	762	287	15.7	13,500
FSM	1,850 a/	105	26	n.a.	n.a.
Kiribati	710	76	4	6.9	150
Marshall Islands	1,670 a/	51	7	4.5	350
Solomon Islands	740	354	12	3.9	496
Tonga	1,530	98	25	6.3	1,624
Vanuatu	1,230	161	44	26.3	1,300
Western Samoa	950	167	47	22.1	1,100

a/ GDP per capita.
Source: Tourism Council of the South Pacific

economic significance in Vanuatu where visitor expenditures account for 26.3 percent of GDP, followed by Tonga and Western Samoa. Tourism's contribution to GDP in the remaining countries—where tourism infrastructure is very limited—is more modest contributing between about 4 and 22 percent of GDP (see Table 3.1). However, all of these countries have increasingly had to turn to tourism to generate export and employment opportunities.

Between 1988 and 1993 visitor arrivals to the East Asia-Pacific Region increased by 8.7 percent per year compared with an annual growth rate of 4.5 percent world wide. Led by the strong growth in arrivals to Australia and New Zealand, the Oceania sub-region experienced an average annual increase of 6.5 percent over the same period. During this time the PMCs performed better with an average growth in arrivals of 6.8 percent per year and exceeding world wide growth by a substantial margin (see Table 3.2).

Destinations and Market Characteristics

Within the PMC group, considerable diversity exists in regard to tourism development. Fiji is a mature destination with frequent air services to Australia and New Zealand and direct access to long haul markets. However, the conventional beach product is no longer proving to attract new markets and repeat visitors and the focus is shifting to its terrestrial and marine environments; increasing emphasis is being placed on cultural heritage. Tonga and Western Samoa have strong cultural identities, but both countries have limited and inconvenient flight connections. Among the Melanesian group, Vanuatu has a well-established tourism industry but is plateauing due to airline and hotel capacity constraints. The Solomon Islands are still at an early stage of tourism development. FSM, Marshall Islands and Kiribati are distinctly different from the five other PMCs because they are far more remote from source markets and their land area is much smaller and more widely scattered—and hence affected by segmentation of access.

Tourism Demand

Market Growth. Over the five years between 1988 and 1993 visitor arrivals to PMCs increased by 39 percent, from 327,000 to 453,000 and holiday arrivals by almost 45 percent, from 217,000 to 315,000 (see Table 3.3). However, the aggregate figures mask two very significant factors. In the case of Fiji, which is by far the most significant PMC destination, accounting for almost two thirds of all arrivals, the political events of 1987 resulted in a severe downturn in visitor arrivals from 258,000 in 1986 to 190,000 in 1987. It was not until 1990 that visitor arrivals again exceeded pre-1987 levels and subsequent growth since 1990 has been very weak, averaging only one percent per year. Similarly, as a result of disrupted air services, perceived political instability and a severe cyclone in early 1987, visitor arrivals to Vanuatu, the third most popular PMC destination, fell from a peak of 32,400 in 1983 to 14,600 in 1987. Visitor arrivals did not recover to 1983 levels until 1990 although, unlike Fiji, they have continued to grow strongly since. Hence, if the increase in arrivals was measured from the previous peak levels experienced in Fiji

Table 3.2: Tourist Arrivals and Receipts by Region 1988 and 1993

Region	Arrivals (Millions)			Receipts US $ Billions		
	1988	1993	Average Annual Increase	1988	1993	Average Annual Increase
Worldwide	402.0	500.1	4.5%	199.3	304.0	8.8%
East Asia Pacific Region	45.1	68.5	8.7%	30.6	45.6[a/]	10.5%
Oceania Sub-Region	4.6	6.3	6.5%	5.7	7.8[a/]	8.2%
Pacific Member Countries	0.33	0.45	6.8%			

a/ 1992 Data.
Source: World Tourism Organization (WTO), PMC National Statistics Offices and NTOs.

and Vanuatu the real increase in visitor numbers since 1988 would be halved from 126,000 to 62,000 representing a net increase of 15.9 percent or 3 percent growth per annum.

Purpose of Visit. Fiji attracts almost three quarters of all holiday visitors to PMCs with 81 percent of visitors to Fiji traveling for holiday purposes. In terms of holiday visitors as a percentage of total visitors, Fiji is closely followed by the Marshall Islands, with an estimated 80 percent, Vanuatu (71 percent) and FSM (66 percent). Holiday visitors are of least significance in Kiribati and Western Samoa with less than 20 percent of arrivals visiting for holiday purposes. Like the Solomon Islands, where holiday visitors have fallen from a half to one third of all visitors, holiday visitors to Western Samoa have fallen in number as well as in percentage terms since 1988. In the case of Tonga and Western Samoa, around half of all arrivals are recorded as holiday visitors. However, it is believed that a significant proportion of these are nationals visiting friends and relatives, who record "holiday" as their purpose of visit on their arrival cards (see Table 3.3).

Visitor Origin. Around 40 percent of arrivals in PMCs are from the short haul markets of Australia and New Zealand. Although arrivals from both these sources have grown significantly over the five years since 1988, Australia's share of total arrivals has fallen by four percentage points and, in the case of Fiji, the number of Australian visitors is well below its peak, which exceeded 100,000 in 1984 and again in 1990 in response to heavy discounting following the events of 1987. However, in the face of increasing competition from Australian resort destinations, resulting from domestic airline deregulation and an oversupply of rooms, plus the increasing competition from Asian destinations, especially Bali which is now serviced by Ansett as well as Qantas and Garuda, the PMCs are finding it increasingly difficult to maintain their share of the Australian outbound market. In the case of New Zealand, renewed economic growth in recent years coupled with improved airline schedules and fare structures and attractive accommodation packages have combined to generate strong growth particularly to Fiji where New Zealand arrivals are now at levels not seen since the 1970s.

The two strongest growing source markets are Europe and Japan. Visitors from Europe have almost doubled since 1988 and their share of PMC arrivals has increased by three percentage points. Fiji, Vanuatu and Western Samoa have registered the highest numerical increases with Fiji recording the strongest growth from the UK and Western Samoa from Germany. From a very low base, Japanese visitors have increased to over 50,000 in 1993 with Fiji and FSM sharing over 90 percent of this growth—Fiji by virtue of its more developed tourism infrastructure and direct air service to Japan and FSM by virtue of its historic links with Japan, the associated wreck diving opportunities, and air connections via Guam.

The major market that has scarcely grown and seen its market share decline by almost six percentage points is North America. This can largely be attributed to the slow economic recovery in the USA and Canada and the reduction of services between the US West Coast and Fiji as US carriers, specifically Continental, withdrew from Pacific routes. Air Pacific's reinstatement of a weekly B747-200 service between Nadi and Los Angeles from July 1994 can be expected to stimulate this market provided that the accommodation preferences of American (and European tourists who are expected to connect with this service) can be satisfied.

Length of Stay. The average duration of stay for all visitors to PMCs is estimated to be 8.5 nights and the average stay for holiday visitors slightly shorter at 8.1 nights. The average duration of stay has fallen since 1988 and will continue to do so. The reasons for this are that the long stay short haul holiday markets of Australia and New Zealand are growing much less quickly than the short stay Japanese and other Asian markets and the long haul European markets, which tend to be multi-destinational with shorter stays in each destination.

Cruise Market. With the exception of Vanuatu, which received almost 60,000 cruise passengers in 1992, and Fiji, which received 30,000 and which also has small cruise ships operating within Fijian waters, cruise ships make a negligible contribution to the economies of PMCs. The North Pacific nations of FSM, Marshall Islands and Kiribati are too remote from the main

Table 3.3 Pacific Member Countries: Total Arrivals and Holiday Arrivals 1988-1993

	Total Visitors					Holiday Visitors						
	1988		1993		Average Annual Increase	1988		1993		Average Annual Increase	Average Length of Stay	
	Numbers	% PMC Total	Number	% PMC Total	(%)	Number	% Country Visitors	Number	% Country Visitors	(%)	All Visitors	Holiday Visitors
Fiji	208,200	63.7	287,462	63.4	6.7	166,560	80.0	233,081	81.1	7.0	8.5	8.0
FSM	14,676	4.5	26,129	5.8	12.2	3,669	25.0/a	17,181	65.8/d	36.2	4.3/d	-
Kiribati	3,465	1.0	4,755/a	1.0	6.5	270	10.0	1,031	15.0/c	30.7	-	-
Marshall Islands	3,578	1.1	7,179/b	1.6	14.9	2,860	79.9	5,743	80.0/c	15.0	-	-
Solomon Islands	10,679	3.3	11,570	2.6	1.6	5,367	50.3	3,917	33.9	-6.1	13.0/e	-
Tonga	19,456	6.0	24,628	5.4	4.8	9,728	50.0/c	13,792	56.0/c	7.2	16.5/e	8.6/e
Vanuatu	17,544	5.4	44,483	9.8	20.5	12,240	69.8	31,565	71.0	20.9	8.7/e	8.7/e
Western Samoa	49,088	15.0	47,071	10.4	-0.8	16,363	33.3/c	8,311	17.7	-12.9	7.8/f	7.1/f
Total PMCs	326,686	100.0	453,277	100.0	6.8	217,057	66.6	314,621	69.5	7.7	8.5	8.1
Total Increase			126,591		+38.8			97,564	+44.9			

Sources: TCSP, National Statistics and Tourism Offices.
a/ World Bank estimate based on average rate of growth 1988-92.
b/ World Bank estimate based on FSM growth rate.
c/ World Bank estimate based on previous or subsequent years.
d/ World Bank estimate based on individual State statistics.
e/ 1992 Data.
f/ 1990-91 Data.

cruising grounds to benefit, as are Tonga and Western Samoa. The Solomon Islands have also previously featured on cruise itineraries receiving up to 5,000 cruise passengers a year until 1992. Although the economic benefit derived from cruise ship visits is limited, the positive aspect is that, apart from berthing or landing facilities, the host countries do not have to provide the infrastructure to support ship borne visitors. Although there are some moves to encourage cruise ships to visit and contribute to the economies of smaller islands, such as the recent "Fairstar" visit to Kioa in Fiji, there are equal concerns about the cultural impacts, litter and pollution problems associated with cruise visits to more remote islands.

Tourist Accommodation

The quantity, characteristics and cost of tourist accommodation in PMCs are illustrative of many of the problems faced by the industry in these countries. There are estimated to be approximately 8,000 guest rooms in PMC accommodation establishments ranging from luxury resorts, standard to simple guest houses (see Table 3.4). In Fiji, 80 percent of guest rooms are found on Viti Levu although not all in a single center. In the other PMCs apart from Fiji, over two thirds of all guest rooms are located in a single town or island in each country, indicating the degree of concentration of tourism facilities. The size of the largest hotel in each country varies greatly but the proportion of rooms found in the largest 3 or 4 establishments in each country also indicates the concentration of the room supply.

Overall, around one third of all rooms are contained in 7 percent of total establishments. Excluding Fiji, the most mature destination, this rises to almost half the rooms (44 percent) in 11 percent of all establishments. The average size of hotels is misleading in that, if the 29 largest hotels are excluded, the average size comes down to 14 rooms, which is scarcely large enough to be financially and operationally viable and too small to be included in most tour package programs. In contrast, the average size of the 29 largest hotels is almost 100 rooms, which usually requires expatriate management and an additional department head level of management (again often expatriate). Moreover, in the more mature destinations, particularly Fiji and Vanuatu, the large hotels are owned and operated by overseas investors and managers. There is considerable debate about the optimum size of operation which would assist in the decentralization of tourism facilities and which: (i) would be within the reach of local investors; (ii) would be operationally viable; and (iii) be capable of being operated by local people.

The optimum size would appear to be between 15 and 50 units (related to the size of the local community). This scale of operation lends itself to local bungalow style accommodation, which matches the expectations of most visitors to the Pacific. At the upper end of the size range, 50 units is about the maximum that can be provided without losing the small scale intimacy associated with such resorts. Subject to adequate management and service levels this is also the scale of operation that can be readily packaged. However, largely as a result of the limited hospitality management and vocational training opportunities available in PMCs, even accommodation establishments of this scale are considered beyond the capability of local operators, thus contributing to the reluctance of domestic financial institutions to finance such projects.

Promotion and Diversification

Prospects. The prospects for tourism to the PMCs appear bright with forecasters predicting that the East Asia Pacific Region is set to be the fastest growing travel market for at least the next decade. By the year 2000, the World Tourism Organization estimates that arrivals in the East Asia Pacific Region will increase to 101 million from 68.5 million in 1993 and that three quarters of these travellers will originate within the region. By 2010, Asia Pacific travel markets will account for 40 percent of all global air traffic.

There are three main reasons why the PMCs have not matched the performance of Northeast and Southeast Asia in tourism development.

- First, from a market standpoint their problems are those of the "tyranny of distance" insofar as, even within the East

Table 3.4: Tourist Accommodation Stock in PMCs

	No. of Establishments	No. of Rooms	%	Size Range (Rooms)	Average Size (Rooms)	Average Occupancy %	Proporation in Major Hotes		
							No.	Rooms	% of Total
Fiji	178	4,573	57.2	1-436	26	65	4	1,311	28.7
FSM	41	620	7.8	4-56	15	45-50	6	202	32.6
Kiribati	6	110	1.4	4-40	18		2	76	69.1
Marshall Islands	14	200	2.5	5-48	14		3	93	46.5
Solomon	55	572	7.1	1-96	10		3	204	35.7
Tonga	44	613	7.7	2-76	14	50	4	216	35.2
Vanuatu	43	751	9.4	1-165	18	65	4	414	55.1
Western Samoa	27	556	6.9	3-156	21		3	301	54.1
PMC Total	408	7,995	100.0	1-436	20		29	2,817	

Source: World Bank estimate based on NTO accommodation inventories, brochures and previous reports.

Asia Pacific Region, they are long haul or verging on long haul destinations from the fast growing outbound markets of Asia. However, the economics of long haul travel dictate the use of wide bodied aircraft which, in most cases, cannot be justified to serve small island tourist destinations. Consequently, with the exception of Fiji, which has a well established aviation infrastructure as a legacy of its former refueling role, the remaining PMCs lie in an ocean vacuum between the major magnets of Guam/Saipan, Hawaii and French Polynesia to the north and east and Australia and New Zealand to the southwest.

- Second, from a resource standpoint, not only are the PMCs characterized by fragile natural environments and susceptibility to natural disasters such as cyclones and tidal waves, but also by a lack of qualified and trained personnel; lack of community awareness about the benefits of tourism; lack of tourism data and lack of adequate funding for tourism infrastructure and marketing. This is further compounded in most countries by complex customary land tenure traditions, which are a deterrent to investment because of concerns about security and duration of tenure.

- Third, whilst most PMC governments appreciate that tourism offers perhaps their only source of foreign exchange and employment they, and in some cases the tourist industry, have yet to realize that their real competitors are outside the region not within it. If the PMCs are going to compete effectively, it will call for a greater degree of regional cooperation than exists at present. The constructive debate and agreements reached on aviation at the 25th South Pacific Forum held in Brisbane, Australia, in August 1994 is indicative of a growing recognition of this need.

Marketing

Recent trends in visitor arrivals to Oceania as a whole and expected future growth from different source markets is likely to result in a very different mix of visitors to PMCs by the year 2000. English speaking Australian, New Zealand and North American visitors are expected to decline to around 40 percent of the total compared with almost 60 percent at present. European arrivals are expected to increase to around 20 percent of all arrivals compared with 15 percent at present as are Japanese and other Asian arrivals. These anticipated trends will have a significant influence on shaping the future tourist product of PMCs. To broaden access into new markets will require a concerted effort to improve aviation arrangements.

The challenge facing the PMCs and other Pacific nations is quite clear and was succinctly expressed in a 1992 ESCAP report on sustainable Tourism Development in Pacific Island Countries. Quite simply it is "to distinguish themselves from (those) other beach destinations in terms of their cultural differences and other unique attractions". "Among themselves they each (i.e. island nations) need to emphasize their unique attributes as a visitor destination and plan the development of new attractions and activities based on these attributes, ... to identify very specialized niche markets ...... based on their unique attractions ......" Marketing these unique tourism attributes to the highest value markets is undoubtedly the path which the PMCs must follow. Together with other PICs they must market their unique shared Pacific identity and, within that framework, promote their own individual cultural identity and unique attractions. Only in this way can they capitalize on the comparative advantage they have over other destinations and compensate for their remoteness. In short, preserving those qualities which make them different is the key to developing a sustainable tourism industry.

With these objectives in mind, Table 3.5 provides an assessment of existing and potential products and markets the PMCs could promote. The listing of an activity or attraction as a “potential” product is not meant to offer that it is not already part of the destination product, only that it has the potential to become far more important. Neither is the list of potential products meant to be exhaustive; instead they focus on those attributes or qualities which, given proper development and adequately resourced and well-targeted

Table 3.5: Existing and Potential Product/Market Match

Principal	Existing Products	Existing Markets	Potential Products	Potential Markets
Fiji	Mainly price driven beach/resort holidays, general interest sightseeing, "Shop Window" cultural displays.	Australian and New Zealand families, older couples, honeymooners.	Scuba Diving Cultural Tourism Eco/Soft Adventure Events	- North American, Japanese Fishermen - North American, Japanese European Divers - Third Age/Special Interest Markets - Young Japanese and North Americans - Australia and New Zealand sports people
FSM	Diving World War II	US and Japanese dive travel market	Cultural Tourism (Yap) Cultural Heritage-Nan Madol/Leluh (Pohpnei, Kosrae) Sport fishing (Blue Marlin)	- Third Age/Special Interest Markets - North American, Japanese, Australian
Kiribati	Sport Fishing	US sport fishing market	Bird Watching (Line Islands)	- Special Interest Groups
Marshall Islands	Diving Sport Fishing	US and Japanese dive travel and sport fishing market	Sport Fishing (Blue Marlin) Inter-atoll cruises	- North American, Japanese, Australian
Solomon Islands	Diving	Australia, New Zealand and US dive travel markets	Cultural Tourism Bird Watching (e.g., Megapodes on Savo) Sport Fishing (Black Marlin)	- Third Age/Special Interest - Special Interest Groups - Australian, Japanese
Tonga	Cultural Sightseeing	Mainly FIT couples, half on multi-destination trips	Marine Ecology (bird watching) Cruising/Yacht Charter, Sport fishing Culture and pre-history	- Special Interest Groups - Third Age, Special Interest, Sailors - Third Age/Special Interest
Vanuatu	Mainly price driven sightseeing, beach/resort holidays	Mainly Australian couples, honeymooners	Cultural Tourism Nature-based Tourism Diving (Santo) Wrecks, Coral	- Special Interest (European) - Third Age/Special Interest - North American, Japanese and Australian
Western Samoa	General Interest, Sightseeing, "Shop Window" cultural displays	Mainly couples, one third on package tours, two thirds FITS.	Cultural tourism Nature based tourism (e.g., Lava fields)	- Special Interest (European) - Special Interest

marketing, have the potential to pull people from half way around the world.

The inadequacy of information services also features as a major shortcoming in several countries. Likewise tour guide services are frequent sources of dissatisfaction with guides frequently not being able to impart anything but the most elementary general information. Eco-tourism, in particular, would call for well trained tour guides who are knowledgeable about each country's natural attractions. This is an important aspect of adding value to the tourist product and, apart from improved tour guide training, may require licensing and/or accreditation to maintain standards.

Marketing of the PMC tourism product merits improvements. Cooperative marketing and packaging with major neighboring destinations presents another opportunity to undertake cost effective marketing. Familiarization trips conducted by Air New Zealand as part of their "Project Pride" program and which included Pacific island countries are a good example of this. Further research of back-to-back fly cruise operations between Sydney and Fiji, re-establishment of the Honiara-Cairns service and joint packaging of North Queensland and Solomon Islands, joint packaging of Tonga and Western Samoa with New Zealand, all represent different ways in which PMCs can "piggy back" on their larger neighbors.

Air Access

Prime among the constraints to tourism development are the lack of direct air services, lack of frequency and generally high cost of travel to island countries combined with the high cost, infrequency and often unreliability of intra-regional and domestic inter-island services.

Airlines in the South Pacific have been plagued by low-capacity utilization rates. This, in turn, has led to severe financial losses, despite high passenger changes for the national carriers of Western Samoa, Solomon Islands, Tonga, FSM and Kiribati. Attempts have been made, however, to improve the financial management of air services by:

- Appointment by a number of governments of experienced managers from outside the relevant country carrier (e.g. Polynesian Airlines, Solomon Airlines, Royal Tongan Airlines);

- Cooperation through code-sharing on a fairly broad range of services between various points; and

- Some rationalization of aircraft fleet, with both Polynesian Airlines and Air Vanuatu disposing of uneconomic craft and routes.

The Relationship between Tourism and Aviation. The two elements are inextricably linked in terms of the nature and potential viability of air services in the South Pacific, although the two are sometimes in total conflict. The basic dilemma is how to provide adequate and efficient air services between and among the various island nations when the level of traffic is so low. The development of tourism to boost the total number of travellers is, in turn, hampered by the lack of services available as well as suitable infrastructure. It is important to note that in most instances, the level of infrastructure could not handle and cater for an overnight stay for a B747 aircraft load.

The financial situation of most of the island nations is such that it is impractical to run services at a loss in order to build up traffic, especially if this is done without a coordinated tourism plan, or else the current situation causing such concern at the South Pacific Forum is the end result. Even in Fiji, with a relatively sound airline and a reasonable tourism market, forming the basis for commercially-stable scheduled services, is dependent on the further development of tourism for its financial well-being and prospective growth.

Broadening Air Access

Only Nadi (Fiji), Faleolo (Western Samoa), Fua'amotu (Tonga) and Bauerfield (Vanuatu) airports have the runway capability to accept wide bodied aircraft, and of these, only Nadi has the terminal facilities, ground transport and accommodation capacity to accommodate a B747 with a full payload. Of the others, only Vanuatu has the volume of visitors to justify developing airport infrastructure to accommodate wide-bodied services to long haul destinations.

Even if they had the financial resources FSM, Kiribati and the Marshall Islands do not have the physical or human resources to accommodate the scale of tourism required to support viable wide-bodied services. Smaller aircraft and greater service frequency is likely to do more for these countries, especially if more competitive "island hopper" fares can be introduced.

The dilemma of insufficient air access limiting resort investment is best illustrated by Vanuatu. There are limits on airline capacity arising from Air Vanuatu's aircraft leasing arrangements with Qantas only for four days per week, but initiatives have been made to increase the frequency. Low visitor numbers, in turn, have discouraged investment in new tourist accommodation in both Efate and Espiritu Santo. Although Bauerfield Airport at Vila can now handle limited movements of B767 aircraft on short haul services and direct services to long haul source countries such as Japan it is constrained because the topography prevents the take-off of fully loaded B767s. There are no such constraints on Luganville Airport on Santo where the runway could be upgraded at an estimated cost of US$9.0 million (plus the cost of terminal improvements) to permit the introduction of direct services to markets such as Japan and Singapore (which is a major hub for European travellers to the Asia Pacific Region). Quite clearly, until investors can see that this constraint on access to long haul markets is being remedied they will not proceed with new tourism projects. Similarly, until airlines can see that there is sufficient accommodation and tourist product being put in place to support a new service they, in turn, will not consider providing the service.

In the case of the Solomon Islands, the quantum of tourism infrastructure and the realistic rate at which it can be expanded suggests that for the foreseeable future the volume of visitors is unlikely to be sufficient to justify wide bodied services. What is important for the Solomons is to develop its intra-regional links and in particular to reinstate the service to Cairns which offers the Solomon Islands the best opportunity to access large numbers of Japanese and European visitors to Far North Queensland which, in 1993, numbered 154,000 and 177,000 respectively. This will be greatly assisted by following the example of Vanuatu and expediting the construction of a new international terminal at Honiara.

In the case of Tonga and Western Samoa access to longer haul markets is likely to be best achieved by expanding code sharing arrangements. This can provide better access to the major South Pacific gateways of Sydney, Auckland and Nadi. It would also improve access through increased frequency utilizing smaller narrow-bodied aircraft, especially between Tongatapu and Apia and Tongatapu and Nadi via Vava'u.

Domestic Aviation Issues. Within individual countries the infrequency of services, the high cost, baggage limits on small aircraft and the perceived unreliability of inter-island services is a major constraint on developing tourism opportunities out of the main centers. The difficulties of operating low volume inter-island services which provide essential passenger and freight services for local people are not underestimated. However, the fact remains that, even if they can obtain seats on inter-island services, FIT tourists are often deterred by the fear that delays or re-scheduled flights may cause them (or their baggage) to miss international connections. Also, tourists or their agents may be advised that inter-island services are over-booked by locals but not infrequently flights depart with empty seats due to "no-shows". Vanair, for example, is now taking a much firmer line on pre-payment at the time of booking to overcome this.

Also in Vanuatu, Vanair is planning to increase passenger and especially freight capacity between Efate and Santo and between Efate and Tanna by the acquisition of a turboprop aircraft. This would facilitate the development of tourist facilities on Santo and Tanna (and even other neighboring islands with additional feeder services using Twin Otters or Islanders). However, it would also require access to other intra-regional routes such as Noumea (currently served by Air Vanuatu's 18 seat Bandierante) and Nadi to be viable and would require the upgrading of the Lenakel strip on Tanna to a 1,400 meters minimum compacted coral standard.

Kiribati inter-island air services are only available in the Gilbert, Line, and Phoenix Groups, and in Western Samoa the destruction of the airstrip at Asau by Cyclone Ofa in February 1990 has curtailed access to the west end of Savai'i. Both the Western Samoa Tourism Development Plan and the WSVB have identified the replacement of this facility as an urgent need to stimulate visitation and further product development opportunities on Savai'i.

Aviation Reform Priorities

The future of aviation in the South Pacific is linked so closely with the future of tourism that any programs of regionalization or rationalization must take into account the urgent need for infrastructure development and investment in the tourism industry, together with a forward-looking marketing and promotions plan to attract not only international visitors but international carriers. One of the most difficult tasks will be to remove the fear of competition which appears to be present in all the South Pacific carriers, even Air Pacific, and to convince both the carriers and their Governments of the benefits of a more open, bilateral system or even some form of pragmatic multilateral arrangements.

Rationalization and Regionalization. There is no question that an essential element for survival for the airlines of the South Pacific is the rationalization of aircraft, routes and services. This needs to be combined with the development of a network of regional routes and routes beyond the individual island countries to serve at least the major markets of Australia and New Zealand other than on a point-to-point basis from each capital.

The major problem facing all the Pacific island carriers, even Air Pacific, is the generally low level of traffic to and between countries. This represents the classic "chicken and egg" situation in aviation terms—whether providing the aircraft and services to cater for a larger volume of traffic will stimulate growth in passenger numbers, or alternatively, whether the number of visitors to the various countries should grow to a certain level before further services or additional or larger aircraft are justified.

Role of Air Pacific. Air Pacific is of the view that there is sufficient inter-island traffic for all regional carriers to consolidate over a Nadi hub, and is attempting to convince the various governments accordingly. While this strategy makes sound commercial sense, its success is likely to be hampered by the attitude and business relations of the various smaller airlines in terms of their dealings with Air Pacific. The very difficult task for Fiji and Air Pacific is to avoid the tag of "interfering" or trying to dominate the region while providing rationalized assistance to other smaller South Pacific airlines via commercial arrangements which cannot always cater for the individual carriers' interests rather than the general well-being of air services in the region.

Cruise Operations. At present opportunities to attract more large cruise ships are limited by the duration of cruises, which are relatively short, apart from the seniors market, and the distance from the home port, principally Sydney. Traditionally the cruise market has been locally sourced (Australia and New Zealand), but the Australian Tourist Commission (ATC) is actively promoting "fly-cruise" business from the USA. Although Fiji has already been down this track without success, there is the potential, with the ATCs interest in this market, to develop Fiji-Australia cruise packages provided airline schedules can be tailored to permit back-to-back cruise operations.

Supporting Infrastructure

Human Resource Development

The low skill levels and poor service delivery are an oft repeated criticism of the tourism industry within PMCs. With the exception of Fiji the scale of the tourism industry in PMCs is too small to support the establishment of training institutions at the national level. A regional approach to formal training supported by in-service training is therefore the most efficient and cost effective approach utilizing means such as the proposed mobile training unit in Western Samoa. At the formal tertiary level the University of the South Pacific offers certificate and degree courses in tourism and the Western Samoa Polytechnic is about to introduce a Diploma Course in Business and Tourism. Vocational training is provided at the Fiji School of Hotel and Catering. In-service training in Fiji is undertaken by the Fiji National Training Council. But more needs to be done in shifting the training function to the industry.

Outside of Fiji, the Tourism Council of the South Pacific has a mobile team which travels around member countries conducting short in-service training courses. Beyond this there are very few training opportunities other than in-house training by tourism operators, scarcely any of whom have a training manager on staff. It is difficult to support a case for national vocational training establishments in that they are difficult to staff with appropriately qualified and experienced teachers and which may run the risk of turning out trained people for whom there are no jobs. A more effective approach may be through extension of the TCSP programs, in-service training programs intensive pre-opening training by operators.

Training initiatives should also focus on guide training in order to add greater value to the ecotourism product of PMCs. This is already happening through proposed NZODA Nature and Adventure Tourism Programs in Western Samoa and AusAID ecotourism guide/interpretation training in Fiji.

Physical Infrastructure

Roads. In many of the PMCs the standard of roads is a constraint to access to many tourism resources. Road standards outside the towns and road networks in general are limited. The principal exceptions are Fiji, where it is possible to circumnavigate Viti Levu on sealed roads for all but 20km of gravel; Western Samoa, where roads on both Upolu and Savai'i permit circumnavigation of the islands plus cross island alternatives on Upolu and Yap State, which has a good quality circuit road. Elsewhere, some of the needs are:

- in Vanuatu the upgrading of the Efate "round-the-island" road from Port Vila to Takara to further improve the tourist potential;
- Solomon Islands, the extension of the sealed road beyond White River in Guadalcanal, and the extension of the road to the southern tip of Malaita, which is being funded by the EU;
- and in Tonga the improvement of access roads and parking at principal attractions as identified in the Tonga National Tourism Plan.

Public Transport. In several of the PMCs there is a need to improve the standard of taxis through more rigorous licensing controls, the availability of taxis (e.g. ensuring that they are available to effect airport transfers regardless of arrival and departure times) and, in the absence of meters, to establish a schedule of standard fares which are well advertised in airports and hotels. Similarly in some countries more rigorous licensing of tour operators is required to eliminate substandard operators who undercut tour prices through the use of substandard, and sometimes unsafe equipment.

Water Transport. Depending on relative proximity water transfers may be the only option, such as transfers within individual coral atolls, or a preferable alternative to air transfers. Where the option for water transfers exists new tourist facilities or access to attractions should be planned with this in mind. For example, Nan Madol, Pohnpei's primary attraction can only be accessed by water and accessibility is dictated by tides. As visitor numbers build up, consideration will need to be given to the most appropriate type of vessel to access this attraction in the least intrusive way, regardless of tides, in order to control visitor flows and avoid over-crowding the site.

Tourism and Environment

The major existing and potential tourist markets for PMCs have certain expectations about the quality of services and products which they use or purchase, and about the environment in which these are experienced. One of the major disappointments for people visiting PMCs is the general lack of cleanliness, the untidy and unkempt appearance not only of towns, villages and even visitor attractions themselves but also of accommodation establishments. In several countries this is compounded by widespread dumping of household refuse, vehicle bodies and other junk. Some countries, such as Western Samoa, seem to manage the problem well through the strength of the village culture and through government incentives. Elsewhere, such as in Chuuk State, where the Chuuk Visitors Bureau has initiated a beautification program, junk removal and garbage collection service, the problem is still acute and will require wider community education to achieve results.

Tourism is also closely related to the quality of the coastal environment. On the one hand tourism development could exert pressure on the coastal environment through for example, contraction, land filling and sedimentation. This points to the need for intensified coastal zone management. On the other hand, a clean coastal environment can enhance the tourism potential considerably.

Role of Government

Planning

Tourism development should take place in the context of an overall tourist strategy or a spatial plan. There are a number of externalities which argue strongly against leaving all decisions related to the location of tourist facilities to the private sector. With limited financial resources, infrastructural facilities cannot be laid on wherever development takes place. Moreover development in some areas should not be allowed to continue to the point where there could be serious environmental damage. Individual investment decisions could clearly impose costs on other parts of the economy.

Planning for tourism needs to be integrated into the broader framework but should not be over-prescriptive. At the same time, however, it should be very strong on protecting prime environmental resources and beware of the cumulative effects of small compromises. Essentially what is required is an inventory of protected sites that have the potential to be tourist attractions of international significance and which should be managed as such. Beyond this governments should not be too rigid about where tourism development should occur other than to actively encourage tourism development where it will support the provision or upgrading of infrastructure services to the community at large. Such simple principles are usually congruent with the needs of genuine investors and operators who want sites that not only have tourist appeal but which can be most easily serviced and which are (or can easily be made) readily accessible to their markets.

Policy and Regulatory Environment

In the face of increasing competition for scarce capital resources, an overriding objective for PMC governments must be to create a policy and regulatory environment which is conducive to tourism development and expansion.

From the standpoint of investors this is a question of confidence—confidence in the certainty, consistency and timeliness of decision making in the investment and development process. From the standpoint of operators they need confidence that infrastructure and services which are rightly the role of governments, or government business enterprises such as airlines, to provide will be provided and maintained and that government fees or charges will not be increased unreasonably, or without notice.

Governments need to be aware that package prices are generally negotiated more than a year in advance and subsequent cost increases cannot be passed on to the customer. Similarly if, for whatever reason (e.g. loss of an air service), an operator is unable to deliver the advertised product, there are increasingly onerous legal liability implications, especially in major growth markets such as the European Union and Japan which have tough consumer protection laws.

Without confidence in the ability of PMC destinations to deliver the product overseas wholesalers and retailers simply will not package or promote them.

Both regionally and individually the role of PMC governments needs to be framed within a consistent set of principles which:

- develops a vision for the future of tourism and its place in the community;
- ensures the timely provision and maintenance of essential infrastructure;
- provides incentives to facilitate changes necessary to develop tourism;
- ensures an equitable formula for the collection of charges and taxes;
- ensures a free and orderly market place; and
- protects the long term interests of society.

Within this framework governments should consider tourism proposals on the basis of five fundamental criteria:

- economic viability;
- environmental sustainability;
- appropriateness to local culture;
- contribution to diversity of the tourism product; and
- preservation of flexibility (i.e. does not overcommit resources to a single project or product).

Country Specific Initiatives

Within this broad framework, individual country strategies will need to be framed. Key country initiatives might include:

- **Fiji**. In order to sustain tourism growth the Fijian tourism product needs to be strengthened and diversified. This includes further expansion of existing activities such as diving and game fishing and a greater focus on nature based and cultural tourism. At present Fiji is caught in a trap where mid-scale accommodation in secondary destinations is achieving poor occupancy levels, and the high occupancy levels are being achieved by up-scale resorts at the expense of returns, hence there is no incentive for new investment. Nevertheless, there is a growing demand for up-market, three to five star hotels. Air Pacific's new long haul services to Los Angeles and Osaka and Air New Zealand's new service to Nagoya via Nadi present an opportunity to break this nexus. More innovative packaging of accommodation products offering a combination of up-scale resort accommodation and mid-scale accommodation in secondary areas with a nature/cultural focus offers two benefits. First, it could improve the performance and encourage the development of more dispersed second tier accommodation and second, by reducing the average length of stay in up-scale accommodation, could assist in improving yields without necessarily increasing package prices. This in turn could provide the stimulus for further investment in new resort accommodation which will be needed to support current and future expansion of Air Pacific services.

- **Tonga**. Tonga urgently needs a catalyst to precipitate action. The recommendation contained in the Tonga National Tourism Plan to nominate the Ha'apai Group for World Heritage listing may be useful. It would attract world attention to Tonga's natural resources; it would also provide a stimulus to the development of tourism beyond Tongatapu.

- **Western Samoa**. Western Samoa is the one country that has recorded a fall in visitor levels over the last five years. However, the tourism prospects for Western Samoa appear more positive than for most other PMCs notwithstanding the problems besetting Polynesian Airlines. There is a positive community attitude towards tourism, a well conceived Tourism Development Plan is in place, and the structure and performance of the WSVB is becoming increasingly professional and is supported by some well targeted bilateral aid from New Zealand. What is lacking is an investment strategy which will facilitate the development of much needed tourist accommodation and other facilities as well as adequate information regarding air connections to Western Samoa in airline booking systems.

- **Vanuatu**. Vanuatu's tourism development could, no doubt, benefit from the upgrading of Bauerfield and Luganville Airports to enable wide bodied air services for long haul markets. This is the catalyst which can be expected to trigger direct foreign investment and which will support government policy to decentralize tourism and economic development especially to Santo and the immediately adjoining islands. This project was estimated to cost around US$15 million, but has recently been scaled-down to an extension of the runway at the Luganville Airport at a cost of about US$9 million. In any event, the project has to be approached with caution since it is likely to cause severe fiscal pressures during the next two years unless other items of expenditures are cut to reduce the deficit. Commercial borrowing in particular will exacerbate the debt service burden and is inappropriate.

- **Solomon Islands**. Australia provides the best avenue for the Solomon Islands to access new long haul markets. Priority should therefore be given to reinstating the link with Cairns, where hotel accommodation is now at a premium, and seeking to develop joint promotion and packaging into markets such as Japan. This will require high priority to be given to the new international terminal at Henderson Airport. If the Cairns link can be re-established and successfully developed, this may be sufficient to trigger the development of long-stalled projects such as the Doma Resort, Anuha Island and the Governor General's residence site in Honiara, as well as new projects in the Western Province.

- **FSM**. Each of the Micronesian States needs to focus on improving the quality, access to and, where appropriate, the interpretation of its prime attractions; in the case of Yap, its unique cultural heritage; in Chuuk, the diving opportunities of Truk Lagoon; in Pohnpei, Nan Madol and in Kosrae its ecology and the Leluh ruins. None of the States can expect to become long stay destinations, other than for special interest visitors such as divers and sports fishermen. Therefore they need to work on developing convenient and economical island hopping packages. In the case of Yap this means capitalizing on traffic between Guam and Palau, and in the case of Chuuk, Pohnpei and Kosrae between Guam and Hawaii.

- **Kiribati**. Given its remoteness, Kiribati has little option but to focus on promoting its special interest attractions. The most urgent need is to improve the frequency and reduce the cost of access. Kiribati should endeavor to achieve this through the proposed rationalization of regional air services agreed to at the 1994 South Pacific Forum in Brisbane.

- **Marshall Islands**. Given it remoteness, limited land resources, shortage of potable water and land tenure problems, as illustrated by the aborted Erikub Atoll resort project, the Marshalls need to focus on the tourism potential of its marine resources. In the immediate future the further development of sport fishing, which is already established, should be the primary focus. The market potential and viability of developing inter-atoll cruises connecting with air services through Majuro and Kwajalein should also be researched.

Priorities for Action

Accessibility. The geographical isolation and dispensed nature of PMCs is a critical constraint making access to tourist markets difficult and costly. Therefore, a fundamental priority is to improve air access, flight frequency and fare levels. This calls for rationalization of aircraft, routes and services combined with the development of an improved network of regional routes (and inter-island routes within countries) and improved links with larger neighboring destinations and source markets (e.g. Australia and New Zealand) other than on a point-to-point basis from each capital.

Product. It is the unique cultures of the South Pacific which distinguish PMCs from other sun, sand and sea destinations. It is therefore vitally important not only to protect, but also to emphasize these unique cultural attributes in marketing the South Pacific. Associated with this is the need to improve the presentation and interpretation of the cultural heritage of the Pacific as a means of adding value to the tourist product. This should be accompanied by improved protection, presentation and interpretation of the natural environment in which these Pacific cultures developed.

Government Role. Globally the competition for development capital is becoming increasingly intense. In order to compete successfully, PMC governments must create a positive investment climate by ensuring that potential investors have confidence in the investment and development process. There must be confidence in the certainty, consistency and timeliness of the decision making process; confidence that government commitments (e.g. provision of infrastructure or air services) will be honored; confidence that there will not be unforeseen or excessive increases in government fees and charges and confidence that regulations will be applied consistently and that there will not be overlapping or duplication of regulations by different levels of government or government agencies.

4. FISHERIES

Overview: *This chapter reviews the status of the fisheries sector in the PMCs, in order to identify key issues which offer the greatest opportunity to increase benefits derived by island populations. The chapter concludes that collective action in management and licensing of offshore tuna resources will be necessary to generate financial benefits to PMCs today, and ensure sustainability of the resource for future generations. Coastal fisheries are very important in terms of food security and their contribution to household income, but appear to be under pressure from excessive exploitation throughout the region. Urgent attention to management of coastal resources is thus needed.*

Background

Fish is the largest single source of animal protein and the fastest growing food commodity in international trade, providing direct and indirect employment to over 100 million people globally. Over 1 billion people rely on fish and shellfish as their main protein source. Of the top forty countries ranked by the share of animal protein derived from fish, thirty-nine are developing countries. World production of fish currently averages about 100 million tons per year, and up to half of the portion consumed by humans is produced by smallholders.

Over the past fifty years global fish catches have grown from about 20 million tons to about 90 million tons in 1989 before dropping off presumably because of overfishing. Underlying this rapid increase in fisheries output, there has been an astonishing increase in the global fishing effort, both in terms of the numbers of vessels and technological capacity—total world gross registered tons of fishing vessels more than doubled between 1970 and 1989. As a consequence of the rapid expansion of fishing effort, all but two of the world's 15 major fishing areas have experienced declines in productivity and entire fisheries have disappeared. The global fishing fleet is excessively large and heavily subsidized—the total operating cost of the world fleet exceeds its revenues by about US$54 billion yearly. The general lack of property rights in fisheries is considered to be a major contributor to over investment and overexploitation.

The PMCs' exclusive economic zones (EEZs) cover nearly 12 million square kilometers. By comparison, their total land area is meager at just under 64,000 square kilometers. Thus, the countries of the region look toward ocean resources as an important means to advance their economic development, through the creation of employment and the generation of exports and income. The fisheries sector in the PMCs is dualistic, consisting of *offshore fisheries* and *nearshore* or *coastal fisheries.*

Fisheries have traditionally occupied an important position in Pacific Island societies, which have relied on *nearshore or coastal resources* for much of their food and subsistence needs. More recently, they have played a role in supplementing cash incomes of coastal communities and in generating foreign exchange. Coastal fisheries are characterized by low-capital, labor-intensive fishing methods targeting reef and lagoon species. Exploitation of offshore resources—mainly tuna—is a modern phenomenon introduced to the region by foreign countries aiming to supply international markets. This is a technology and capital-intensive activity, employing modern methods and equipment in which few PMCs, with their scarce resources, are able to participate directly.

The main issues facing the PMCs in ensuring the sustainability of and increasing the returns to fisheries are:

- How best to maximize resource rents derived from fishing access fees;[1]

- How to protect offshore resources to ensure that they are not over-fished;

- How to manage investment in the sector, particularly foreign investment, and further define the appropriate roles of the public and private sectors;

- How to protect vulnerable coastal resources from overexploitation, given the fragility of coastal ecosystems, and the strong socio-economic links of this sub sector with nutrition and broad-based income generation; and

- Identifying and exploiting income-generating opportunities for coastal fisheries.

Economic Contribution

Fisheries development in the PMCs encompasses a diverse range of activities—from purely subsistence activities relying on traditional methods, to commercial fishing, and downstream industrial activities in processing. Fishing is clearly an economically important activity, especially since in all PMCs a significant share of households participate in some form of fishing, often on a part-time basis.

The fisheries sector appears to have a modest share of GDP in most PMCs, averaging about 7 percent in the Solomon Islands and the Marshall Islands and only about 2 percent in Fiji.[2] This distribution is in keeping with Fiji's diversified economic base relative to the other PMCs. These national accounts statistics clearly understate the economic importance of the sector because they usually fail to account adequately for artisanal and subsistence production.

In most Pacific Island countries, fisheries make an economic contribution through employment generation, import substitution, the receipt of access fees and through exports. Figure 4.1 shows the export shares of fisheries for the PMCs for 1988 and 1993. Most remarkable is the large increase in the share of fish in total exports for FSM and the Marshall Islands. For FSM the share of fish in total exports nearly doubled to 86 percent and for the Marshall Islands it increased five-fold to over 80 percent. This transformation is due to the relatively recent entry to export markets of these two countries, coupled with much untapped resource potential. Thus, fish exports were growing from a small base, while other export commodities remained unchanged. The performance of fisheries exports in the remaining countries has been stagnant over the 1988-93 period, largely because of the poor prices prevailing in world markets. The relatively low shares for countries such as Tonga and Western Samoa mainly reflect their poor resource endowment compared to the other countries. Nevertheless, fish exports are important in all the PMCs.

All PMCs receive access fees from licensing foreign fishing vessels. A comparison of these fees

Figure 4.1: FISH EXPORTS (% OF TOTAL EXPORTS)

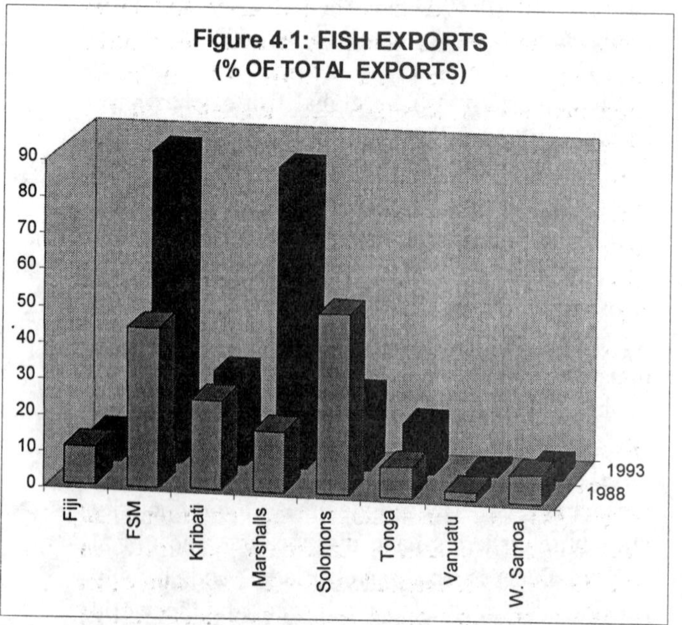

Source: National sources.

[1] Issues in rent collection are a complex area, covered in greater detail in a background paper.

[2] Based on detailed sectoral information compiled by country.

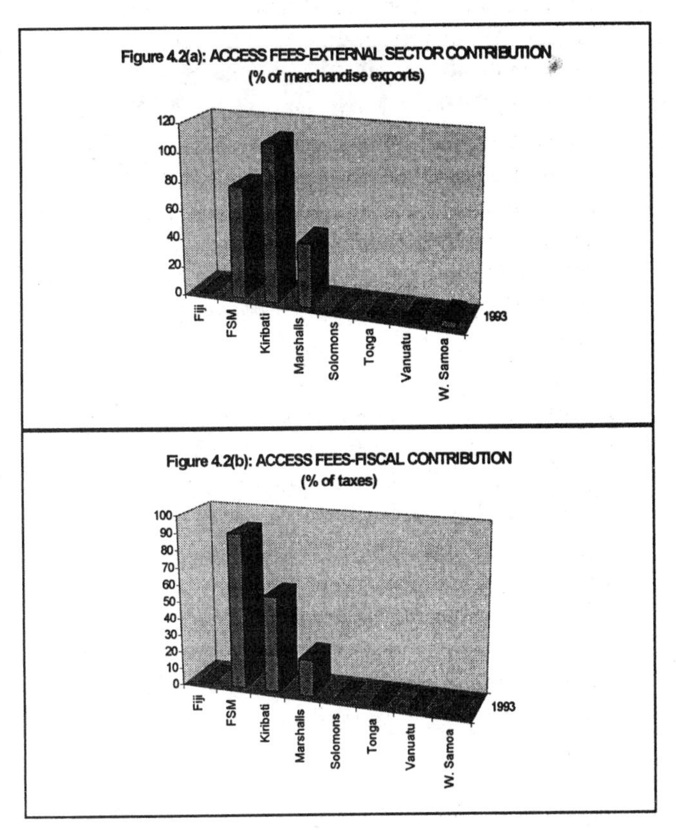

Source: National source, FFA and estimates.

in terms of their balance of payments and fiscal contributions across countries is quite illustrative (see Figures 4.2(a) and 4.2(b)). As might be expected access fees are very important in the three countries with the best tuna resources and catching conditions—FSM, Kiribati and Marshalls. In the remaining countries access fees are much less important. Thus, the PMCs are characterized by great variation in the distribution of offshore resources and consequently in the economic importance of the sector.

Table 4.1 compares key characteristics of the fisheries sector and the environment within which it must operate in the PMCs. The table also highlights key institutional and environmental factors which constrain fisheries development in the Pacific. These include the relatively high costs of labor and other inputs, and the prominent role of the public sector, which often serves to crowd-out private investors. Moreover, public sector involvement in commercial activities in the Pacific, as elsewhere in the world, has a poor financial track record, usually necessitating scarce budgetary resources being expended in support of financially ailing enterprises. Other factors include the scarcity of management capacity, skills, entrepreneurial spirit and research services.

Exploitation of coastal resources in the PMCs is well developed and varies widely across countries, with activities concentrated in *bêche-de- mer* (dried sea cucumber), shell-gathering and processing, reef fish and some aquaculture. Table 4.10 presents a summary of activities in the sector for the PMCs. From the available data, it is clear that coastal fisheries are significant compared to offshore fisheries in terms of output value and employment, but to a much lesser extent in terms of export value (see Table 4.2).

More important than this, however, is the role that fisheries play in generating broad-based benefits for local communities and guaranteeing food security. As many as 83 percent of the coastal households of the Solomon Islands, 35 and 99 percent respectively, of the rural households of Vanuatu and Kiribati; 87 percent of the households in the Marshall Islands; and half of the rural households in Upolu (Western Samoa) fish, primarily for local consumption. In the Solomon Islands, moreover, about 17 percent of all households integrated into the cash economy sell coastal fisheries products. By contrast, the industrial and commercial sector provided full-time employment to 1,097 fishers in 1992, or less than 4 percent of formal employment.

Nearshore fisheries, including deep-slope demersal resources, also account for approximately 65 percent of total fisheries exports in Kiribati, about 10 percent in Fiji, Marshall Islands, and Solomon Islands, and less than 5 percent in FSM. The two most important nearshore export commodities are bêche-de-mer and trochus products, followed by finfish and aquarium fish. Seaweed exports are also important in Kiribati.

Table 4.1: Selected Attributes of Fisheries Sector in the Pacific

	FSM	Marshall Islands	Kiribati	Fiji	Solomon Islands	Vanuatu	Tonga	Western Samoa
Resource endowments:								
Offshore	•••	•••	•••	••	•••	•	•	•
Deepslope	••	••	••	•••	••	••	••	•
Nearshore	••	••	••	•••	•••	••	•	•
Economic importance	•••	•••	•••	••	•••	••	••	•
Inputs/labor costs	•••	•••	•	••	•	••	•	•
Transportation development	••	•••	•	•••	••	•	••	•••
Infrastructure development	•••	•••	•	•••	••	•	••	••
Foreign invest. climate	•••	•••	•	•••	••	••	•	••
Role of public sector	•••	•••	•••	••	•••	••	••	•••
Role of private sector	••	••	•	•••	•	•	•••	••
Training services	••	•	••	••	•••	••	••	•
Information/Research Services	•	•	•	•••	••	••	••	••
Marketing support	•	••	••	••	••	•••	••	•
Customary tenure systems	√	√	W	√	√	√	N	√

Note: •=Low, ••=Medium, •••=High, √=yes, W= Weak; N=No.
Source: World Bank staff.

Table 4.2: Artisanal & Commercial Nearshore Production, 1989-92
(US$ million, average per year)

	Fish	Shellfish	Other	Total
FSM	0.9	0.6	0.0	1.5
Fiji	11.7	3.0	4.3	19.0
Kiribati	3.6	0.0	1.2	4.8
Marshall Islands	0.3	0.4	0.0	0.7
Solomon Islands	0.1	1.7	2.6	4.3
Tonga	2.7	0.1	0.0	2.8
Vanuatu	0.5	1.0	0.1	1.5
Western Samoa	0.3	0.0	0.0	0.3
Total	**20.0**	**6.7**	**8.2**	**35.0**

Excludes subsistence production.
Source: Dalzell and Adams, 1994.

Table 4.3: Subsistence Fisheries in Selected Pacific Island Countries, 1992

	Volume (thousand MT)	Value to Consumer (US$ mill.)	Foreign Exchange Savings (US$ mill.)
Fiji	16.4	6.3	8.2
Solomon Islands	12.7	7.8	7.7
Vanuatu	3.1	2.2	1.3
W. Samoa	3.1	0.5	2.6
Total	**35.2**	**16.8**	**19.8**

Source: World Bank staff estimates.

Despite increasing commercialization of the catch, subsistence fisheries remain a vital source of animal protein in the region. This is particularly true in isolated and small islands, among coastal communities, and in areas where sources of cash income are scarce. While their importance is generally recognized among PMC governments, the value of subsistence fisheries is largely unknown and tends to be ignored in national accounts. Table 4.3 presents estimates of the value of subsistence fisheries in terms of the output, import savings, and value to consumers.

While these estimates are subject to a certain degree of uncertainty, they suggest that subsistence fisheries play an important role in the economies of PMCs. In Fiji, their value to consumers is equivalent to 54 percent of the retail value of the total artisanal catch; and in Vanuatu, their value to the consumer is equivalent to more than three times the retail value of the commercial and artisanal fisheries in Port Vila and Espiritu Santo.

Significant foreign exchange savings can also be attributed to this activity, which reduces the need to rely on food imports. For Vanuatu, these savings were equivalent to the value of all fish and meat products imported during 1992. In Western Samoa, the foreign exchange savings exceeded the value of imported preserved fish in 1991/92 by 35 percent. In the Solomon Islands, the value of subsistence fisheries was equivalent to more than 60 percent of the value of canned fish exports. The protection of subsistence fisheries should therefore remain a high priority for PMC governments.

Offshore Fisheries

Introduction. The main offshore fish resources in the region are tuna, especially *albacore, bigeye, skipjack and yellowfin.* Although not as sought after as bluefin tuna, these species are nevertheless quite valuable. The two major end-uses of this tuna are the fresh fish markets of Japan and increasingly the US and Europe, and canning in water and oil. This area represents one of the richest tuna fishing grounds in the world supplying over one-half of the world's canned tuna, and a significant proportion of fresh tuna.

Tuna are a highly migratory and mobile species. As a result the tuna resources cannot be apportioned out by any one country but consist of several regional stocks. This gives rise to a number of important issues concerning both the management and exploitation of the resource.

The total tuna catch in the region has been increasing steadily over the past decade, as indicated in Table 4.4 which shows the catch for the statistical area served by the South Pacific Commission (SPC). According to this, the total tuna catch rose to over 1 million metric tons (MT) in 1991 and declined thereafter. The PMCs' share of the regional catch is relatively small, approximately 13 percent in 1993, reflecting both their endowment of tuna resources and the fact that the SPC region covers 26 countries.

In 1993, over 90 percent of the PMC tuna catch was attributed to three countries—FSM, Kiribati and Marshalls. The bulk of this fish was captured by purse-seine vessels which increased significantly in number, from 1980 to 1992. The resultant increase in purse-seine activity has been the main factor behind the increase in the regional catch.

In the SPC region, the purse-seine fishery represented about 84.2 percent of the total volume and 50.6 percent of the total value in 1992, whereas the long-line fishery with only 9.6 percent of the volume accounted for 41.1 percent of the value. The final destination of purse-seine tuna are canneries, and of long-line tuna mainly the Japanese *sashimi* (raw fish) market.

In addition to the Oceanic Fisheries Program of the SPC (OFP), which represents 26 member countries and is responsible for tuna stock assessment and information processing, the South Pacific Forum Fisheries Agency (FFA) with headquarters in Honiara, is the lead regional agency providing management and logistical assistance to its 16 member states in licensing, management, control and surveillance. All 8 World Bank PMCs are also members of FFA.

Table 4.4: Catch in the SPC Statistical Area, 1984-93
(thousand metric tons)

	Albacore	Bigeye	Skipjack	Yellowfin	Total
1984	19.6	32.2	437.7	138.3	627.9
1985	27.5	40.9	371.3	129.4	568.6
1986	32.4	32.1	436.7	129.2	632.3
1987	23.5	41.2	407.5	187.7	659.9
1988	33.3	35.4	542.6	133.7	744.9
1989	47.6	33.9	527.0	184.3	794.8
1990	30.6	53.8	579.7	208.8	872.8
1991	24.9	41.1	754.7	231.1	1051.7
1992	41.8	45.0	689.9	272.4	1049.0
1993	40.9	46.7	552.3	291.7	931.7

Source: South Pacific Commission, Tuna Fishery Yearbook, 1993.

Maximizing Rents from Offshore Tuna Fisheries

Need for Management Strategy. The market-led growth of the tuna fishing effort in the Central and Western Pacific during the last few years is becoming a matter of concern. Much progress has been achieved to date to enhance regional management of the resources through a variety of agreements—most notably Minimum Terms and

Conditions under the Nauru Agreements, the Niue Treaty, the Palau Agreement which attempts to limit purse seine licenses, the Regional Register which has proven an effective enforcement tool against violators, and the recent trends towards multilateral agreements. Despite this, there are several major decisions that still need to be taken by the Pacific Island countries if an effective *fisheries management regime* (FMR) is to be established at the regional level.

Based on the best available information, the tuna stocks in the wider Pacific region are not believed to be biologically overexploited at this time. However, the levels of under reporting are believed to be high. In addition, the practice of illegal fishing and discard of by-catch may bias catch statistics which together with tagging work form the basis for stock assessments. Perhaps most importantly, the large capital investments in the sector would preclude a rapid adjustment of effort should stocks suddenly decline. Active management of the stocks is therefore required even before there is evidence of overexploitation.

Experience throughout the world shows that regardless of how healthy fish stocks may appear, sooner or later they will be over-fished if an *open access fishing policy* prevails and/or if regulation is inefficient. Under these conditions, technological improvements in vessels and gear result in a greater fishing intensity than is economically efficient. It should be noted that the maximum economic yield of a fishery usually occurs at levels of effort below the biological maximum sustainable yield (see Box 4.1).

Thus, it is possible that the tuna fishery in the region may be overexploited in relation to the maximum economic yield even if it is not biologically threatened at this time.[3] A compelling argument to effectively limit entry to the fishery is the fact that vessels from *distant water fishing nations* (DWFNs) will be willing to pay higher access fees if total fishing effort is limited to the point where their net revenue per-unit-of-effort is maximized. Coastal states will therefore need to balance this willingness to pay with the total number of vessels required to optimize the *total* net revenue they can extract from the fishery.

Essentially the Pacific Island countries need to be aware that there is no substitute for a well designed regional FMR. If tuna resources collapse, there are no substitute offshore resources capable of providing the same level of revenue to coastal states. West African coastal states as well as many developed countries are plagued with excessive fishing effort and depleted resources. Fishing grounds such as the Grand Banks off the west coast of Canada once considered an inexhaustible source of cod fish supplies are now in their second year of a complete moratorium without any visible sign of a resource recovery. This is costing the Canadian Government over C$1.5 billion per year in subsidies to the fishermen. Inappropriate management policies which allowed *inter alia* overcapitalization of the catching capacity was one of the principal factors which led to this situation.

Two other reasons favor entering into a regional management arrangement which would limit entry to the fishery: (a) at present, most of the known global tuna habitats are being exploited so that the supply appears to be relatively fixed; and (b) over the last two decades the tuna markets have experienced tremendous expansion. Canned tuna has increased 300 percent and demand for fresh tuna has also grown rapidly. Both these markets are expected to continue expanding. At the same time the lack of new fishing grounds mentioned above should constrain supply. Together these two forces should exert upward pressure on prices in the medium to long term.

---

[3] Work is currently underway to answer this question, but the results will not be available for some time.

Box 4.1: Maximizing Economic Returns from a Fishery

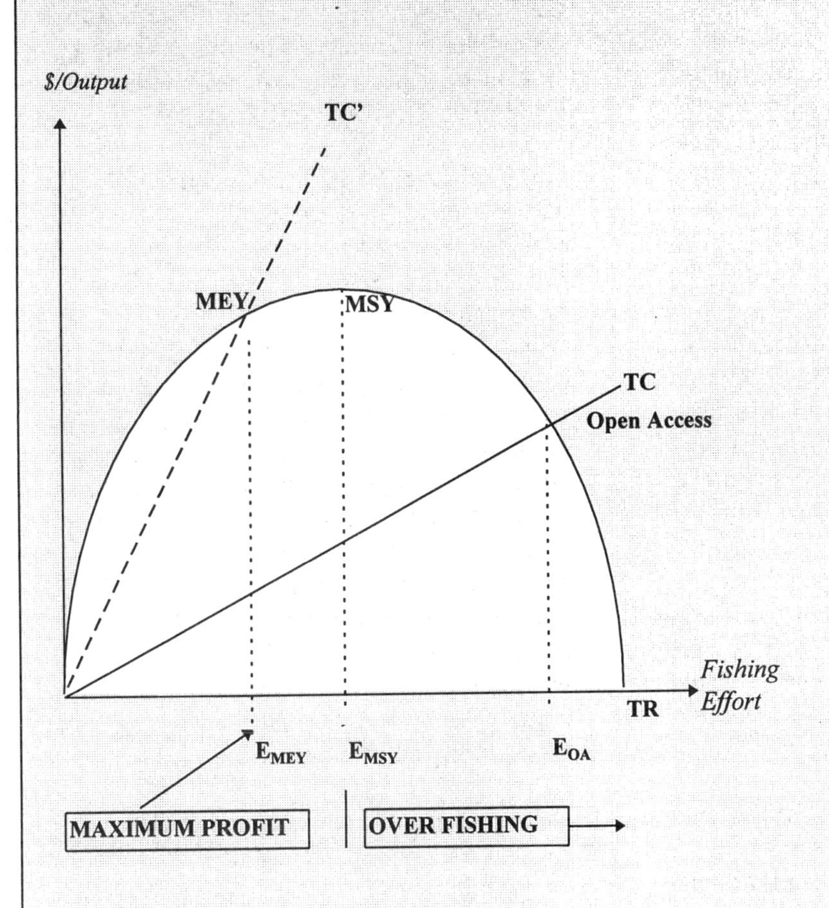

The curve in the figure represents the output or catch of a fishery as fishing effort is increased. This shows that as effort is increased, the output of a fishery keeps increasing up to a point known as the *Maximum Sustainable Yield* (MSY) at which point the biological regeneration of the fish cannot keep up with depletion. Beyond MSY, increasing the fishing effort (by say adding additional vessels) will lead to declining output. This will therefore also be the shape of the *Total Revenue* curve (denoted TR) as revenues will rise with increasing effort and then fall beyond MSY.

The curve TC represents *total costs,* which are seen to increase as effort is increased. Thus the vertical distance between the *total revenue* and *total cost* curves represents profits.

In an unregulated fishery, under an *open access regime,* as long as profits are positive there is incentive for additional vessels to enter the industry. This continues until profits are dissipated which is the point at which *total revenues* equal *total cost.* This point is denoted the *open access equilibrium* E_{OA}. As the figure shows, this is clearly an inefficient outcome as the level of fishing effort is beyond MSY, and results in overfishing.

The efficient point of exploitation is that at which the *maximum economic yield* (MEY) or profit is obtained. This occurs at the point where the vertical distance between the total revenue curve and the total cost line is greatest. Note that in this depiction, the MEY occurs before the MSY and the open access equilibrium. Regulating a fishery through limiting access could therefore aim to shift the cost curve upwards to TC' in order to stabilize fishing effort at the point of maximum economic yield or profit.

It should be noted that the outcome of this simple model of a fishery is dependent in a dynamic sense on the discount rate held by society as well as individuals engaged in fishing. If this rate is sufficiently high, MEY can approach the level of the open access equilibrium and occur at levels of effort beyond MSY.

Tuna migrate widely across the EEZs of the Pacific Islands, Asian Pacific countries and the area between EEZs known as *High Seas.* Therefore they cannot be properly managed unless the coastal states understand that the resources should be managed at the regional level, both on their behalf and under their mandate. If the region wants to maintain a major role for itself as a tuna supplier to world markets in the years to come, the implementation of a regional FMR with its three components—a fisheries management system appropriately supported by solid research, monitoring control and surveillance, and a fisheries judicial system—becomes a matter of urgency.

Recommendations. An effective FMR operating under a limited access policy has the potential to

Box 4.2: The Fishery Management Regime-FMR

To be effective an FMR requires three components—*a fishery management system* (FMS) strongly supported by research, a *monitoring, control and surveillance* component (MCS), and a *fishery judicial system* (FJS).

The FMS specifies the regulatory framework for fishing. It encompasses both fishery management rules—such as requirements concerning fishing licenses and catch quotas—and less crucial ones—such as gear and area restrictions. It relies heavily on information provided through research, particularly regarding the health of the stocks and the seasonal determination of the total allowable catch of the particular resources.

The primary task of the MCS function is to enforce the management system that has been adopted. Its secondary—but nevertheless very important task is to generate data that can be used to improve both the fishery management and judicial systems, as well as monitoring, control and surveillance. The FJS is usually part of the general judicial system. It issues sanctions to those alleged to have violated the fishery regulations and thus complements the MCS activity.

The three components of the FMR are strongly interdependent. For example, the fishing rules specified by the FMS define the scope of the MCS and the focus of the FJS. The MCS places demands on the FJS, and both activities in turn suggest modification of the FMS.

Each of the three components of the FMR is crucial to its success. To attain full economic benefits from the fishery, all three components must be appropriately designed, well coordinated and fully functional. This point cannot be overemphasized. Any one or two components of the regime, regardless of how well designed and managed, will generate limited social benefits unless integrated with and supported by the other two components.

Establishing an FMR is basically an exercise in social engineering. It involves not just technical, biological and economic aspects, but a range of social and political considerations. For optimal results it is very important to pay attention to as many of the socio-political aspects of the situation as possible. These include public attitudes, regional conditions, power relations, interest groups, and traditional social values and methods of production. Some of these aspects may justify important modifications of the components of the FMR. Others, if not attended to in time, may develop into serious obstacles to the implementation and the eventual success of the FMR.

In view of the large number of independent states that comprise the region, the establishment of an FMR for the Central and Western Pacific is indeed a challenge. In spite of all the difficulties that may be envisaged to implement such a system, the potential benefits to the region are such that they outweigh the costs. On the other hand the region cannot afford the cost and consequences of maintaining the *status quo* and postponing adoption of an FMR.

be self-policing. (See Box 4.2 for a discussion of the key attributes of an effective FMR.) In order to move to an effective FMR it is recommended that the PMCs in conjunction with other FFA member countries :

- Establish a moratorium on the issuance of new licenses until appropriate economic evidence related to the rapid expansion of long-line fleets is properly evaluated;
- Seek and obtain additional financial assistance to support scientific efforts undertaken by OFP to assess the health of the tuna stocks;
- Undertake the necessary institutional restructuring to allow the FFA in conjunction with the OFP to become effective regional tuna fisheries management institutions on behalf of the coastal states;
- Strengthen the *limited access policy* to further restrict the number of vessels operating in a given fishery;
- Introduce catch limits by species in order to protect the resources;[4]
- Conduct an in-depth assessment of the environmental impacts of the shore-based fresh tuna long-line fishing vessels which have recently proliferated in some parts of the region, and appear to be polluting coastal lagoons, in

---

[4] This is in keeping with the conclusions of the Forum Heads of State meeting, 1994.

the course of transshipment operations and other port calls; and

- Support the implementation of a satellite tracking system for fishing vessels operating in the area, complementary to ongoing aerial and surface surveillance. Transponders should be required for those vessels which have proven unreliable in their compliance with the established management system.

Issues in Rent

Introduction. Tuna fishing is conducted by vessels from DWFNs who pay access fees for the rights to fish in waters under national jurisdiction. The major DWFNs are Japan, Korea, the Peoples Republic of China, Taiwan, and the United States. Contrary to PMC expectations, two decades of DWFN participation in offshore fisheries has not generated much economic activity in their domestic economies through downstream processing or support activities. Offshore fishing has remained very much an offshore activity and the pay-off for the PMCs has been limited largely to the collection of access fees. Thus, the PMCs face a dilemma in terms of how to translate their vast offshore fishery resources into significant domestic value-added, in order to generate employment and incomes.

Current Access Fees. At the present time the PMCs derive access fees through a number of mostly bilateral arrangements with individual countries or operators. The exception to this is the case of the United States which in 1987 negotiated a single multilateral treaty with the FFA member states. Under the terms of this treaty, all FFA members receive a minimum payment whether or not any part of the U.S. catch comes from the waters. The balance is tied to actual catch.

Table 4.5: Access Fees—Major Fishing Nations, 1993

	Access Fee (Share of catch)
USA	10.0%
Japan	5.0%
Taiwan	3.7%
Korea	2.2%

Source: World Bank staff estimates based on FFA and national sources.

Although the U.S. Treaty specifies a lump sum payment, it is customary practice to express the fee as a proportion of the value of the catch as all other agreements are tied to paying fees, based on the catch. In 1993 total access fees for the region were about US$56 million compared to a total catch valued at approximately US$1.2 billion. Thus the average access fee was about 4.4 percent of the value of the catch (see Table 4.5). Access fees from the U.S. represent about 10 percent of the value of the catch. Exclusion of the US from these estimates reduces the average access fee to about 3.7 percent of the value of the catch. This seemingly low level of fees received by the coastal states has generated much debate, with the PMCs feeling that their resources are being under priced and the DWFNs claiming that this is a fair rent given the price volatility of tuna and the high capital requirements of the sector.

Figures 4.3a-c present the distribution of access fees, catch volumes and catch value by fishing nation for 1993. Comparison of these suggests that after the U.S., Japan appears to be paying the most, relative to the output value while Korea and Taiwan appear to be the most serious underpayers—for example, Korean vessels paid 11 percent of total access fees, for catch which was worth 21 percent of the total catch value. Thus it appears that there is a fair degree of variation in fee payments across countries.

Two further points should be noted. First, over 25 percent of the total access fees in the region went to non-PMCs in 1993. Second, of the total access fees received by the PMCs in 1993, approximately 96 percent went to just three countries—FSM, Kiribati and Marshall Islands.

Rents. Rent can be defined as the difference between revenue and costs, where the latter represent opportunity costs, or the returns that inputs in fishing would have earned in their best alternative use.

A number of difficulties arise with the application of this simple definition of rent to the fishing industry. The first is associated with the ownership of the resource itself. Fish are not owned until they are caught. Given time and the existence of open-access conditions, all rents will be driven to zero because of open access. Rents can only be maximized if there are controls placed on the entry of vessels into each EEZ. Thus, the actual level of observed rent tends to bear little relation to potential rents. For this reason the appropriation of *optimal rent,* rather than the observed rent, should be the ultimate goal for coastal states. It should be noted, however, that only in rare circumstances are the economic and biological data easily available to calculate the optimal rent.

The second difficulty concerns the biological nature of the resource. As noted previously, tuna in the South Pacific are either highly migratory or highly mobile. Their abundance fluctuates between seasons and from year to year. The optimal economic rent for a tuna fishery in any country's EEZ is therefore a biological variable with a large magnitude of uncertainty. Moreover, prices, costs and international exchange rates are subject to large random variations and cyclical movements. Resource rent is therefore also an economic variable which exhibits considerable fluctuation through both time and space.

This uncertainty adds to the magnitude of the problem more than just in its calculation. It means that this industry has a number of facets which contribute to the very high level of risk associated with harvesting. The logical conclusion is that fishing companies must be allowed a rate of return above the normal in good years, in order to compensate for the years when returns are low. Thus these rents should be shared between the DWFNs and the resource owning coastal states.

Resource rent in the tuna fishery was estimated for U.S. tuna purse-seiners for the period 1989-92 and for Japanese long-lining vessels for 1992. The estimates were repeated varying the most important factors—such as price, costs, catch per unit of effort (CPUE), and days fished. These are summarized in Tables 4.6 and 4.7. An interesting conclusion to emerge from this analysis is that medium-sized (100-200 MT) Japanese long-line vessels are unprofitable under most scenarios. Clearly it is inappropriate to shift the costs of operating inefficient vessels to coastal states in the form of lower license fees.

Figure 4.3a: Access Fees Paid, 1993

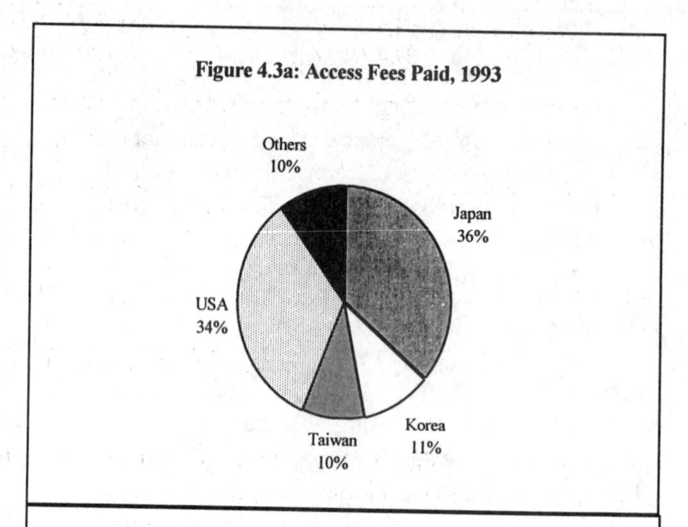

Figure 4.3b: Volume of Catch, 1993

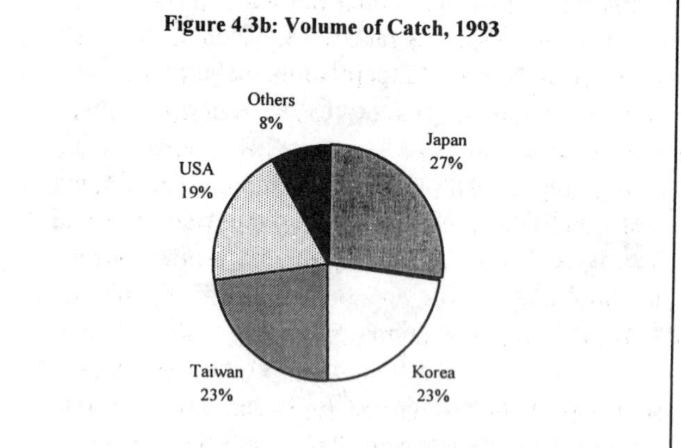

Figure 4.3c: Catch Value, 1993

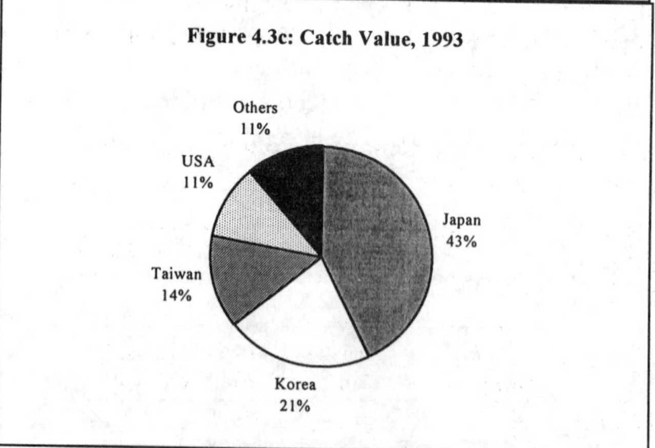

Source: World Bank staff estimates based on SPC, FFA and national sources.

Table 4.6: Rent For U.S. Purse-Seiners Under Various Scenarios, 1992
(% of catch value)

	Days Fished Per Year (CPUE fixed @ 24.4 MT/day)				*CPUE (MT/day) (Days fished fixed @ 180/year)*				*Days Fished Per Year (CPUE fixed @24.4 MT/year)*				
Price (US$/MT)	*140*	*160*	*180*	*200*	*18*	*22*	*26*	*30*	*CPUE (MT/day) (Price US$800/MT)*	*140*	*160*	*180*	*200*
600	-21	-16	-12	-9	-52	-24	-5	9	*18*	-23	-18	-14	-11
700	-4	0	4	7	-30	-7	10	22	*22*	-1	3	7	10
800	9	13	16	18	-14	7	21	32	*26*	15	18	21	23
900	19	23	25	27	-1	17	30	39	*30*	26	29	32	34
1,000	27	30	33	35	9	25	37	45					

Source: USITC 1990, South Pacific Commission 1993 and World Bank staff estimates.

The analysis shows the high sensitivity of rent to both prices and CPUE, as other factors are held constant. For example, under the various scenarios presented in Table 4.6 rent for U.S. purse-seiners varies widely from -52 percent to +45 percent. A number of conclusions can be drawn from this analysis. First, in poor years, vessel owners will make losses, which tend to be compensated during good years. Second, the wide variations in rent illustrate the high degree of risk in the industry. Very low rent figures are obtained when the major determinant factors combined (price, total effort, and CPUE) are low in magnitude. Under the most likely simulated scenarios, however, rents range between 7 and 30 percent. This analysis therefore suggests that there is scope to raise the access fees beyond the present level of about 4 percent of catch value.

Table 4.7: Rent for Japanese Longliners Under Various Scenarios, 1992
(% of catch value)

Price (US$/MT)		*3,000*	*5,000*	*7,000*
CPUE:	*1.5:*			
	50-100 T	-55	-23	10
	100-200 T	-61	-29	4
	200-600 T	-48	-16	16
CPUE:	*1.9*			
	50-100 T	-42	-1	40
	100-200 T	-48	-7	34
	200-600 T	-35	6	46
CPUE:	*2.3*			
	50-100 T	-29	20	70
	100-200 T	-35	14	64
	200-600 T	-22	27	77

Source: Statistical Yearbook, Ministry of Agriculture, Forestry & Fisheries, 1992, Japan, and World Bank staff estimates.

Issues in Collection

DWFNs generally point to low profit levels, calculated for taxation purposes with high capital costs and high depreciation rates to argue that their ability to pay is low. Inappropriately low license fees create many problems. First, they may encourage inefficient fishers to participate in the industry. More importantly, by driving down costs they encourage entry into the sector and exploitation beyond economic and biological sustainability, leading to overcapitalization and overfishing. Thus rent capture by the coastal states is a mechanism to automatically reduce overexploitation.

Under reporting of catch was a serious problem in the past but is much less a concern since the advent of compulsory transshipment in port in 1993. The problem of illegal fishing is believed to be serious but there is little evidence to support or refute such an assertion. Both of these must continue to be addressed through monitoring and enforcement with increased collaboration between coastal states. The present method of fee collection, for example, encourages under reporting since the access fee is based on the value of the expected catch—which is derived from prior years' output.

Alternative Collection Methods. The best method is, in theory, one which collects the rent, or the profits earned, with an appropriate allowance for some sharing between DWFNs and the coastal states. *Auctioning the fishing rights* works best in theory in terms of market efficiency, flexibility, ease of implementation, enforcement, and rent collection. However, it requires a competitive market in order to function, which at present does not reflect the state of the industry. Thus collusion between vessel operators could ensure minimum returns to the coastal states.

Much interest has recently been generated in *Individual Transferable Quotas* (ITQs) as a form of fisheries management. ITQs are presently being used in Australia, New Zealand and the United States. Although these have enjoyed a certain degree of success a number of problems have emerged. First, ownership is transferred to the fishers who may sell their access rights freely. Second, there has been no satisfactory way of dealing with multi-species fisheries and by-catch. This simply means that when species not specified under an ITQ are caught, they are routinely discarded at sea. Finally, in spite of ITQs, it has proven very difficult to reduce fishing effort when a stock is threatened. In the case of southern bluefin tuna in Australia, the industry, which had invested heavily in vessels, fought vigorously and vociferously against a reduction in fishing effort, despite overwhelming scientific evidence that the stock was severely depleted.

Taxing the value of access is another idea generating interest. The two principal drawbacks to this approach are: (a) determining the value of access would not at this time be practical in the region; and (b) in bad years such as those associated with low prices, this method could yield zero rents for coastal states.

Present Fee Method. The lump sum method of charging in advance is the most widely practiced method in fee negotiation, and is probably the best method available for the South Pacific tuna fishery at the present time. The formula used can be expressed as:

FEE = EXPECTED CATCH *X* EXPECTED PRICE *X* FEE RATE

The expected catch per vessel can be derived from historical records. The lump sum fee, based on the formula above, is paid in advance of operations. The FFA keeps current records of prices, allowing the expected price to be estimated with ease. The difficulty is that the burden of an unexpected fall or rise in value of catch, either due to environmental factors or economic factors, falls directly on the DWFNs. To the extent that distant water fishermen are risk averse they will be willing to pay only a lower fee in advance. It is nearly certain that higher fees could be easily negotiated based on actual value of catch—the obvious difficulty is the direct incentive this gives for under reporting, with immediate cash returns to those fishing.

The most serious drawback of the present method of assigning fishing rights and access is that there is no element of regulating catch by species. Under this system, once fees are negotiated, the incentives are for fishers to maximize their catch. Consequently, pronouncements on the sustainability of the fish stocks under the current fishing effort are only made *ex post.* There is therefore an urgent need to introduce an element of management into the licensing as discussed previously.

Value of Aid. The U.S. pays an access fee of about 10 percent of value of catch, of which, only about one-quarter is paid by the U.S. Tuna industry, the balance being paid by the U.S. Government. One cannot then argue that the U.S. Treaty with its generous access fee of 10 percent reflects the willingness-to-pay of the fishers and therefore reflects their profitability.

There is ample precedent for these types of agreements—the *Protocols* between the EU and West African coastal states consist of low value license fees paid by the fishers compensated by a direct contribution by the EU to the coastal state. These agreements, however, have the disadvantage of subsidizing the industry, allowing vessels to remain profitable at low levels of revenue. Thus fishing effort tends to increase beyond the optimum economic level. At the next revision or renewal of the U.S. Treaty, the PMCs should work to raise the portion of the access fee paid by the tuna industry as there is, on average, rent to be earned.

It is often claimed that although Japanese fees are low, there is a large amount of Japanese aid flowing to the region that should be taken into account. It has been shown, however, that total aid over the period 1983 to 1987 was US$79.3 million to South Pacific countries with Japanese fishing agreements, compared to US$78.8 million for countries without fishing agreements, over the same period.[5] This provides no support for the argument that Japanese fees contain an aid component: this aid is, and should be considered as, distinct from negotiated fees.

Payments in Kind. The practice of payments in kind should in general be the least acceptable method of payment. Access to fishing grounds often generate a number of benefits—other than financial—such as grants of goods and services, provision of scientific data, technical assistance, aid, provision of capital investment including infrastructure, domestic processing, and access to markets for fisheries products. These benefits can be called *de facto* royalties if, in the absence of a fishing agreement, the particular aid in kind would not have been an expenditure for the DWFN.

The provision of technical assistance to processing plants under joint venture agreement, no matter how valuable, cannot be considered a *de facto* royalty. Nor can access to markets, or the provision of infrastructure if its primary goal is to serve the DWFN in marketing or during port calls. Such payments in kind are part of normal operating costs for the DWFN. Since it is so very difficult to sort out what is aid, what are *de facto* royalties, and what are normal operating costs, it is preferable to negotiate all fee agreements in financial terms. Aid ought to be considered separately.

Negotiating Agreements

If lump-sum financial payments in terms of value of catch are seen as the optimal strategy, there still remains the issue of which is the best method of negotiating the fee. Under the present negotiating regime which is largely bilateral, the DWFNs are able to play off one Pacific Island state against another in order to obtain concessions and to lower the access fee as much as possible. There is clearly substantial room for improvement in this practice by resorting to collective action. The endorsement of the *multilateral approach* by the Heads of State at the Brisbane Summit in August 1994 is a first step in this direction.

Present Approach to Negotiations. Under the present system, all but the U.S. access agreements are negotiated bilaterally between the fishers, DWFN fleets/DWFN governments, and the individual countries.[6] Fisheries and foreign affairs officials usually represent the coastal state. The FFA may be invited to participate as advisor to the country concerned. In any event they usually provide logistical and technical assistance to the negotiations whether or not they serve as participants. As an important repository of information on catches and prices their services during the negotiations are invaluable.

Proposed Approach to Negotiations. It is recommended that the PMCs along with the other FFA members take further steps to collaborate in moving to a system of collective or multilateral negotiations for licensing fisheries access. Notwithstanding the principal attraction that this should result in an increase in the rents going to the Pacific Island states, there are a number of compelling reasons that argue in support of such a course of action. First, it reduces the costs of negotiations considerably because, at most, it only requires one negotiation per fishing country rather than the present system of multiple negotiations with different companies. Second, this would considerably reduce the costs of monitoring, control and surveillance (MCS) by introducing regional economies of scale. Finally, scarce resources in fisheries departments would be freed up, allowing them to be deployed in other priority areas such as management of nearshore resources.

---

[5] See Uwate R. *Japanese Aid and Access Fees to FFA Member Countries,* FFA Report 89/37, 1989.

[6] The Nauru Agreements were also multilateral agreements but were focussed on establishing Harmonized Minimum Terms and Conditions of Access among member countries.

A successful regional strategy for conducting negotiations will depend crucially on stock assessments and the ability to relate these to desirable fishing levels. Thus the advice and expertise of the OFP and FFA will remain vital. In particular the role of MCS will be more important than before because the effectiveness of the new strategy will rest squarely on the ability to determine compliance and to penalize offenders (see Box 4.2). Another key requirement will be the effective incorporation and enforcement of the Harmonized Minimum Terms and Conditions of Access in all new agreements.

This new strategy will require concerted effort and cooperation between the Pacific Island countries on an unprecedented scale. The essence of it is that a strong commitment will be required from all parties for this effort to be successful. As a first step the countries of the region will need to design and agree upon a comprehensive long-term negotiating strategy that lays out the steps required to achieve a specific rent target over a period of time. This will require countries to make plans regarding all aspects of fishing access and development, for example, where ports, trans-shipment facilities and other infrastructure should be located.

Such plans should be formulated with the major markets and shipping routes in mind and will require close collaboration and agreement between Pacific Island countries. Clearly it is not optimal for each and every country or island to have a transshipment facility. These decisions will require access to the best possible technical advice. The potential gains from implementing such a far-reaching strategy would seem to far outweigh the costs.

The second part of this strategy concerns the institutional and technical requirements of a multilateral strategy. The negotiations themselves will need to be carried out by specialized professional negotiators who would be identified and recruited by Pacific Island countries. Moreover, they should be utilized extensively in the first stage—to design the framework for a regional strategy on negotiations.

Efforts will need to be made to ensure that coastal states with richer fishing grounds are not made worse off through the negotiation of multilateral agreements. A possible safeguard in this respect, would be a guarantee system to ensure that no country would receive less under any future multilateral agreement than it presently does under bilateral agreements.[7] This could be ensured by formula or other appropriate method. The PMCs could move gradually to full multilateral agreements, initially grouping adjacent states or a few resource-rich states.

Managing Investment Effectively

Pacific Island countries are keenly interested in developing domestic fisheries capacity to participate in the harvesting and processing associated with tuna operations. Yet this goal has remained largely unattainable and generated high costs for governments across the region. This section examines the issues underlying such participation and tries to determine whether governments with limited capital resources should invest in off-shore fisheries development, given the high opportunity costs of other domestic activities, such as health, education and infrastructure. Micronesian countries, in particular, have adopted that path, whereas countries like Vanuatu have chosen to focus their resources on the development of inshore fisheries.

Investment in fisheries development is a highly capital-intensive undertaking—be it in vessels, loining facilities, or canning plants—and given the high risk and technical requirements of the sector, success is not easy to achieve. Most PMCs simply lack the private savings which would be required to finance such investments. Consequently, in many PMCs the government has undertaken such investments directly, in the process utilizing scarce public savings. The macroeconomic consequences of these decisions are significant and may have long-term repercussions (see Table 4.8). Public investment in a tuna cannery, for example, would amount to nearly 20 percent of GDP for FSM. Thus the opportunity cost of such an investment,

---

[7] This was agreed to in principle at the 1994 Forum Heads of State Meeting.

Table 4.8: Illustrative Costs of Investment in Fisheries, 1992

	Purse-Seiner *(% of GDP)*	Cannery *(% of GDP)*	GDP per Capita *(US$)*
FSM	3	19	1,554
Fiji	0	2	2,128
Kiribati	7	44	944
Marshall Islands	6	38	1,717
Solomon Islands	2	12	763
Tonga	3	20	1,626
Vanuatu	3	16	1,236
Western Samoa	3	20	925

Note: Purse-seiner assumed to cost $US5 million and a cannery $US30 million.
Source: World Bank staff estimates.

especially given its riskiness, should not be taken lightly.

The outcomes of these past investments are easy to quantify—not a single financially viable public enterprise is known to exist in the region. This has usually meant that in addition to the initial capital outlay, many governments have remained burdened by a continuing call on their budgets to keep these enterprises running, on the grounds of maintaining employment or income. Thus, it is vitally important for governments in the region not to become involved in direct public investment in the sector, when it requires a financial contribution. This applies equally to foreign and domestic investment.

In addition to the high capital costs already mentioned, there are a number of other factors which argue against direct government participation in the sector and help explain some of the past failures in this area. Modern fishing is a highly skill-intensive occupation. These skills presently exist in the PMCs in a limited fashion. Furthermore, investment in vessels is not a cost effective way to create employment, as a typical purse-seiner will employ 15 people for an investment of upwards of US$5 million.

Canneries may be able to provide significant employment, but require even larger outlays, in excess of US$30 million. The requirements for a successful canning operation are also hard to meet in the region. These include the existence of substantial supplies of fresh water which is scarce in some of the PMCs, and the availability of internationally competitive unskilled labor. Conditions in world markets are such that even after meeting these conditions many canneries are in financial distress—several canneries in Thailand and Indonesia with some of the lowest labor costs in the world, for example, are running financial losses. These losses, however, are being borne by their private operators.

In the short term, PMC governments are advised to reduce their presence in these purely commercial activities. This calls for a strategy to cover the transition from publicly managed public assets to privately managed public assets and will require joint-venture partnerships with foreign investors. However, governments should be cautioned against making any direct financial contribution. On the contrary, foreign investors should be charged a fee to manage these enterprises within a framework which allows for the possibility of future ownership. Thus, the government concerned is relieved of the immediate financial burden and receives a fiscal contribution.

Over the long term PMCs will have to rely on attracting foreign direct investment (FDI) while continuing to encourage domestic investment in activities with low-capital requirements, such as fish smoking and loining (see Chapter 2). Such FDI should once again not be the basis for government financial contribution. Rather investors should be required to bear the full commercial risk associated with their investments, thereby maximizing the potential for success.

The role of the government needs to be confined to creation of an enabling regulatory framework and conducive business environment for private sector participation, both foreign and domestic. Additionally, it will need to ensure adequate provision of infrastructure. This is one of the prime factors behind the success of the domestic tuna longline fishery in Fiji. In this instance the Government has taken a basically hands-off attitude toward the private sector operator, allowing expansion and consolidation to take place unfettered. This success has generated some

Box 4.3: Transfer Pricing in the Pacific

Transfer pricing appears to have been practiced in the fisheries sector in the Pacific region at various times. Examples of firms in two different PMCs which have operated for long periods of time without showing consistent accounting profits but have failed to exit the industry are outlined here.

The first concerns the prawn fishing industry in one country in the 1980s during which three firms operated. A comparison of two of these—a foreign joint-venture with the Government and a Government-operated company, is quite illustrative.

The joint-venture was established with large amounts of debt from its parent companies and consequently had significant interest expenses—as high as 8 percent of sales through the mid-1980s. The firm also generated massive exchange losses which by 1986 had escalated to 22 percent of sales in contrast to the government-run firm which showed no evidence of such exchange losses in spite of selling the same product in the same market. Both firms maintained technical assistance agreements with companies in the same foreign country but the joint-venture paid a much higher fee for these—an average of 30-40 percent of sales throughout the 1980s. Finally, the joint-venture company received a price for its prawns consistently below that of the government-owned venture. Thus it appears that the firm was inflating its costs and reducing its revenues in order to report losses and avoid paying corporate taxes.

The second example of reported losses concerns a foreign joint-venture established in the early 1970s to produce and export frozen fish, canned fish, and fish meal. This company has operated under a series of joint-venture agreements with the Government—three to date—the first two of which gave almost no incentive to make profits. Over two decades the company failed to earn a consistent profit, making an operating profit on just eight occasions up to 1993, accumulating enormous losses in the process. The firm last paid corporate taxes more than ten years ago. Despite these massive losses, the firm entered into a third joint-venture agreement recently rather than closing down an apparently unprofitable operation. Like the company in the first example this firm appears to have had a high-cost structure on sales, management fees, and commisions which were all handled through subsidiary or related firms in the home country. The effective rate of sales commission was nearly double the existing 1.7 percent paid as sales commission for similar canned tuna entering the U.K. market. Finally, intra-group debts have ballooned nearly nine-fold over the last five years.

While definitive conclusions are difficult to draw from such aggregate information, the preceding examples are highly suggestive of transfer pricing practices which generate accounting losses for the purpose of tax avoidance. In addition to the revenue losses generated by these practices, there may be significant efficiency losses due to the up-front withdrawal of surplus rather than a *bottom-line* approach to profits.

regional interest and the Solomon Islands has entered into an arrangement with the Fijian operator to try to replicate the model.

Participation in foreign joint-ventures has been the most common vehicle by which governments in the Pacific Islands have encouraged foreign investment in a host of activities ranging from vessel purchase and operation to processing plants. This is an area that needs careful attention and much caution as some joint-venture agreements are especially unfavorable to the host country and poorly crafted agreements are often the cause of other more serious difficulties, such as revenue leakage due to trade malpractice or transfer pricing manipulation.

Transfer pricing is the term used to describe the internal sale of goods and services between different divisions of a business enterprise. Transfer pricing usually occurs when a firm operates in more than one country—international trade permits transactions beyond the jurisdiction of the home country tax authority and creates the necessary conditions for transfer pricing to take place. The existence of tax havens and low tax areas encourages firms to manipulate prices and costs so as to reduce profits in the higher tax jurisdiction thereby reducing the tax liability of the firm. This can be done in various ways, for example, by raising prices and costs. Although transfer pricing is associated with multi-national enterprises it is not limited to such firms. Domestic firms may also indulge in this practice through double invoicing of exports or imports. This practice is believed to occur in both the forestry and fisheries sectors in the Pacific Islands[8] (see Box 4.3).

Policy Response to Transfer Pricing. In the Pacific the most common response to the perception of transfer pricing has been to employ *ad valorem* export or turnover taxes in lieu of company taxes. The problem with this approach is that it loads a company, that already suffers from distortions to its balance sheet, with up-front costs which further decreases profit generating potential.

Another option is for governments to auction resource development rights and abolish all taxes. The lack of a competitive market in the region would render this unviable as would the lack of monitoring capacity. Privatized market monitoring through a company such as Société Général de Surveillance is an option that several developing companies have employed successfully but at a cost. In general joint-ventures should rely on profit sharing arrangements and not on *ad valorem* commissions as the latter gives no incentive to minimize costs.

In particular, transfer pricing may be best avoided if governments impose taxes on companies that fail to generate a profit. Economic theory suggests that the only form of tax that is efficient is a lump sum tax, one that cannot be avoided by any action apart from closure. Government can and should impose taxes based on estimates of what a *best practice* firm would achieve in the market and establish the tax liability accordingly.

The strategy outlined in the preceding section for limiting access to the fishery and raising access fees through collective action should, over the medium term, have a positive effect on raw material prices and raise the value of fishing rights in the region. At the same time it should forge closer links between the Pacific Islands and the DWFNs. The PMCs should rely on attracting investment from this pool of foreign investors already operating in their midst. From the point of view of foreign participants, shore-based processing facilities have the potential to reduce costs by virtue of the closeness to the raw material resource, which can be used to offset lack of labor competitiveness.

Coastal Fisheries

Coastal fisheries are influenced by the general socio-economic trends which occur both within and outside the Pacific Island region. In many PMCs, the traditional role of the government in fostering coastal fisheries development is increasingly being adopted by the private sector. There is therefore a need to redirect public services to the management of overexploited resources and to focus public resources on the provision of adequate infrastructure, training, and creating a favorable environment for stable investment.

PMC governments have identified the following goals for coastal fisheries development: (a) protection of food security; (b) utilization of coastal fisheries as a substitute for imported protein; (c) maximization of foreign exchange from coastal resource exploitation; and (d) generation of local employment. Many PMCs have thus focused on developing relatively unexploited fisheries, and in creating the national infrastructure necessary for development of domestic markets. The experience to date has been disappointing. Diseconomies of scale, inappropriate maintenance, poor management of collection and distribution centers, lack of entrepreneurial spirit and socio-cultural factors discouraging full-time participation in the sector have been but a few of the factors responsible for the high failure rate of these programs.

---

[8] See *Commission of Inquiry into Aspects of the Forestry Industry*, Prime Minister's Department, Port Moresby, 1989.

Changing Patterns of Resource Exploitation

Future strategies for nearshore fisheries development in the Pacific need to be based on a good understanding of the socio-economic trends affecting the sector. There is evidence, for example, that in many areas the reliance on subsistence fisheries is declining due to increased commercialization of the catch at both village and national levels. The sales of fisheries products is currently practised by 31 percent and 17 percent, respectively, of the income-earning households of Kiribati and Solomon Islands; 40 percent of the fishing households of Vanuatu, and 36 percent of the fishing households in Upolu, Western Samoa. Village sales appear to be replacing traditional bartering systems in many areas.

Box 4.4: Trends in the Use of Coastal Fisheries-The Case of Vanuatu

	1983	1993
% of Rural Households Collecting Fish	50%	35%
% of Rural Households Collecting Trochus	10%	19%
% of Rural Housholds Collecting Green Snail	8%	13%
Average Fishing Trips/Week	1	7
% of Fishing Households Selling their Catch	n/a	40%
% of the Above Selling Within their Village	n/a	70%
% of Households Purchasing Fish from Formal Outlets	n/a	31-33%

Source: Department of Agriculture, Agriculture Censuses 1983 and 1993.

Some of these trends are highlighted in Box 4.4, which indicates an overall decrease in the number of households involved in fishing in Vanuatu over the last decade, but a rise in the proportion of households collecting shells—an important source of cash income. Average fishing effort has also increased, suggesting that fishing activities are being concentrated in the hands of fewer, but more intensive, operators.

While domestic sales are expanding, there is little evidence that public programs are responsible for this trend. The most rapidly expanding markets have been informal village outlets, unstructured road-side sales, and direct sales to private outlets in major urban areas, often at the expense of public and municipal outlets. In Fiji, for example, the share of domestic sales held by non-municipal market outlets has increased from 50 percent in 1978 to nearly 80 percent at present. In Vanuatu, similarly, 67 percent of the seafood consumed in Efate is sold through private outlets.[9]

In countries such as Tonga, Western Samoa and, to a lesser extent, Vanuatu, the role of seafood products in the total protein supply has declined (Table 4.9). While this trend is not apparent in other PMCs, where fish is a more important component of animal protein supply, the consumption of alternative products to fresh fish—in particular canned fish and meats—has been rising in the region. As much as 80 percent of the fish consumed in Honiara, for example, is frozen or canned.[10] The lower price and non-perishability of these processed foods plays a major role in influencing consumer choice.[11]

The introduction of new technology and targeted demand from export markets, tourist outlets and urban centers is increasing pressure on high-value nearshore resources, especially near urban centers. In Western Samoa, commercial sales of inshore fish at the Apia Fish Market decreased by 90 percent from 1986 to 1991, largely as a result of overexploitation.[12] This fishing pressure cannot be easily reduced by re-directing effort to less exploited areas or alternative species. Remote areas, while well endowed with resources, are often commercially unprofitable due to lack of economies of scale. Changes in target species, similarly, are not easily compatible with either tourist or export markets. Where it exists, pressure

9 MacAlister Elliot & Partners (1992).

10 Crossland and Philipson (1993).

11 For Vanuatu, it has been estimated that for the same value, a consumer in Port Vila could obtain three times as much caloric content, and four to six times as much protein from canned mackerel as from fresh reef fish. (See David and Cillaurren, 1992).

12 Other causes include the destruction of reefs caused by cyclone Ofa, coastal degradation, and shifts in the location of sales in favor of private outlets.

Table 4.9: Trends in Per Capita Supply of Fisheries Products, 1974/76-92

	1974/76	1985	1992
Kg/year			
Fiji	24.9	42.5	40.7
Kiribati	51.4	72.6	74.6
Solomon Islands	55.7	58.3	53.9
Tonga	11.5	30.5	15.5
Vanuatu	45.7	39.4	31.7
Western Samoa	44.2	45.2	43.2
% of Animal Protein Consumed			
Fiji	33.0	35.4	28.9
Kiribati	70.0	71.3	68.2
Solomon Islands	70.6	67.1	73.6
Tonga	21.0	32.9	17.9
Vanuatu	39.0	35.3	30.9
Western Samoa	46.6	39.2	31.8

Figures reported are averages for the years 1985-92.
Source: FAO, Agrostat Database.

on target nearshore resources is thus likely to remain high for the near future.

Because of their proximity to land, coastal fisheries are vulnerable to the environmental impacts of rapid urbanization and poor land management. These include urban pollution of reefs and lagoons, increased sedimentation of reefs, lagoons, and nearshore ecosystems (e.g., through logging), and direct alteration of coastal environments.[13] The present levels of *fecal coliform* contamination of shellfish in the Tarawa lagoon, for example, are of special concern, since contaminated shellfish was the primary cause of the cholera epidemic of 1977. Alterations of vital coastal habitats such as estuaries and mangroves can also have long-lasting negative impacts on coastal fisheries.

Environmental effects on fisheries are difficult to quantify. It has been estimated that in Upolu, Western Samoa, fishing yields around degraded urban reefs average 28 kg/ha/year, compared to an average productivity of 120 kg/ha/year for the island.[14] Assuming that urban reefs have similar productivity, the costs of urban pollution in terms of productivity losses could amount to WS$415/ha/year, or nearly US$170/ha/year.

In view of the above trends, and considering the important socio-economic role of coastal fisheries in Pacific Island economies, management of coastal resources should become a matter of national priority. Given the limited capacity of most fisheries departments in the region, it will be important to ensure that management strategies are supported by community action and effective enforcement mechanisms, and that they are adequately linked to broader environmental and nutritional strategies.

A Management Strategy for Coastal Resources

What justifies management of coastal resources? In general, overexploitation of fisheries occurs as a result of market failure due to the lack of incentives to exploit the resource sustainably, commonly associated with unclear property rights or lax enforcement. It can also result from poor understanding of the benefits of management in ensuring sustainable extraction. The introduction of cost-effective management regimes can enable resource custodians to capture resource rents that would otherwise be dissipated. Pacific Island communities know this all too well; in many PMCs, customary leaders imposed *taboos* (temporary closures) on fishing grounds to allow stocks to recuperate prior to a ceremony requiring a large harvest.

The absence of adequate management, has meant that exploitation of sedentary species for export markets have been characterized by *boom-and-bust* cycles. Figure 4.4 illustrates this pattern for bêche-de-mer exports. During the late 1980s, Fijian exports expanded rapidly to a level of 717 MT in 1988, valued at nearly US$2.0 million, only to drop abruptly in 1989 to US$1.3 million (365 MT). Subsequently in the Solomon Islands, exports of bêche-de-mer peaked in 1992 at 715 MT, but fell by over US$2 million in 1993 to 315 MT. Local traders attribute these declines to

---

[13] See World Bank, *Managing Urban Environmental Sanitation Services in Selected Pacific Island Countries,* February 1995.

[14] Zann (1991).

overexploitation.[15] The depletion of the Melanesian fishing grounds is reportedly causing a shift in trade to Micronesian and Polynesian countries, as indicated by recent export trends in Tonga and Western Samoa.

Figure 4.4: Beche-de-Mer Exports from Selected PMCs, 1984-93

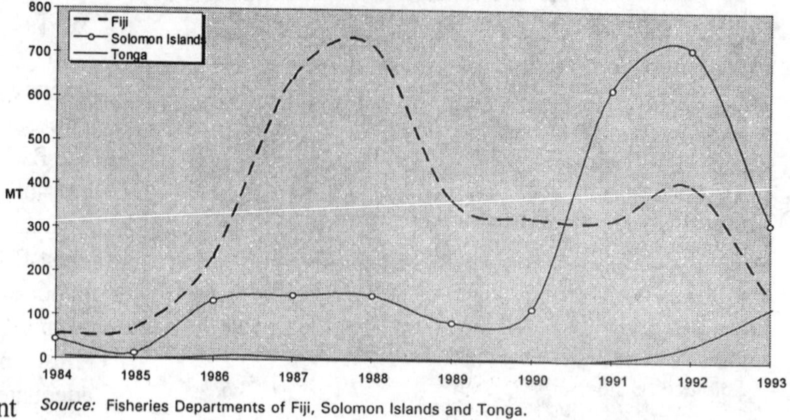

Source: Fisheries Departments of Fiji, Solomon Islands and Tonga.

From a national standpoint, boom-and-bust cycles can result in the sudden loss of an important source of income for households involved in collection and processing—in Solomon Islands an estimated 7 percent of households in the cash economy participate in bêche-de-mer collection. There may also be investment losses in the case of trochus, where button-processing facilities have been established. Wide fluctuations in the availability of raw material are not conducive to stable investment. Furthermore, boom and bust exploitation can, in some cases, drive the resources to extinction. This has happened in the Kiritimati Islands of Kiribati, where pearl oysters never recovered from the heavy exploitation inflicted last century.

All PMC governments have adopted fisheries management legislation for key coastal resources, ranging from size limitations to closed seasons, and gear restrictions for certain species. The most important constraint to the implementation of these measures is, however, the poor enforcement capacity of PMC governments.

Recognizing the difficulties of managing complex multi-species fisheries with limited budgets and staff, several PMCs have recently shown a renewed interest in establishing collaborative management regimes utilizing traditional resource custodians. In Aitutaki (Cook Islands) and Arnavon Islands (Solomons), this collaboration has resulted in the drafting of joint resource management plans. In Aitutaki, trochus resources are managed by the Island Council through a strict management regime that includes a limited open season, individual transferable quotas, and inspection upon landing.

Another form of collaborative management consists of using *customary marine tenure systems* (CMTs) to implement village-based fisheries management. The role of the government is here limited to facilitation and provision of technical advice on management issues. One of the most successful examples of the above has been the resurgence of village-based management in Vanuatu, through separate efforts initiated by the Fisheries Department and the Environment Unit (Box 4.5).

Perhaps the most radical of the current experiments in reviving CMTs is the initiative by the Government of Fiji to grant property titles for coastal areas to custodian communities (*yavusa*). In preparation for this, all customary marine areas (*qoliqoli*) are being mapped and registered, and titles are expected to be granted in 1995-96. Granting of titles and settlement of disputes will be handled by a board, similar in function to the Native Land Trust Board, and economic activities in the titled areas would require the written consent of all resource custodians in the communities.

There are cases where village-based management cannot be implemented. These include areas where CMT has never existed or has been weakened, by proximity to urban areas, in-migration, or by the weakening of traditional authority. Moreover, CMT does not provide a practical means for

---

15 In Fiji, the introduction of size limitations and the improvement of general socio-economic conditions may also have contributed to the decline in exports after 1988. (Adams 1992).

Box 4.5: Collaborative Management of Coastal Resources—The Case of Vanuatu

By the late 1980s, it was evident that fishing pressure on coastal resources was leading to resource depletion, especially of trochus, a commercially important coastal product.

The Department of Fisheries and the Environmental Unit launched public awareness campaigns to encourage village-based conservation. Village education programs were started by the Environmental Unit with the purpose of encouraging communities to propose and publicly announce traditional conservation measures for coastal resources.

Staff from the Fisheries Department used radio broadcasting to announce their willingness to advise villagers on optimal measures for trochus management, and survey their fishing grounds. The response from villagers was enthusiastic and widespread, and led to informal discussions on management options. The final decision was, however, left to coastal communities.

Since 1990, closed seasons or taboos—an ancient practice related to traditional ceremonies—have been reinstated by villages throughout the country. Their success in improving catch rates have led villagers to extend closed seasons from trochus to other species, such as green snail, reef fish, sea cucumber, and lobsters, and to adopt further conservation measures such as bans on gillnetting and night spearfishing. The recent national strike has restricted village visitation by fisheries extension workers, but local traders and retailers in Efate and Santo confirm that the practices have been sustained to current times.

Among the lessons suggested by this experience in collaborative management are:

- Government staff visiting coastal villages should have enough technical expertise to be credible advisors on management options;
- The communication media chosen should be appropriate to local socio-cultural conditions;
- Extension staff should act as facilitators, limiting their role to offering options for management—the ultimate management decisions should be left to local communities;
- The success of village-based management is higher where traditional authority remains strong, in rural, rather than peri-urban areas; and where populations have alternative sources of cash income and food to rely on during the closed seasons.

Source: Johannes (1994).

protecting pelagic species or coastal species whose seasonal migrations take them in and out of tenured waters. Finally, some communities may simply not have the incentive to conserve.

Recommendations. In order to improve coastal fisheries management, PMC governments should:

- **Improve the effectiveness of enforcement**. Penalties for violations of fisheries regulations should be punitively high to act as effective deterrents,[16] and should target both fishers, and those linked to them in trade. Legislative ambiguity in the form of exceptions granted by Ministries should be avoided. Fisheries officials should assist customs officers in conducting regular inspections of export shipments. New laws and regulations should be developed and discussed with traditional resource custodians to facilitate future compliance.

- **Exchange information.** In the process of revising fisheries regulations, it is important that PMCs review and take account of regional experience in this area. Regional organizations can play an important role in disseminating this information, namely through the recently created Pacific Islands Marine Resources Information System.

- **Re-train extension services in fisheries management principles**. In many fisheries departments, extension services need to shift focus from development to management goals. Collaborative management, for example, is unlikely to succeed if not supported by solid

[16] In Vanuatu, for example, the Fisheries Act specifies severe penalties for use of poison or explosives—fines of up to Vt. 10 million (US$91,000) for fishers and traders employing these practices. This probably accounted for the recent decline of such activities.

technical back-up from extension services. National governments should ensure that coastal fisheries management goals are included in national strategies, and that re-orientation of extension services is adequately supported by incremental budget allocations.

- **Foster collaborative management with resource custodians.** Collaborative management regimes should be attempted in areas where strong customary leadership and CMT exist. A stronger collaboration between Fisheries Departments, Environmental Units and NGOs could help ensure that field support is adequate. Fisheries staff involved in collaborative management need to have the complementary scientific knowledge that villagers need in order to improve resource management in their area. Management decisions, however, should be formulated and enforced by the resource custodians themselves. Field visits should be complemented by awareness raising of conservation issues through appropriate media.

- **Develop management plans for key areas and resources.** Area specific and/or species specific management plans should be prepared in consultation with resource users, and implemented so as to involve them in decision making and enforcement (e.g., through the engagement of village wardens). Legal backing can be conferred through by-laws but care must be taken to keep management options flexible and adjustable to changing conditions.

- **Publicize good examples of local management.** In almost every PMC, there are good examples of local-level management that should be disseminated through the media, through the granting of awards during national conservation days, and through cross-visitation by local chiefs. The recording and dissemination of traditional resource management practices should also be encouraged. In particular, the financial gains from resource management should be highlighted, as there is often scepticism and ignorance on this subject. The link between resource management and increased profits needs to be publicized.

- **Use cost-effective ways to monitor field conditions.** Full-fledged stock assessments are rarely effective for the tropical multi-species conditions of the Pacific region. Often, the type of information required for management decisions can be obtained by low-cost rapid ecological surveys and participatory rural appraisal techniques. These surveys should be complemented by structured resource utilization surveys implemented at a national level. Additional effort should also be chanelled into developing regional *rules of thumb* regarding for example, stock abundance, which can be effective in guiding local level management efforts, particularly in the absence of national or other public support.

A Development Strategy for Coastal Fisheries

Development objectives for coastal fisheries should focus on their role as suppliers of urban and export markets. Improved access to market information, and an emphasis on competitiveness, quality control, and consistency of supply should be integral parts of export strategies.

National strategies for the development of coastal fisheries should be reviewed to include a re-evaluation of how public funds can be used to achieve national goals. At the present stage of development the role of PMC governments in coastal fisheries should focus on the following objectives:

- management and regulation of key fisheries;
- collection and processing of cost-effective information to back policy decisions;
- provision of supporting infrastructure where economically justifiable;
- provision of key services such as training and extension;
- creation of an enabling environment for stable investment, both foreign and domestic; and
- development of quality control and grading for export products.

Substantial public investment has been devoted to the establishment of marketing and distribution centers in many countries, such as Solomon Islands, Tonga and Vanuatu. Given the level of private activity taking place outside these outlets, it is doubtful whether these investments are necessary. Privatization of selected marketing and distribution facilities should therefore be considered.

In order to develop small-scale tuna fisheries, many PMC governments have invested in fish aggregation devices (FADs). Typical deep-water FADs cost between US$3,000-12,000, and last 3 to 14 months. For the most part, these costs are borne by government with no cost-recovery. Such an approach is not justified, particularly in Vanuatu, Western Samoa, Fiji and Kiritimati (Kiribati) where publicly-financed FADs are extensively used for sports fisheries. There is now sufficient experience with FADs in the region to promote their privatization, and/or introduce mechanisms for cost-recovery, particularly if exclusive access rights are granted, and enforced.

PMC governments have devoted considerable public funding to promoting new fisheries. These fisheries may in fact be commercially unexploitable because the ex-vessel price in remote areas is too low to encourage fishers to raise effort levels and take advantage of economies of scale. New fisheries should not be seen as a panacea for reducing pressure on overexploited coastal resources, and public funding should only be directed to new fisheries if their economic viability has been proven.[17] In any event, the development of new fisheries should not be carried out at the expense of improved management of existing fisheries.

Training, extension and research functions should be re-evaluated to focus on those activities where national fisheries departments have a comparative advantage over the private sector or regional fisheries institutions. In Fiji, for example, the Fisheries Department is shifting the emphasis of extension services from development to management. A strengthening of regional collaboration in research could also avoid duplication of basic research in fields as hatchery techniques for aquaculture species.

Creating an enabling environment for private investment will require streamlining procedures for license applications. With the recent resurgence of interest in fisheries investment in the Pacific, however, many of the proposals received are new to PMCs, and investment boards and fisheries departments often lack the capacity to evaluate their feasibility. At the same time, there is a need to distinguish between long-term proposals and short-term investors who generate little benefit to the countries. Due to the inherent fragility of coastal resources, it is important that technical departments be consulted on both the feasibility and the conditions of proposed investments.

In general, PMCs hold relatively small shares in world markets of coastal products. Under these circumstances, competitiveness in world markets will depend on consistency of supplies, high quality, and ability to access marketing information. Export marketing strategies should be formulated with a solid knowledge of their current prospects in world markets. These are outlined briefly below:

Bêche-de-mer. In 1992-93, Fiji, the Solomon Islands and PNG supplied about 14 percent (930 MT) of the total exports of bêche-de-mer to Hong Kong, the principal world market. Approximately 30 percent of this production was re-exported, primarily to China. The Pacific Island region also contributed about 15 percent of the total exports to Singapore. A recent review of the Asian market for bêche-de-mer indicated that the long-term demand prospects appear favorable in the expanding Chinese market, but that demand is likely to decline in up-scale Asian markets such as Hong Kong, Singapore and Korea.[18] These prospects favor the continuing extraction of lower valued species such as tiger fish, sandfish, and lollyfish.

[17] In some instances, such as in the case of Tonga, exploitation of a new fishery has been a significant source of economic growth and employment.

[18] See Kriz (1994); Conand (1993).

Trochus. The main export destinations of trochus products are Japan—to which the Pacific Island countries contributed 70 percent of the supply in 1990—South Korea, and Europe. In 1991-92, prices of trochus products declined significantly, in part, as a result of stockpiling of raw supplies by button processors. Button manufacturing industries in the region have also been severely affected by industry over-capacity relative to the availability of raw supply. Future demand prospects are uncertain, and will depend to a large extent on regulatory changes in Indonesia, where trochus is currently protected, and supplies from other Southeast Asian countries; the efficiency of management regimes in the Pacific; and the advent of possible substitutes for trochus buttons.[19]

Deep-Slope Finfish. Exports of deep-slope finfish such as snapper from PMCs have expanded in recent years to end markets in Australia, Hawaii, Japan, and New Caledonia. Returns to exporters are heavily dependent on freight rates, the species composition and quality of the catch, and the landed prices of fish in the place of origin. Moreover, the long-term prospects for deep-slope finfish exports are constrained by the fragility of the resources even in areas where the fishery is economically profitable. This has led to a substantial reduction in the size of the commercial fleets in Tonga and Fiji, in part, due to a shift to the more profitable tuna long lining. Given these constraints, the recent granting of exploratory licenses to large-scale foreign vessels, in Western Samoa and Vanuatu, should be strongly discouraged.[20]

Aquarium Products. Many PMCs export live aquarium products, which are air-freighted to markets in the U.S. and the U.K. The industry presently suffers from rising freight costs—40 percent of gross revenues for an operation in Fiji, and stagnating export prices, typically only 5 percent of the retail value in export destinations. Aquarium fish extraction can be sustainable if low-impact gear—such as collector nets—are used. However, operations in Southeast Asia make extensive use of stun poison to increase catch rates. It is therefore important for PMC governments to favor long-established operations with a record of poison-free guarantees and low mortality.

Live Fish Exports. A recent development in the Asia-Pacific region has been the growing market for live reef fish to serve restaurant outlets in Hong Kong and Singapore. To date, operations have been set up in PNG and Palau, and an application has recently been approved by the Investment Board of the Solomon Islands. Despite the financial attractiveness of these ventures, they have been associated with severe negative impacts, including: (a) violation of local agreements prohibiting the use of hookah gear (PNG); (b) poaching in areas where access was denied by customary leaders (Palau); (c) widespread use of cyanide poison leading to extensive coral reef damage poison (Indonesia and the Philippines); (d) depletion of breeding aggregation sites; and (e) lack of compensation of customary owners for the capture of by-catch. Given this experience, live reef fish operations should be discouraged in the region.

Black Pearl. Following the success of French Polynesia, pearl culture is presently being considered in the Marshall Islands, FSM, Fiji, Kiribati, Solomon Islands and Vanuatu. French Polynesia has based the success of its South Pacific pearl on an emphasis on high quality and volume control. Nonetheless, the average price of black pearls decreased by nearly 30 percent between 1991 and 1992 as a result of over-supply. The Cook Islands venture has been plagued by poor quality, overstocking, and poor technology development.

Future prospects for pearl farming appear stable, but favor low-cost producers such as China and Indonesia. The market may, however, be able to absorb highly differentiated brand name products such as the South Pacific pearl and white pearls particularly in view of the significant declines in Japanese production. Competing in this dual environment will not be easy for PMCs, and will require a careful start to avoid over-stocking.

---

[19] See Fao (1992); Nash (1992).

[20] These vessels, are a product of surplus capacity in the New Zealand fleet which resulted from the granting of exclusive marine rights to the Maori population.

Other Aquaculture Products. Giant clam aquaculture has been constrained, until recently, by the focus on an end-product food (adductor muscle), which was not cost effective. A recent breakthrough in Palau and Solomon Island has been the production of 2-year old clams for the live aquarium trade and local handicraft trade. The aquarium market, however, is expected to become saturated in the short term. *Tilapia* aquaculture has been successfully developed in Fiji for home consumption and sales at local markets. This type of small-scale aquaculture operation should be encouraged in countries with sufficient freshwater resources, but care should be taken to closely monitor the introduction of exotic species.

Seaweed culture in Kiribati is estimated to have produced export revenues of US$0.9 million in 1993. The seaweed—*Eucheuma*—is used in the production of *carrageenan,* a food additive. Current trends appear favorable, especially for low-cost extensive culture, but PMCs will face severe competition from major producing countries such as the Philippines and Indonesia. Despite strong support from both local fisheries departments and donors, most other aquaculture activities have been unsuccessful in the region.

Recommendations. Experience has demonstrated that socio-cultural traditions of engaging in fishing as a part-time, opportunistic occupation must not be ignored. Coastal fisheries development programs should be designed with the understanding that these unstructured fisheries are likely to remain the prevalent pattern in the near future, and build upon these traditions to maximize their potential contribution to Pacific Island economies. PMC governments should therefore:

- Move towards privatization of selected marketing facilities and distribution centers, such as the regional fisheries extension centers in Vanuatu, the Natai Fish Market in Port Vila, and the provincial fisheries centers in the Solomon Islands;

- Devise cost-recovery mechanisms for the use of FADs, and promote private sector involvement in FAD construction and operation, in conjunction with the allocation of exclusive fishing rights;

- Introduce quality control and grading standards for bêche-de-mer, as any extra return from this fishery is likely to come from improving the presently low quality of the product, and adopt best practice regulatory measures to stabilize supply (e.g. closed seasons);

- Carry out an updated trochus marketing study to assess the competitiveness of Pacific Island products and re-assess the viability of trochus button industries in the region, with a view to formulating appropriate policy decisions. These may include: (a) strictly enforcing export restrictions for raw shells; (b) restricting the number of processing licenses to the availability of raw supply; or (c) lifting raw shell export restrictions in areas where the industry is found to be non-competitive;

- In the Solomon Islands and Vanuatu, further economic analysis should be carried out on deep-slope finfish to determine the optimal number of vessels that could be licensed in areas showing evidence of over-capitalization.[21] Rotational fishing on sea mounts should be strictly enforced to allow stocks to recuperate. No licenses should be granted for the operation of foreign vessels because of the fragility of the resources;

- Poison-free guarantees should be established for aquarium fish producers and traders;

- Licenses for live reef fish exports should not be granted in the region in view of the limited capacity of PMC governments to enforce contract agreements, and the potential for negative socio-economic impacts;

- PMCs should encourage low stocking rates for new black pearl culture operations in order to avoid over-capacity and gain technical experience. Stronger regional collaboration in

---

[21] Recent MEY estimates for Vanuatu are believed to be considerably over-estimated as they are based on older, less reliable estimates of MSY.

quality control and grading is encouraged to ensure that the quality reputation of Pacific black pearls is not undermined;

- Given the high rate of failure of aquaculture projects in the region, it is recommended that governments refrain from direct participation in this area, and ensure that proposed new ventures be subject to rigorous economic, technical, and market analysis; and

- A fisheries investment advisor position should be established at FFA, with the explicit objective of assisting member governments in evaluating fisheries investment proposals, and to disseminate information on their potential impacts. A regional register of investors and investment proposals should also be maintained.

Table 4.10: Main Uses and Markets for Nearshore Fisheries Products in the Pacific

Products	Utilization	Main Producers	Markets	Status and Potential
Reef Fish	Food, fresh/chilled	All PMCs	Subsistence use, and domestic trade	In general, overexploited near urban centers; export market constrained by susceptibility to overexploitation; domestic market constrained in ciguaterra-prone areas.
Small Pelagics	- Bait for large pelagics - Food	-Fiji, Solomon Islands, Tonga - Most PMCs	- Generally caught by industrial tuna operations through payment of royalties; - Subsistence use and domestic markets	Fishery believed to be sustainable, but small pelagics are naturally susceptible to wide variations in abundance; small pelagic stocks in Micronesia generally insufficient to support pole and line tuna fishery.
Sharks	- Dried Fin - Food, fresh	Fiji, Vanuatu, FSM, RMI, Solomons - FSM, Kiribati, Tonga, Solomons, Vanuatu	- Generally caught as a by-catch of longline fishery, fins exported to SE Asia for food; past attempts at squalene extraction from deep-sea sharks recorded.	Generally unknown, but believed to be sustainable; potential exists for the exploitation of shark liver oil (squalene) for the cosmetic and aerospace industries; the use of skin for leather; and further development of sports-fishing.
Deep-slope Finfish	- Food, fresh/ frozen	- Fiji, Solomons, Vanuatu, Tonga - Micronesia	- Domestic market, limited exports to Australia, Hawaii - Subsistence and artisanal use	Overcapitalization of the fishery led to shifts to other fisheries in Fiji, Tonga, and Vanuatu. Potential exists for expansion of the fishery in the Solomon Islands and FSM if carefully managed, but resources are limited and susceptible to overexploitation. Can provide an alternative to reef fish in ciguatoxic areas.
Aquarium Products	- Live fish, algae, corals, giant clams, and other shellfish	- Tonga, Fiji, Solomon Islands, Vanuatu, RMI	- Exported to US, Australia, New Zealand, Japan, UK	Status generally unknown, but believed to have low impact if number of operators is limited, and coral breaking and use of poison is effectively prevented. Need strict guidelines to ensure compliance and respect for customary tenure.
Live Finfish	- Live groupers, coral trout, cod, wrasses	- None known at present; one license recently approved for Solomon Islands	- Exported live to restaurant markets in Hong Kong and Singapore	Similar operations in Palau, PNG, and Indonesia have led to extensive coral damage localized stock depletion, and social conflicts; not recommended for PICs due to difficulties of monitoring operations and interactions with subsistence and artisanal fishery.
Trochus	- Shell used for buttons; flakes used for lacquer, shampoos; meat consumed	- Solomons, Vanuatu, Fiji, FSM, RMI	- Exported to Japan and Korea - Meat consumed for subsistence	Button blank factories have been established in Vanuatu, Fiji, Solomons, Pohnpei, but profitability has been eroded by uncontrolled licensing and overexploitation of raw material; future prospects will depend on the success of national and community-based management initiatives and future world demand.
Pearl Oyster	- Mother-of-pearl used for buttons, jewelry, handicrafts - Wild stock used for spat collection for pearl culture - Meat used for subsistence consumption	- Solomon Islands, RMI, Fiji, FSM (Chuuk) - RMI, Solomon (experimental spat collection and grow-out)	- MOP exported, mostly to Japan - Round and half pearls exported to Japan	Black-lip resources substantially reduced in the Solomon Islands and Fiji. Trial surveys in Kiribati and RMI revealed insufficient stock densities for pearl culture, with the exception of Namodrik, Marshall Islands. Current experiments in the Solomon Islands and RMI should take into consideration quality and over-supply problems experienced by the Cook Islands and French Polynesia.
Giant Clam	- Meat and adductor muscle eaten; - Shell used for artifacts - Live giant clam used for aquarium culture	- Solomon Isl., RMI, FSM, Fiji, Vanuatu, Tonga - FSM - Solomons, Tonga,	- Meat consumed for subsistence - Meat and abductor muscle exported to Southeast Asia, American Samoa - Shell used for artifacts in tourism resorts - Live giant clam exported to U.S.	Wild stocks are highly vulnerable to overexploitation. Giant clam farming has been attempted in Micronesia, Solomon Islands and Tonga, but export meat market has not shown to be profitable due to the long grow-out cycle required. Promising developments are the export of live giant clams for the aquarium trade, but this market is limited and expected to become saturated shortly.
Lobster	Food	- Solomons, Vanuatu, Tonga, FSM	- Domestic Market (restaurant, hotel outlets) - Subsistence Use - Limited exports to Guam, Saipan	Little potential to sustain export-oriented fishery due to difficulty of applying intensive fishing methods (e.g. traps)
Crabs	Coconut crab used as delicacy food Other crabs used as food	Coconut crab - Solomons, Vanuatu,RMI, FSM (Chuuk) Other crabs - Most PMCs	Coconut and mangrove crab used for subsistence and restaurant consumption;- Other crabs used mainly for subsistence	Status poorly known; coconut crab is in high demand in urban centers, and is very susceptible to overexploitation.
Sea Cucumber	-Dried, boiled product used as specialty food, aphrodisiac, and homeopathic medicine in Asia -Subsistence Consumption	- Solomons, Fiji, Vanuatu, Tonga - FSM	Exported to Hong Kong, Taiwan and Singapore. Approximately half of exports into Hong Kong are re-exported to China	Likely overfished in the traditional producing centers of Solomon Islands, Fiji, and Vanuatu. Exporters will likely expand trade to Micronesia and Polynesia (e.g. Tonga), as prices remain high.

Source: FFA Fisheries Profiles,and World Bank staff.

5. FORESTRY

Overview: *This chapter identifies key issues to be addressed in improving conservation and management in the forestry sector. It focuses on those Pacific Islands Member Countries which have significant forest resources, namely Solomon Islands, Fiji, Vanuatu and Western Samoa. Recent developments in the sector, the current status of the resource, factors affecting trade in forest products and issues surrounding the effective management of these resources are discussed. Recommendations are made on how management of the sector could be improved by focusing on: protection and conservation of natural forests, better management of natural forests for production purposes and achieving a more equitable distribution of economic rents.*

Introduction

Tropical rainforests, a valuable economic resource, are rapidly disappearing throughout the Pacific Islands. Deforestation and forest degradation, resulting from agricultural activities and commercial logging, are widespread. Not only are timber harvesting rates unsustainable but harvesting is being done in a highly destructive manner, causing unnecessary damage to natural forests and negligible to slow rates of regeneration. In addition, in recent years logging companies have been extracting windfall profits during a period of high prices, and often depriving governments and landowners of additional revenues through various malpractices, such as transfer pricing or under-reporting of both log values and volume of exports.

Recent Developments in the Sector

The recent ban imposed on log exports from Sabah and reduced logging quotas in Sarawak and Western North America, which were responsible for the marked increase in timber prices in 1993, led to an increase in the number of overseas logging companies moving into the Pacific in search of new sources of supply. Many of these companies have contracts to supply logs to plywood and veneer mills in Japan and Korea.

These companies have actively sought timber licenses in order to avoid the substantial losses which would be incurred if they failed to meet their supply contracts. In addition, logging licenses granted by Pacific Island countries have generally given most of the economic surplus to logging contractors, providing them with windfall profits. These gains are so lucrative that companies and individuals have been willing to use very aggressive tactics in order to obtain logging licenses.

Consequently, over the past few years, timber licenses have been issued and logging agreements made far in excess of annual sustainable yields in the Solomon Islands and Vanuatu (see Table 5.1). It has been estimated that, at the 1994 rate of harvest (approximately 700,000 m^3 per annum), the Solomon Islands' remaining commercial forests will be logged out within 15-20 years. This period will be reduced to 8 years if the harvest rate increases to 1,300,000 m^3 per annum. The sharp increase in the rate of timber harvesting since late 1994 indicates that this is the more likely scenario. The jump in the approved timber license quota from 1,300,000 m^3 per annum to 3,400,000 m^3 per annum since 1993 means that the country's production forests could be liquidated in an even shorter period of time, with very serious economic and environmental consequences.

In the Solomon Islands, areas which have been logged heavily are not regenerating. As Poole (1993) has noted, forests in the wet tropics, along with their associated plants and animals, are very easy to destroy completely. In most other parts of the world forests can be destroyed while most of the tree species will survive. This does not seem to be the case in the wet tropics which is why he argues that exceptional care is required in developing these lands to ensure that their many valuable resources are not wasted and destroyed.

It is estimated that an annual cut of 286,000 m^3 per annum could be sustained in perpetuity, if this level of cut is implemented in 1996. If this is not achieved by that date, the sustainable cut figure reduces as excess cutting continues.

In Vanuatu, early in 1994, following lifting of the log export ban imposed in 1990, logging licenses were issued which would allow logging of timber volumes 5-6 times that of the estimated annual sustainable yield of 52,000m^3. Without firm government action it is predicted that the country could be logged out of all commercial stocks of timber within five years. Realizing the seriousness of the situation the Government reimposed the log export ban in June 1994, and commenced to renegotiate logging licenses, starting with those that had been issued on the timber rich island of Erromango.

Because of growing unease about developments in the forestry sector, agreement was reached between Australia, Fiji, New Zealand, Papua New Guinea, Solomon Islands, and Vanuatu to:

- work towards a common code of conduct governing logging of indigenous forests, to which companies operating in their countries will have to adhere; and

- urgently increase monitoring of logging and exports of timber.

Subsequently, a South Pacific Forum Regional Forestry Meeting in Port Vila, Vanuatu in October, 1994, began work on drawing up a code of conduct on logging of indigenous forests. The meeting agreed on a set of "guiding principles" and "best management practices" for logging.

Role of Forests

Forests play an important role in Pacific Island societies. Their functions include:

- to protect and conserve the environment (including soil, water and biodiversity resources);

- to provide cash income to landowners, timber processors and governments;

- to produce wood and other forest products;

- to provide cultural, recreation and tourism opportunities; and

Table 5.1: Timber Production from Natural Forests[a/]

Pacific Island Nation	Estimated Sustainable Annual Cut in 1995 (m^3)	Actual Annual Cut in 1993 (m^3)
Solomon Islands	286,000	650,000
Vanuatu	52,000	27,000
Western Samoa	12,600	22,000
Tonga	NA	NA

[a/] The term 'natural forests' is used in contrast to forest plantations which are forests in which naturally occurring tree species have been totally replaced by planted trees. Natural forest includes a range of types which have been subjected to varying degrees of modification by humans and which grade into one another (Poole, 1993).

Sources: Forest Department Reports, Forest Inventory Reports and World Bank Reports.

- to sequester carbon. (This role is gaining prominence as the world's forests are being depleted and concerns are growing regarding the potential impact of climate change).

The importance of forestry in Pacific Island economies varies as shown in Table 5.2. For example, forestry plays a significant role in the Solomon Islands' economy, accounting for nearly 55 percent of total merchandise exports in 1993 and 20 percent of total government revenues. It plays a much lesser but still quite important role in the economies of PNG, Vanuatu and Fiji accounting for 16 percent, 13 percent and 7 percent respectively of their total value of exports.

Fiji embarked on an ambitious program of reforestation in the early 1960s with mahogany in the wetter indigenous forests and pine, *Pinus caribaea* in drier areas on degraded grasslands. Its plantation program was supported by grant aid primarily from New Zealand, the United Kingdom and Australia. These plantations are expected to support a large, export-based forest products industry. Forest products exports have grown from 2 percent of Fiji's exports in 1990, to 7 percent in 1993, and this is anticipated to increase substantially as the mahogany plantations come on stream.

While the Solomon Islands, Fiji and Vanuatu have timber resources surplus to their needs, most other countries in the region, including Western Samoa, Kiribati and Tonga are net importers of timber products.

Table 5.2: Trade in Forest Products in Selected Pacific Islands Countries (1993)

Pacific Island Nation	Annual Forestry Exports (mill. US$)	Annual Forestry Exports as % of Total Export Value	Annual Forestry Imports (m^3)
Solomon Islands	69.7	55	NA
Fiji	32.9	7	6,500
Vanuatu	2.6	13	500
Western Samoa	Almost nil	<1	7,500
Tonga	Almost nil	<1	5,000
Kiribati	Almost nil	<1	NA

Sources: Country Economic Reports and UNDP/FAO South Pacific Forest Development Program.

The Forest Resource

Current Status

Forests in the region are in decline. Recently completed national forest inventories in the Solomon Islands, Vanuatu and Fiji, which define the extent and condition of their forest resources, support this finding. While much of the international media attention has focused on deforestation occurring in the Amazon and jungles of South-East Asia, small countries, like Western Samoa which has one of the highest deforestation rates in the world, have been overlooked. Western Samoa's rate of deforestation, approaching 3.5 percent per annum during the past decade, exceeds the average annual rates for Brazil (0.6 percent), Malaysia (2.0 percent) and Indonesia (1.0 percent) for the period 1981-90[1]; see Table 5.3. Clearing for agriculture is the main cause of deforestation in Western Samoa and Tonga. Remnant patches of hardwood forests are all that remain of Tonga's natural forests.

In **Vanuatu**, the introduction of large scale cattle ranching by colonial settlers has contributed to a steady decline in forest cover. Even on abandoned grazing sites, forest has not returned. The most common vegetation type in Vanuatu is that dominated by *Hibiscus tiliaceus,* a herbaceous shrub which effectively inhibits the development of forests by successfully out-competing trees for soil, water and light resources on disturbed sites. In the Solomon Islands there are many forest areas dominated by single pioneer species, believed to have been degraded by cyclones and clearing for cultivation. In Fiji and Western Samoa, poor, degraded and non-commercial forest types dominate the landscape.

Deforestation has been endemic in the Pacific since first human contact and along with cyclones is responsible for the development of secondary forests, savannah grasslands and a degraded fern-grassland. It is also probably the main cause of the extensive anthropogenic grasslands of highland Papua New Guinea, the xerophytic *niaouli (Melaleuca lewucadedron)* savannah of New Caledonia and the highly degraded "sunburnt lands" or *talasiga* lands found throughout Fiji (Thaman, 1993). It has been suggested that deforestation may have been responsible for the collapse of the pre-European contact megalithic culture on Easter Island (Fenley and King, 1984).[2]

Deforestation rates alone do not provide an accurate indicator of the severity of forest loss. Forests are also being rapidly degraded (i.e. the number of trees, the diversity of species, the portion of crown cover, and soil quality, are declining), often due to poor logging practices. The area of non-commercial forest increases every year, as logging and relogging further erode the growing stock.

While deforestation in Fiji is moderate (<1% per annum), degradation of natural forests is continuing at a rate which should be cause for

[1] FAO, *Forest Resources Assessment,* 1990.

[2] The Pascuans, a tribe of Polynesians who in 700 AD settled on small Easter Island, proliferated in 900 years from 200 to 70,000 people, before succumbing to a lack of resources due to overpopulation. (Jacques-Yves Cousteau, "The Global Challenge", *First Annual Conference on Environmentally Sustainable Development*. World Bank 1993)

national concern. The Department of Forestry has tended to focus its attention on the development of plantations of exotic species, while paying little attention to the management of native forests. Decisions to continue "enrichment" plantings of mahogany in natural forests are not justifiable when cleared or degraded lands are available for afforestation.

A review by the New Zealand Ministry of External Relations and Trade, of New Zealand development assistance to the Fiji hardwood plantation program, noted its concern about the loss of biodiversity as a result of planting in natural forests.

As illustrated in Table 5.3, in most of the countries covered, production forests form only a small portion of the total forest estate (600,000 ha versus 4.4 million ha in total). The definition of what constitutes a "production forest" varies across countries, but generally conforms to a standard FAO description which describes these as areas having productive, merchantable forest cover and located on accessible terrain of less than 30 degrees slope. In theory, even when all of the production forests have been logged, large areas of "non-production" forest should remain (ranging from 30 percent in Fiji to 80 percent in the Solomon Islands).

However, these forests are not "self-protecting", nor are they protected by legislation in most countries in the Pacific. They are often at risk from fire and encroachment for agroconversion. They are also under pressure from logging, particularly once the more accessible production forests have been logged. In order to protect these areas of "non-production" forest, which may include important watersheds and land which is too steep to be successfully logged or farmed, governments need to introduce and enforce land use zoning which defines permissible land use practices in sensitive ecological areas.

In most Pacific Island nations forest areas outside those classified as production forests provide an opportunity for setting aside larger, more viable conservation areas involving complete catchments or mountain to coast continua. The presence of these locational opportunities could be useful in setting protected area priorities in these countries.

Not shown in the comparative figures of forest extent in Table 5.3 are the significant differences in forest structure, diversity and quality. Generally, forests in the Pacific Islands are much less diverse in species numbers and in structure than the forests of South-East Asia. The vegetation is also less developed compared to the neighboring countries of Papua New Guinea and New Caledonia, both of which are older geologically and less subject to cyclones. A typical Malaysian

Table 5.3: Extent of Forest Cover in Selected Pacific Island Nations in 1993

Pacific Island Nation	Total Land Area (mill. ha)	Area of Natural Forest (mill. ha)	Natural Forest % of Total Land Area	Production Forest Total Area (mill.ha)	Forest Virgin (mill. ha)	Area Logged (mill. ha)	Change in Forest Cover (%/Year)
Fiji	1.83	0.821	45	0.27	0.16	0.11	-1.0%
Kiribati	0	0	0	NA	NA	NA	NA
Solomon Islands	2.75	2.20	78	0.254	0.124	0.13	NA
Tonga	0.07	0.004	6	0	NA	NA	NA
Vanuatu	1.20	0.900	75	0.055	NA	NA	NA
Western Samoa	0.28	0.215	77	0.016	NA	NA	-3.5%
Total	6.13	4.43	72	0.59	NA	NA	NA

Sources: South Pacific Forestry Development Program and Individual Country Forestry Reports.

dipterocarp[3] forest will have several hundred species of trees. Heights of trees emerging from the forest canopy range from 50 to 70 meters. In contrast, the richest forests in Melanesia have about 60 tree species, with emergent tree heights of 30 to 40 meters.

It is believed that most of the flora and fauna of the region originated from the centre of diversity in the Indo-Malayan region and spread eastward. This may account for the fact that diversity drops progressively east of Papua New Guinea. The barrier presented by large expanses of the Pacific Ocean combined with the fact that the island groups become smaller and more dispersed are factors which have limited colonization and restricted development of biodiversity - and in particular, hampered development of Pacific Islands' forest structure.

However, the Pacific Islands are thought to contain the highest proportion of endemic species per unit of land area or per human inhabitant in the world. High levels of endemism occur throughout the region due to the isolated evolution of island species. Fiji, Solomon Islands, Vanuatu and Western Samoa are particularly important for their wealth of biodiversity.

The biological diversity of islands is amongst the most critically threatened in the world. Isolated and endemic species can be lost in a few months through the destruction of habitat and the introduction of exotic species. The terrestrial biodiversity review commissioned for the South Pacific Biodiversity Conservation Program cites birds "as an outstanding example of depletion resulting from the impact of human actions on South Pacific environments. Worldwide, the largest number of documented extinctions (28 between 1600 and 1899 and 23 this century) have occurred on islands of Oceania, which now has more threatened species (110) than any other" (Dahl, 1984). These factors support placing a high priority on biodiversity conservation in the South Pacific.

Forest Ownership

Unlike many other tropical forest countries, the forests of the Pacific Islands are largely controlled by communities, not governments. In some countries formerly under colonial administrations, a small proportion of the land was alienated, mostly within the main urban areas and in the fertile coastlands. The proportion is small, however, with 83 percent of land in Fiji, 82 percent in Western Samoa and 97 percent in the Solomon Islands under customary tenure as illustrated in Table 5.4.

Customary land tenure is advantageous in that it puts control over the resource in the hands of those who would stand most to benefit from its sustainable management. However, the fragmented, scattered ownership pattern can also be a hindrance to national level planning for the sector and leaves landowners vulnerable to pressure from logging companies.

Table 5.4: Extent of Customary Land Tenure in Selected Pacific Islands

Pacific Island Nation	Land Ownership (% Custom)
Solomon Islands	97
Fiji	83
Vanuatu	98
Western Samoa	82
Tonga[a/]	-
Kiribati[b/]	40

[a/] In Tonga all land is owned by the Crown. But user rights have been vested to private families.

[b/] In the Line and Phoenix Islands, most land is owned by the Government; in the case of Kiritimati, all land is owned by the Government

Source. UNDP/FAO South Pacific Forestry Development Program and individual country statistics.

Disputes often arise among customary land owners over clan boundaries; the composition of a particular land owning group; who has the right to decide whether or how a resource is utilized and

[3] Dipterocarp Forest is the major forest type in South-East Asia, the term coming from the name of the dominant tree family found in these forests - the Dipterocarpaceae family. These forests are of greater height and merchantable timber value than any other broad-leaved tropical rainforest in the world.

how the proceeds should be distributed. While it is often stated that governments have little control over what landowners do with their lands, they can and often do exert strong influence on landowners. In the quest for increased incomes, by both governments and landowners, the longer term national interest frequently suffers.

Forest Products Markets

Pacific Island producers of forest products will remain price takers in the major markets in which they sell their output. This means that they are subject not only to changes in international demand and supply but also to political factors related to environmental concerns in those markets.

Most of the export trade in forest products from the Pacific has been in the form of logs. With a few notable exceptions, primarily in Fiji (Fiji Forest Industries, Tropik Wood and Pacific Green Furniture Company), most wood processed in the Pacific Islands nations is for local consumption. The Solomon Islands, Vanuatu and Fiji are self-sufficient in wood products and have some surplus for export. The remaining countries of the region produce only a portion of their wood requirements and imports of timber are generally increasing.

In 1993, log prices were 30 percent to 90 percent above their 1992 levels. Forest products prices also increased, but their increase was not as pronounced. This situation led to an imbalance in the normal relationship between log prices and wood product prices - placing downward pressure on log prices. In 1994, prices for tropical logs decreased by 10 percent to 35 percent from their 1993 highs while prices of plywood (made in Japan) were down by 20 percent from 1993. Sawn timber import prices (cif Japan), have decreased by 10 percent - high quality sawntimber decreased from US\$730/m^3 in 1993 to US\$660/m^3 in 1994.

One factor which contributed to the log price decreases of 1994 is substitution of other products which are beginning to make inroads into markets traditionally dominated by wood. Examples of this include steel and waferboard. Steel construction components are being substituted for wooden building framing materials (joists, rafters, studs, etc.).

The steel industry is offering attractive prices - competitive with sawn timber components at wood prices of more than US\$400 per 1000fbm.[4] Sawn timber prices in 1993 and early 1994 were above this level. Steel suppliers are offering purchasers who place advance orders, guaranteed prices for up to two years. Steel also enjoys a competitive advantage in fire insurance rates. North American steel manufacturers have set a target of taking over 25 percent of the home framing market by the year 2000. Similarly, waferboard is being substituted for plywood, due to its 30 percent lower price.

Some indicative reference prices of logs are shown in Table 5.5. Prices for processed wood products are consistently down from their 1993 high levels - the degree of price decline ranges from 3 percent for North American sawntimber; to 10 percent for Russian and Chilean softwood sawntimber; to 20 percent for plywood. Log prices are generally down by more than processed wood products, ranging from 10 percent for North American conifer logs: to 30-35 percent for logs from South-East Asia, PNG and the South Pacific Islands.

Prices for wood products, and their substitutes, control the price of logs. Price restraints on logs and their wood product derivatives are being imposed through market resistance and substitution, and therefore further increases in log prices are not likely in the near term.

Pressures in developed countries to eliminate tropical timber from the market, as a means of slowing tropical deforestation, if successful, could further depress tropical timber prices. In a 1994 paper, *Global Forest Products Trade,* Sedjo, Wiseman, Brooks and Lyon concluded that removal of forest land from timber production for environmental reasons would result in a modest 5 percent increase in log prices in the long-term. However, the paper noted that short-term price increases of up to 36 percent over normal market trends could occur, under buoyant demand, during the first decade after forest land is set-aside.

---

[4] fbm - foot board measure = 12" x 12" x 1".

Table 5.5: Indicative Reference Prices for Logs in 1992, 1993 & 1994

CIF (Japan) Price in US$/m³

Source	Species/ Grade	1992 Log Price	% Change	1993 Log Price	% Change	1994 Log Price
South-East Asia	Hdwd High Qual. Plylog	NA	NA	420	-35	275
South-East Asia	Hdwd Med. Qual. Plylog	197	+56	309	-32	210
South-East Asia	Hdwd Sawlog	132	+70	229	-35	150
North America	Conifer High Quality	165	+40	233	-11	207
North America	Conifer Med. Quality	136	+33	181	-12	160
North America	Conifer Low Quality	NA	NA	174	-10	156
PNG/Solomon	Mixed Light Hdwd	92	+90	175	-23	135
Chile/NZ	*Pinus radiata* Plantation	94	+38	130	-30	91
Russia	Conifer Low Quality	97	+10	106	-16	89

Note: CIF (Japan) prices may be somewhat understated as some importers may not include the export taxes charged by the country of origin. This is done to minimize import taxes paid on imported value in Japan.

Sources: ITTO statistics and World Bank International Trade Division.

Several end-use niches have been identified where tropical hardwood products are likely to remain competitive at higher prices. In general, the market niches for tropical wood tend to be where some or all of the following conditions are met: surface structure and color are of aesthetic value to the user; natural durability and superior strength to weight are demanded; and product value is high to allow for transportation costs. These characteristics are met in the following products: fittings and joinery for marine applications; downstream products such as moldings; and reconstituted wood products such as laminated veneer lumber, which offer the same special appearance and natural durability as solid tropical sawnwood. The product-specific market niches have to be researched from the point of view of a technology-specific end use and distribution system.

Japan, the world's largest importer and consumer of tropical hardwood logs, accounting for more than 40 percent of the world's imports, is also the largest importer of tropical hardwood from the Pacific Islands. Imports of tropical logs have been declining in recent years due to restrictions on exports in many former supplier countries (Philippines, Indonesia, Malaysia).

Japan's imports of tropical logs have declined from a peak of 27 million m³ in the early 1990s to 17 million m³ in 1994. Sources have also shifted - Philippines, Indonesia and Peninsula Malaysia and the East Malaysian State of Sabah, which once accounted for the majority of tropical log imports, have now withdrawn from the trade. This leaves the East Malaysian state of Sarawak and PNG as Japan's major source of tropical log imports. Recently Japan's search for new log sources, in conjunction with their traditional suppliers (Malaysian logging companies), has expanded to Africa, South America (Suriname, Guyana, etc.) and the Pacific Islands (Solomon Islands, Vanuatu, Western Samoa).

Increased exposure of Pacific Island countries to the international market for forest products highlights the need for comprehensive forest sector strategies designed to maximize economic returns while preserving the natural resources that produce them.

Forestry Policies and Management

Background

Throughout the Pacific, in those countries with significant forestry resources, the forestry sector has operated within a very loose and often ineffective policy framework. Until quite recently there have been few attempts to develop comprehensive national forest policies or forest sector strategies. Legislation governing forestry management has generally been weak, of limited coverage and unduly complex. (Reviews of forestry related legislation have recently been conducted in the Solomon Islands and Vanuatu.)

As pressures increase on remaining forestry resources in the Pacific, governments are slowly beginning to develop more comprehensive forestry policies. However, they will have to be prepared to back up policies with firm action before it is too late to preserve the resource along with its associated biodiversity.

Professionally staffed national forest services were established in the Pacific Island nations along typical European/North American lines. In general these forest services have been primarily involved in overseeing the exploitation of forest timber resources, collecting royalties and the establishment and maintenance of forest plantations. Most forest services have not focused on the sustainable management of native forests or on conservation of natural forest areas. This lack of involvement in the conservation of natural forest areas can be partly attributed to a failure to provide for this in enabling legislation.

In relation to logging, most forest departments have developed standard logging agreements, which spell out the main conditions to be specified in logging contracts between timber companies and landowners. These are mainly designed to ensure that the rights and interests of landowner communities are not violated.

Unfortunately, logging contract conditions covering treatment of the forest, both during and after logging are quite weak. In most cases there are no requirements for reforestation or protection of logged lands and often nothing prohibits landowners from contracting for relogging of their lands to another operator, who will remove trees (of lesser quality and size) not removed by the first logging company. This pattern results in degradation and in some cases complete loss of the forest resource.

Loss in Economic Rent

The economic rent associated with a standing stock of trees is the difference between the sale value of the timber and the costs of harvesting it, including a reasonable profit margin to the logger or concessionaire. This rent approximates the maximum amount a logger would be willing to pay for the concession.

Low rates of rent "capture" by Pacific Island landowners and governments have several important effects. The first is to limit government revenues and returns to landowners leading to benefits foregone. The second is to leave the rent available to other parties, giving rise to "rent seeking" by concessionaires. This means that there is pressure to harvest large areas in order to obtain quick profits. The net result is an acceleration in the rate of forest depletion as concessionaires rush to secure their share of profits. Finally, high profit margins permit concessionaires to sell quality timber products at low prices, even though the practice may not be economically sound.

Governments and landowners in the Pacific are forsaking economic rents, to which they are entitled, to logging contractors. There are three areas in which countries in the region have unnecessarily foregone timber revenues. The first is the revenue lost in the way logging contracts/concessions have been awarded, the second is the way in which timber revenue is distributed under the existing form of the logging contract and the third is losses which they may have suffered due to malpractices by parties to the logging contract. An approximate estimate of the distribution of income from logging in four countries in the region is shown in Figure 5.1.

The graph illustrates that resource owners consistently receive the smallest portion (10 percent-15 percent) of the log value, while loggers consistently receive 30 percent-50 percent in the form of excess profits. Government taxes and levies vary, from 30 percent-35 percent in PNG and Solomon Islands to 5 percent-15 percent in Fiji and Vanuatu.

There is latitude for increasing both the amount collected by landowners, in the form of royalties, as well as that collected by government in the form of taxes and other levies. The positive impact of a higher rate of government taxes would be that a lower level of timber harvest would be required to meet government revenue requirements. Based on current log prices and logging costs, the combined revenue collected by

Figure 5.1: Indicative Distribution of Income from Logging of Natural Forests

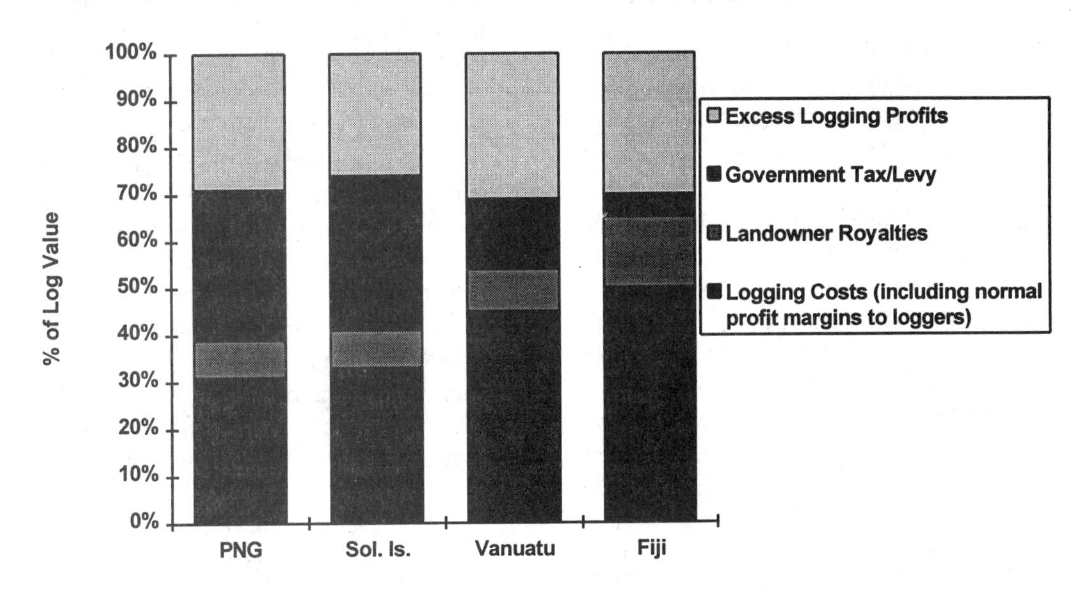

Note: PNG is included as a comparison. Data for Western Samoa were not available.
Source: World Bank estimates.

landowners and governments could be increased to 50 percent of log value - while still providing reasonable profit margins to loggers.[5]

Increasing royalty payments directly to landowners might lead to increased logging rates, if landowners find it increasingly attractive to harvest their forest resources. One approach which has been applied in Scandinavia to counter this trend is to establish a *forest development fund* into which a portion of landowner royalties are placed. Forest landowners who do not log their forests in a particular year can receive payments from this fund. This leads to improved forest management, since the decision on whether or not to log can be based on principles of forest management rather than the immediate cash needs of particular landowners. This concept can also apply to logged, regenerating forest areas whose owners opt to maintain their forests, rather than liquidate the forest and convert the land to other uses. Assets from the fund can also be used for extension services to advise landowners on improved forest management practices and on how to negotiate more equitable logging contracts.

The contracts between logging contractors and customary landowners are similar in the four countries. Agreement is usually reached for logging of specified volumes and species over a set period. Royalties are usually paid to owners on a log volume basis.

The share of log revenue going to landowners is in the form of:

- a small guaranteed payment or royalty;

- a payment in the form of infrastructure of uncertain quality and value e.g. roads and bridges which are usually designed to last as long as the logging; health centers and community centers;

[5] Evidence that this distribution of log value is workable can be found in the East Malaysian State of Sabah, where Government (which owns all forest land) in 1990 collected 56 percent of export log sales revenues in the form of royalties and other levies. It should be noted that in order to promote domestic processing, Sabah collected only 20 percent on domestically processed timber. The net effect was that 50 percent of combined (export and domestic) log sales value was collected by Government.

- an additional premium or goodwill payment which may vary with the price of the logs.

The share of revenue going to government is in the form of small guaranteed levies, licenses and export taxes, which are levied as a percentage of the f.o.b. log price.

In a recent report, Duncan (1994) estimated the economic surplus lost to logging contractors in Melanesia during the 1993-94 timber price boom. For PNG the loss was estimated to be around K193 million in 1993 and for 1994 a loss of K32.5 million was projected. The loss of economic surplus to loggers in the Solomon Islands in 1993 was at least SI$36 million. There is also evidence that the Solomon Islands has been losing large sums of money through under-reporting of log prices. In 1993 the loss from under-reporting of log prices alone could have been SI$94 million. Thus the Solomon Islands total loss in economic surplus in 1993 is estimated to be SI$130 million. Logging contractors have been allowed to appropriate most of the economic surplus from logging and this has been considerable, particularly in the past two years of high log prices.

Forestry Legislation and the Role of Government Agencies

Fiji is unique in the Pacific Island countries in having two institutions developing forest policy and legislation - the Forestry Department within the Ministry of Agriculture, Fisheries and Forests, and the Native Lands Trust Board (NLTB). The NLTB is a statutory body created by the Native Land Trust Act which empowers NLTB to control and administer all native lands on behalf of their Fijian owners. Native lands are leased out for various purposes including agriculture, tourism and forestry.

Since the Native Lands (Forest) Regulations were revised in 1985, the NLTB which previously had little influence on forest policy, has become very actively involved - even to the extent of mounting its own limited but focused research into natural forest management. In 1985 the NLTB adopted a set of proposals and policies for rationalization of the timber industry, protection of the native forest resources and for accelerated involvement of land-owners in the industry. The NLTB also at this time adopted a much more pro-active role in designing legislation and legal instruments for controlling logging.

Fiji's forest policy, written in the 1950s remains relatively unchanged and forest legislation is currently under review. Several reports on the sector have pointed to the need to update the policy to reflect current realities. Over the years the Department of Forestry appears to have focused most of its attention on the development of plantations, while failing to recognize the changing public expectations of the forest resource. Commenting on the situation in 1988, an FAO environmental scientist stated that:

> *...The Department of Forestry still functions in a scarcely derived form from that which operated 25 years ago,...In the intervening period there have been major changes in requirements from the forest resource at both the national and landowner level. Only the plantation sector has developed apace. Management of the native forest has not developed at all, exploitation is effectively demand generated, the resource is being "mined" ....the environmental implications of this are serious. Management of the native forest is in urgent need of a new direction. Principles of conservation and sustainable use will have to be adopted, if the native forest is not to degenerate into degraded 'bush'.*

The situation regarding natural forest management has not improved significantly since 1988. The Forestry Department was not able to provide information on the portion of natural forest which remains unlogged and little attention is being given to forest degradation resulting from overlogging and poor logging practices. Logged coupes may remain open for several years allowing relogging with impunity. When logging coupes are finally closed there are no legal requirements for post-logging management of the forest by loggers, Department of Forestry or landowners.

In the **Solomon Islands,** forestry has recently become the largest foreign exchange earner. Timber exports have jumped from SI$110 million (36 percent of total merchandise exports) in 1992 to SI$230 million (55 percent of total merchandise exports) in 1993.

The main Act governing forestry is the Forest and Timber Utilization Act (1969). This Act is regarded as inadequate, and due to its many amendments, complex and difficult to apply. A draft for a bill to replace the present Act was formulated with FAO assistance in 1989 and is generally regarded as a significant improvement on the present Act. A new forest policy framework was submitted to Cabinet in 1989, in anticipation of new legislation going forward. However, to date the legislation is still pending.

In July 1993, a further "Statement of Policy" was issued setting out the Government's policy priorities for the sector. While these statements of policy refer to the need for inter alia sustainable management, biodiversity conservation, equitable sharing of benefits, and minimization of environmental damage, successive Governments have been very slow in taking any effective policy and legislative action.

Recent policy actions to improve management of the sector have included the establishment of a price monitoring system in July, 1993 to prevent under-invoicing and transfer pricing. In an effort to increase the capture of economic rents the log export tax was increased in July, 1994 to 35 percent on the log price up to SI$250.00 per m^3 and 65 percent on the value of the log above SI$250.00 per m^3. The new Government which assumed power in November, 1994 reduced the log export tax, effective from January 1, 1995, to 32 percent on the value of a log up to SI$250.00 per m^3 and 35 percent on the value of a log above SI$250.00 per m^3. This change will result in a high proportion of timber rents once again accruing to logging companies (See Figure 5.1).

With the finalization of the national forest inventory, sustainable yield estimates can be made for different areas and sustainable management plans developed. The Timber Control Unit within the Forestry Division of the Ministry of Forests, Environment and Conservation is completing a review of the inventory data to provide options for the Solomon Islands Government to reduce license levels in order to achieve sustainable forest management. Their findings will be presented to the Government in May/June, 1995. However, the ongoing granting of logging licenses far in excess of the sustainable yield figure strongly indicates a weak commitment by Government to sustainable management of the nation's forestry resources.

In **Vanuatu**, forestry has been a relatively minor economic activity and, unlike the Solomon Islands, the Government is not dependent on forestry as a source of revenue. In 1993 Government revenue from forestry in the form of export duties on logs and sawn timber was only 0.4 percent of total Government revenue.

The Department of Forestry is responsible to the Minister of Agriculture, Livestock, Forests and Fisheries for the development and management of the forestry sector under the Forestry Act. In particular it is responsible for monitoring and control of logging operations, establishment and maintenance of plantations and forestry research.

There are two legal documents which govern logging. The Memorandum of Understanding (MOU) between the Government and the logging company sets out the terms and conditions which the logging company has agreed to, such as royalty rates, volume of logs to be felled, time period of permit, infrastructure to be constructed (e.g. roads, bridges and jetties) and requirements for environmental impact assessments. The Second Schedule is an agreement between the logging company and the landowners. This agreement specifies conditions such as sizes and species of trees to be felled, royalty rates, compensation payments for environmental damage and measures for resolution of disputes. A forestry officer must explain the terms and conditions of the Schedule to the landowners and witness its signing.

In order to obtain cutting rights to forests on custom owned land, a company must negotiate for a logging license from the Department of Forestry, which will also monitor and control timber harvesting operations. In addition to paying royalties to land owners, logging companies must pay a production based reforestation fee, which is placed in a special fund controlled by the Department of Forestry for reforestation work.

Logging companies and some landowner groups have been lobbying for the Government to lift the ban it placed on log exports in June, 1994. The Government needs to develop a comprehensive forest sector management strategy, which carefully controls the amount of timber exported, since the country is not rich in timber resources.

The forestry sector in **Western Samoa** has in the past operated within a relatively loose policy framework. Forest policy has been derived from the following four main sources:[6]

- objectives of specific projects such as those funded by NZODA, ADB and FAO/UNDP;
- legislation - principally the Forests Act of 1967, the Forest Regulations of 1966, the National Parks and Reserves Act of 1974 and more recently the Lands, Surveys and Environment Act of 1989 Part VIII, and the Watershed Protection and Management Regulations of 1992;
- the triennial Government development plans- Development Plan 7 (DP7) completed in March 1992 covering the period 1992-94. DP7 uses a strategic approach to development planning, rather than the project by project approach used in previous development plans; and
- internal directives - some have originated from Cabinet instructions, and others from within the Forestry Division.

Recognizing the rapid decline in indigenous forests and the inability of the plantation sector in the medium term to replace the indigenous resource, as the main source of wood supply for sawn timber and wood, the Government of Western Samoa instituted a policy review in 1991.

The main objective of this review was to address and resolve national forestry issues and formulate a policy framework to be approved by the Government in order to ensure sound forest management. This comprehensive review was submitted to Cabinet in late November, 1994. It is a serious attempt to deal with issues surrounding forest management and to develop a national policy framework and strategies to responsibly manage the forest resources of Western Samoa.

Although the formulation of this policy is a promising start, the success of any national policy will ultimately depend upon the commitment of Government to the principles of conservation and sound forest management. Failure to enforce sound policies will lead to the inevitable loss of remaining natural forests, biodiversity and species unique to these islands. The Government of Western Samoa like other governments in the region has been slow in developing and enforcing policies to protect and preserve remaining indigenous forests.

The Role of Plantation Forestry

In most countries of the region forest plantations have been developed - usually with the assistance of grant funds from bilateral donors - with objectives such as promoting rural development, increasing rural employment, diversifying the national economy and substituting for sawn timber imports. (See Table 5.6) They have often been promoted as a more productive alternative to supplying timber than natural forest management. However, returns on investment in plantations in the Pacific have been too low to attract significant private investment, reflecting similar experience in South-East Asian countries. Forest plantation development in South-East Asia has been characterized by distorted incentive structures and management inefficiencies.

---

[6] Government of Western Samoa, *Draft National Forest Policy: Forestry Situation Outlook and Strategy: Background to the National Forest Policy*. 1994.

Although there have been few studies conducted on the economics of plantation development in the Pacific Islands, Fiji Pine Limited estimates that large pine plantations in Fiji are producing a return on invested capital of 3 percent to 4 percent. It is expected that the mahogany plantations will produce an 8 percent return on capital invested due to the higher value of timber.

Experience in **New Zealand** and **Japan** has shown that forest plantations do not always produce the anticipated benefits and may cause unforeseen environmental problems. In 1919, the New Zealand Forest Service (NZFS) was formed and began establishing plantations of softwood species on land not suitable for agriculture in order to create a wood supply for the future needs of the country. By 1984, despite huge investments and vast areas of forest established, these forests did not provide any significant monetary dividends to New Zealand.

Forty percent of Japan's forest estate consists of plantations - primarily two coniferous tree species - cedar and cypress established in the post World War 2 period. They replaced rich mixed forests of oak, maple, and conifers. Now, with a virtual monoculture, negative health and environmental effects are being felt. Every year a large portion of the population suffers from severe allergy problems (pollenosis) as a result of unprecedented concentrations of mature cedars. These forests are also relatively poor in environmental values compared to the mixed forests which they replaced.

In the Pacific Islands, plantations have been almost exclusively comprised of exotic species, with few attempts to trial native species. This has had a negative impact on biodiversity, particularly where plantations have been established in natural forest areas. In some cases, industrial forest plantations have been established on non-productive grasslands, as in the case of Fiji's *Pinus caribaea* plantations. However others have been established on logged over natural forest areas, many of which could have been naturally regenerated at far less cost and ecological disruption through a combination of careful planning, control and execution of logging and post-harvest protection.

Fiji has the most extensively developed plantation sector in the region. Softwood plantations, primarily comprising *Pinus caribaea,* now cover 55,000 ha. Fiji's pine plantations are managed by Fiji Pine Limited, a corporation in which the Government is the main shareholder, while landowners are minority shareholders through Fiji Pine Trust.

Initial studies on whether to export pine logs or processed wood showed that the poor quality of plantation wood would not enable Fiji to capture premium prices. It was considered that investment in "in country" processing would allow Fiji Pine Limited to maximize the value from its resource.

Table 5.6: Forest and Tree Crop Plantations (1993)

Pacific Island Nation	Coconut (ha)	Softwood (ha)	Hardwood (ha)	Total (ha)
Solomon Islands	60,000	0	25,000	85,000
Fiji	65,000	55,000	40,000	160,000
Vanuatu	100,000	not significant	2,655	102,655
Western Samoa	47,000	not significant	3,106	50,106
Tonga	34,500	not significant	500	35,000
Kiribati	35,000	NA	NA	35,000

Source. UNDP/FAO South Pacific Forest Development Program.

In 1987 a timber processing complex and export shipping facility were established on Viti Levu for the *Pinus caribaea* timber. Since additional transportation costs have prohibited the processing of timber from Vanua Levu, an additional 12,000 ha of softwood plantation area are now required on Viti Levu.

The hardwood plantations, consisting principally of the introduced hardwood, mahogany, *Swietenia macrophylla,* now cover an area of approximately 40,000 ha and the Forestry Department plans to expand this to 85,000 ha over the next 15 years.

Western Samoa's industrial plantation forestry program began in the late 1960s, with the area devoted to plantations reaching almost 4500 ha in 1989. However, severe cyclone damage in 1990 and 1991 resulted in a large portion of W. Samoa's forest plantations being written off, leaving 2200 ha remaining in 1992. The recent severe cyclones significantly increased the assessment of risk associated with plantation investments and significantly reduced the expected rate of return and economic viability of large scale plantation forests.

In the **Solomon Islands** 25,000 ha of hardwood forest plantations have been established, all on Government land. The Kolombangara Forest Plantation Ltd (KFPL) is the only private company involved in forest plantation development. Their plantation estate is approximately 3600 ha. Problems facing the plantation sector include:- poor market prospects, uncertain stocking, inconsistent annual planting rates by species and locations, and difficulties in obtaining large contiguous areas of land for plantation development.

Pacific Island nations should not regard forest plantations, particularly those of non-indigenous species, as a replacement or substitute for natural forests. The establishment of plantations on bare land is rarely an attractive financial proposition to private investors, who usually require financial incentives, often subsidies, to undertake significant new plantings. Plantations require high levels of investment in capital and labor, in general produce low returns on invested capital and provide only a portion of the environmental services of the natural forests. If governments want to avoid having to subsidize expensive plantation programs they should pay more attention to conserving natural forests and managing them on a sustainable basis.

Key Issues to be Addressed in Improving Forest Conservation and Management

Those Pacific Island nations with forest resources are now facing the prospect that unless governments and people are willing to develop and enforce coherent forestry policies based on sustainable management principles, the forest resource along with the products and environmental services it provides will be lost within 15-20 years. Many associated endemic species will also be lost, leading to a reduction in biodiversity. The costs of environmental management are likely to rise while the potential revenues from tourism will be reduced as tourists seek more physically attractive locations.

If the above trends are to be slowed or reversed and forest resources preserved and managed on a more sustainable basis, action is urgently required in the following three key areas: protection and conservation of natural forests; improved management of natural forests; and a more equitable distribution of economic rents.

Protection and Conservation of Natural Forests

Governments in the region have been slow to recognize the social, cultural, environmental and economic importance of conserving their unique flora and fauna for future generations. There have been few detailed conservation needs assessments and ecological surveys conducted with a view to designating areas of high conservation value. The areas set aside for protection of biodiversity and endangered flora and fauna in Fiji, Solomon Islands, Vanuatu and Western Samoa are quite inadequate.

In **Fiji,** no serious attempt has been made to preserve a representative sample of its varied ecosystems, placing many endemic species at risk. Although large areas of protection forest have been designated, in practice there are few, if any, restrictions on the development of these areas.

Western Samoa was the first Pacific island nation to create a national park, O Le Pupu-Pue in 1978. Nevertheless the country has had one of the highest rates of deforestation in the world and actions to conserve the nation's biodiversity have not been pursued.

In the **Solomon Islands,** although some attempts have been made to identify and protect culturally significant areas, there has been little effort made to identify and protect environmentally important areas, leaving the Solomon Islands with no protected forests. Consequently, important habitat areas and species may be lost through logging operations or through agrodeforestation. One of the two forest reserves, the Queen Elizabeth National Park has been degazetted; and the other, a forest reserve on the island of Kolombangara, has been logged (WWF, December, 1993). Two areas, the island of Rennell and the Marovo Lagoon in the Western Province have been proposed for World Heritage listing.

Vanuatu established its first forest reserve on the island of Erromango in 1995. The reserve covering 3200 ha will protect stands of kauri, *Agathis macrophylla*, which are only found in Vanuatu, Fiji and the Santa Cruz group of islands in the Solomon Islands. Apart from this reserve there are no other terrestrial protected areas or restrictive management categories in Vanuatu. While there have been attempts to pass National Park legislation, the bill has not yet been passed. There are currently proposals to establish national parks in the Big Bay area on the Island of Santo; in the Lolihor watershed on Ambrym and at Wia Wia on the Island of Malekula. However, there has not been a comprehensive assessment, based on sound ecological principles, of what areas should be protected.

Urgent action is required to conserve natural forests and the remaining biological diversity of the South Pacific region. Recent initiatives such as the South Pacific Biodiversity Conservation Program funded by UNDP and the Global Environment Fund are beginning to address this issue on a regional basis. In addition, the recent completion of State of the Environment Reports and National Environment Management Strategies by countries in the region provide governments with the groundwork for developing more specific strategies and policies aimed at protecting biological diversity.

Six Pacific Island World Bank member countries have signed the United Nations Convention on Biological Diversity. The overall objectives of the Convention include: the conservation of biological diversity; the sustainable use of its components and the fair and equitable sharing of the benefits accruing from its utilization, including genetic resources.

In approaching biodiversity conservation, the Convention focuses on a number of development issues, including integrating biodiversity concerns into national decision making. Article 6 of the Convention calls for parties to prepare national strategies, action plans or programs and to integrate biodiversity considerations into sectoral and other national plans.

Since many of the remaining forest areas with high conservation values are found on custom owned land, conservation agencies must convince landowners of the need to conserve particular areas. Approaches might include establishing alternative income generation projects or providing some form of compensation to landowners.

In their 1994 study, *The Socio-economic Assessment of the Erromango Kauri Protected Area*, Tacconi and Bennet attempted to determine the economic incentive for forest landowners to enter into conservation agreements. They started by comparing the net present value (NPV) of a 75 year lease at the current rate at which government agencies lease unimproved agricultural land from landowners - 100 vatu (US$1) per hectare per year - with the NPV of logging royalties in order to see if the proposed lease payment was sufficient compensation for logging income foregone by landowners. The results showed that, although the total value of lease payments over a 75 year period exceeded the royalties foregone, when the payments were subjected to discounting - even at a low (social) discount rate of 4 percent - the NPV of the lease payments fell short of foregone logging royalties. To bring the NPV of the lease payments in line with foregone royalties the lease payment was increased over time. By increasing the lease rate by 25 percent each decade, the NPV of the lease at 4 percent was equal to that of foregone royalties.

NGO Initiatives. In Western Samoa, in an effort to conserve areas of custom owned land with high conservation values, a number of NGOs have developed four private conservation agreements with landowners in four villages. Although these agreements are understood not to be enforceable under Western Samoan law, they are written in a manner that forms a moral contract between the parties involved. Agreements of this type have had problems with landowners reneging on the agreement after accepting compensation payments or making additional demands for increased compensation payments after the agreements were finalized.

In contrast, the Western Samoan environmental non government organization, O Le Siosiomaga Society Inc., in an effort to protect the biodiversity in an area of cloud forest bought the logging rights to an area of about 6 square miles from the custom owners for a period of twenty years. This agreement which was signed in March, 1994 is legally enforceable, unlike the abovementioned private conservation agreements. This represents one of the first moves by an environmental NGO to purchase logging rights in the Pacific. Other conservation organizations are also considering this approach.

A few international NGOs including World Wildlife Fund, Maruia Society, Conservation International and Foundation for the Peoples of the South Pacific are working with local groups and organizations to develop alternative income generating opportunities in order to encourage landowners to protect their forests.

In the **Solomon Islands,** the Isabel Provincial Government passed three Conservation Ordinances which were drafted with the assistance of the Maruia Society of New Zealand. This legislation arose out of landowner concerns over their inability to control natural resource exploitation through traditional decision making mechanisms. Their concerns were based on a perception that unless firm action was taken to protect their forests, they could be lost for future generations.

Recommendations for Protection and Conservation of Natural Forests

Proposed Government Action

- **Biodiversity.** Countries, which have not already done so, should establish the extent and scope of their biodiversity resources by conducting conservation needs assessments and detailed ecological studies.

- **Protected Areas.** Effective systems of protected areas should be established urgently to preserve biodiversity. This should be done in close consultation with communities and landowners and could include conservation areas, national parks, and ecological reserves.

  Since many of the remaining forest areas with high conservation values are found on custom owned land, it is imperative that approaches and agreements are developed which will convince landowners of the need to conserve particular areas. These approaches may involve establishing alternative income generating projects or providing some form of compensation to landowners.

- **Public Awareness Programs.** Develop programs to create public awareness of the need to conserve forest resources to protect coastal areas, stabilize watersheds and maintain biological diversity (e.g. media, community extension programs and school curricula).

- **Institutional Capacity.** Streamline institutional capacity and government structure to achieve cost effective management of protected area systems.

Donor Involvement

- **Donors** should provide grant aid in support of conservation of natural forests, since this is an area which has been neglected in the past in favor of programs aimed at exploitation of natural forests and promotion of plantation development.

  Multilateral and bilateral donors generally are not equipped to mount small-scale community-based programs. There is scope for these donors to support local and international non government organizations, which are working with local landowners, to develop feasible and socially acceptable approaches to forest protection and conservation.

Improved Management of Natural Forests

The forestry sector is a significant source of income to national governments and to rural landowners in many Pacific Islands nations. In spite of this, there is little understanding of the principles and benefits of natural forest management. Typically forestry operations are treated as "mining of a non-renewable resource". There is a vital need to improve the way logging is carried out to reduce the unnecessary damage to forests, improve their regenerative capacity and to reduce the financial and economic costs of logging. Landowners, governments and logging companies all have a vested interest in improving logging practices.

While sustainability is a concern of many policy makers, what is meant by sustainable yield can vary quite significantly, even among foresters. The concept of sustainable yield in forestry arose under the conditions existing in Germany in the mid-nineteenth century and transferred, with little adaptation, to humid tropical forests. The concept originated and has continued to the present with the idea of supplying raw material - largely logs of various sizes - in perpetuity for the benefit of users. Since German forests had experienced a long history of management, old growth trees and their ecosystem equivalents were absent from these forests. These conditions did not apply initially to many of the forests in North America, Australia and the tropics, which contained extensive areas of old growth forests, with timber volumes accumulated over centuries (Cassells et al, 1988).

Today the concept is shifting away from just being associated with sustainable yield of products to embrace forest ecosystems including biodiversity, soil and water values and recreation and amenity values. Recent statements on sustainable forest management (Poore et al., 1989; ITTO, 1991, 1992a; IUCN, 1992) suggest that for timber production from natural forests to be considered sustainable, it should only occur in a land planning context that allocates forest lands for the total protection of biodiversity and the protection of fragile environments such as steep slopes and critical watersheds (Cassells, 1994).

However, theoretically and practically, doubts exist as to whether sustainable forestry is possible in tropical, natural forests (German Bundestag, 1990). Advocates of sustainable forestry in the tropics admit that managed forests are depleted biologically and lose some of their diversity. They nevertheless maintain that long-term constant yields are possible under certain conditions. One of the main conditions being that the volume of timber harvested annually be limited to the rate of commercial timber volume increment. However, the small amount of practical work that has been done does not permit such an optimistic assessment. What is regarded as one of the best examples of forestry in tropical forests, namely that in North Queensland, Australia, has not been assessed over a sufficiently long period to demonstrate sustainability. However, if sustainable timber yields are possible from these systems they are likely to be low by world standards and are only likely to be economically viable in the long term if they are directed at high value specialty products.

Since the likelihood of practicing sustainable forestry in tropical natural forests is poor, where commercial logging does occur it is essential to reduce canopy opening to a maximum of 25 percent to 30 percent in a given forest stand and to minimize damage to residual forest from felling, skidding and construction of roads, skid trails and log landings. This is necessary to ensure an appropriate environment for regeneration of valuable commercial tree species required for subsequent harvests. Sufficient canopy must be maintained to ensure germination and development of seedlings and to inhibit the growth of vines, herbaceous plants and pioneer tree species, which often out-compete commercial tree species for light, nutrients and moisture.

It is also important in the islands to retain a sufficient portion of forest cover to control water runoff and reduce soil erosion. For example, excessive sedimentation, when deposited on coral reefs inhibits, and in extreme cases destroys, the productive capacity of near shore ecosystems upon which the livelihoods of many Pacific Islanders depend.

A number of donors are supporting programs aimed at improving management of natural forests and reducing damage from logging.

In Fiji, the Australian supported **Forest Resource Tactical Planning Project** is providing assistance to design and implement improved logging licenses; more environmentally sound coupe-level logging plans (selected harvesting on a small area basis); and sustainable yield management plans for larger areas. Fiji recently introduced a National Code of Logging Practice designed to improve the efficiency and safety of logging operations, while reducing adverse environmental impacts.

The **National Forest Management Pilot Project** supported by the German Government in Fiji aims to develop management systems for natural forests, which stimulate growth and regeneration of the residual species, to provide sustainable yields of timber and other forest products. The field work on this project was completed in June 1994 and results are now being assessed. This project has addressed a previously neglected area and one requiring further research if the management of Fiji's natural forests for production purposes is to be improved.

In the Solomon Islands, Australia is supporting a **Timber Control project** which is assisting the Government to establish Timber Inspectorate Control Units and provide training for monitoring the activities of logging companies. The project is also helping develop a regulated export pricing scheme through the Commercial Unit, improve quality of sawn timber and assist landowners with information and awareness of their rights and management of the forest resource.

The **Profitable Environmental Protection Project** managed by Foundation of the Peoples of the South Pacific and funded by USAID has supported the introduction of portable sawmills in Vanuatu, Solomon Islands and Fiji. They argue that portable sawmills give landowners a means of converting trees to cash without harvesting large tracts or using heavy equipment and provides an alternative to the wasteful exploitation typical of large-scale commercial logging. Concerns have been expressed that proliferation of these sawmills could accelerate logging in many areas and that their use could lead to loss of log value as a result of poor milling. A recent evaluation of the project found that greater emphasis should be placed on teaching landowners the principles of sustainable forest management.

Carbon Offset Funding for Investment in Improved Forest Management. Tropical forests have a role in the global carbon cycle and the rising atmospheric concentrations of carbon dioxide. Uncontrolled logging results in unnecessary emissions of CO_2 and decreases the forest's capacity to regenerate and sequester carbon. Recognizing the potential of improved forest management for reducing greenhouse emissions, electric utilities are prepared to provide funds to forest managers to implement Reduced Impact Logging (RIL)[7] and other forestry measures aimed at increasing carbon storage.

Improved forest management will entail some costs and if it is to be realized in the Pacific Island nations it will have to be accompanied by a more equitable distribution of economic rents, which is discussed in the following section. ITTO[8] recently reviewed the costs of achieving sustainable forest management in Indonesia, Malaysia and the Philippines and concluded that internalizing the additional costs of moving from the present "liquidation" forestry to sustainable forest management will increase wood production costs by US$25 to US$50 per m^3 - equivalent to US$1,000 to US$1,500 per ha. Using a different approach, the World Bank[9] arrived at a similar figure for Costa Rica, where it is estimated that the net present value (NPV) of payments required to ensure sustainable forest management are between US$717 and US$1,573 per ha.

Based on the foregoing estimates and the forest areas shown in Table 5.3, the cost of achieving sustainable forest management on approximately 600,000 ha of production forest in Fiji, Solomon Islands, Vanuatu and Western Samoa would be US$750 million. To achieve this on the remaining unlogged production forest area of approximately 300,000 ha, would cost US$375 million. Whether or not this amount of funding can be raised from readjusting the distribution of economic rent is important in determining whether the forestry industry alone can finance sustainable forest management.

The four countries referred to above have a combined annual harvest from natural forests of

---

[7] Experience has shown that to achieve a 50 percent reduction in damage to soil and residual forests costs US$350 per ha. In paying for these costs electric utility companies can claim the carbon retained in these forests against their carbon emissions.

[8] ITTO *Tropical Forest Update,* December, 1994.

[9] Nalin Kishor and Luis Constantino, *Sustainable Forestry Can it Compete?* Finance and Development, World Bank, December, 1994.

approximately 1 million m^3. Assuming an average log sales price of US$150 per m^3, this harvest has a value of US$150 million. As illustrated in Figure 5.1, 30 percent to 50 percent (US$ 50 - US$75 million) of this currently accrues to logging companies in the form of excess profits. If, through improved rent capture, these four countries were able to decrease these excess profits to 10 percent to 30 percent by increasing their royalty and taxation collection by 20 percent (US$30 million), the cost of achieving sustainable forest management on the entire production forest estate could be recovered in 25 years. This is approximately the cutting cycle upon which native tropical forests are managed. To recover the cost of sustainable forest management on the remaining unlogged production forest area would require a period of 12.5 years.

Recommendations for Improved Management of Natural Forests

Proposed Government Action

- **Landowner Involvement.** Governments should explore ways of more actively involving landowners in the management of natural forests, including the monitoring of logging operations.

- **Forest Management Plans.** Detailed plans for management of natural forests for sustained timber production should be established in consultation with landowners. Areas of natural forest should be set aside for production purposes only after the conservation needs of the area have been met.

- **Sustainable Yields**. Under internationally accepted guidelines on sustainability such as those adopted by ITTO for tropical forests, timber production can only be considered sustainable if it is practiced in a land use context that allocates forests for the total protection of biodiversity and protection for environmentally sensitive areas such as riparian forest, steep slopes and erosion prone areas.

  Harvesting should also not exceed the best available estimate of sustainable yield. The allocation of the national total harvest should be sustainable within regions. Any new permits or licenses should only be granted if they are within the national and regional sustainable yield limit. Proper landowner representation and consultation should be ensured during the allocation of any new permits or licenses.

- **Research.** Further research should be conducted into areas such as the development of appropriate silvicultural systems for the sustainable management of natural forests and the increased use of native trees in agroforestry and plantations.

- **Extension.** The extension services of forestry departments in the countries studied should be reoriented and strengthened to ensure that due emphasis is placed on natural forest management and that they have the capacity to work closely with landowners in improving the management of their forests.

- **Logging Practice Codes.** National Codes of Logging Practice, which seek to minimize the destructive impacts of logging should be developed, incorporated into logging contracts and enforced with realistic penalties. Ongoing training should be provided to both logging contractors and those charged with monitoring and enforcement. (The use of penalties and ongoing training for both Queensland Forestry Service personnel and industry operatives was an essential ingredient in making the environmental guidelines for the North Queensland rainforest work in practice.)

- **Performance Bonds and Surveillance/ Inspection** should be considered as approaches to ensure that logging companies comply with Codes of Logging Practice and with their contractual obligations.

  For example, in the early 1990s the Philippines Government awarded rights to harvest trees through competitive bidding. The bidding process was used to determine the level of a performance bond which loggers would be willing to deposit with the Forest Department to guarantee that they would observe provisions of sustainable forest management plans. Five such areas were awarded covering a total of 50,000 ha. The average performance deposit paid was US$1,000 per ha. If a company failed to comply with its performance agreement an amount would be deducted from its bond. Conversely, if it met the agreement conditions the bond would be returned with accrued interest.

Donor Involvement

- Donors can assist further in improving the management of natural forests by supporting initiatives relating to the recommendations outlined above.

A More Equitable Distribution of Economic Rents

There is substantial scope for increasing both the royalties collected by landowners and the revenues collected by governments in the form of taxes and other levies. Recent Bank research indicates that, based on current log prices and logging costs, the combined revenue collected by landowners and governments could be increased to 50 percent of f.o.b. log value without endangering the profit margins of loggers.

Recommendations for a More Equitable Distribution of Economic Rents

Proposed Government Action

- In order to obtain a more equitable distribution of economic rents from forestry operations, governments are urged to consider the following measures, bearing in mind that all have certain strengths and weaknesses:

  Stumpage Taxes. There are several types of stumpage fees. They all tax what is cut and not what is exported or processed. The conventional field stumpage system which operates throughout most of Asia uses individual marking of trees for felling, followed by measuring, scaling and grading of extracted log volume (usually at a log dump or pond) to calculate fees payable by loggers. This approach is time and resource intensive. It is also subject to abuse: officials operating alone in the forest are subject to bribery or coercion. Logs can be removed from other areas and given false documentation and evade detection by field officers who are involved with measuring logs at the official dump site. In these circumstances loggers are free to high-grade the resource (i.e. to take only the most valuable trees, rather than all commercial volume) and illegally log a much larger area than covered by their license agreement.

  Export Taxes. They are the most convenient means of raising revenue from forest operations in the short term. These can be set to recover a significant part of the difference between existing revenue collection and what could be collected on the basis of market price and cost information. The simplicity of export taxes, the fact that they can be assessed at convenient check points making it difficult to bypass the system and their appeal to important economic ministries has to be traded off against the fact that they can be intersectorally distortionary and can facilitate discrimination between products within the sector. In addition, if they are set on a simple *ad valorem* basis they cannot maximize rent recovery from international markets in which prices are highly volatile. This problem can be overcome to some extent by a two tiered system. Such a system is designed to collect as tax a large proportion of the price beyond a defined threshold. The threshold, which can be adjusted periodically, is based on industry costs and on a reasonable return on capital invested.

  Export Bans. Bans on log exports have been proposed or are in force in PNG, Solomon Islands, Fiji, Vanuatu, and Western Samoa. This has usually been done to promote domestic processing. High export taxes or bans may play a useful role in the short term to allow governments time to develop more appropriate policies for sustainable forest management. Log export bans seem to have been quite successful in slowing the rate of deforestation in countries such as Vanuatu and Fiji. However, a major concern regarding the use of high log export taxes or outright log export bans to promote domestic processing is that they push the domestic price of timber below world prices and therefore transfer income from log owners to the processors. Devaluing the price of logs, which may already be undervalued if the price does not reflect the true replacement cost, lowers returns to the producer and forces trees to be used for less valuable purposes or cleared to develop agricultural land.

Independent Inspection of Exports. Independent inspection firms and surveillance can help to ensure that sustainable management objectives are achieved and that rents accrue to government and local owners. Inspection firms should be engaged when the uncaptured resource rents they are likely to recover significantly exceeds their costs of operation.

Merging Field Based and Export/Output Tax Measures. It is possible to blend aspects of an export tax system with some elements of a field based stumpage system. PNG will trial an approach to this system which will require logs to be tagged as they emerge from logging sites, and then measured and graded at export points. Thus, it will be possible to reconcile the number of logs coming from particular logging sites with those arriving at export points. This system will produce at least some of the benefits of a field based system, while preserving the export tax approach to revenue collection.

Summary

In summary, a long-term forestry strategy requires the protection and conservation of natural forests as a first step, in the interests of future generations. Second, natural forests need better management including improved logging techniques, to reduce unnecessary damage to forests, improve the regenerative capacity and to reduce the financial and economic costs of logging. Third, a more equitable distribution of rents is required through a combination of increased royalties to landowners, stumpage taxes, export taxes, and independent inspection of exports. Prompt action is imperative to save the forests. The scope for regional cooperation on these and other issues is discussed in the next chapter.

6. PRIORITIES FOR REGIONAL ACTIONS

Background

Regional cooperation has long been attempted and implemented in the Pacific Island countries. In principle, cooperation can increase market size, optimize on the use of scarce technical capacity to manage complex undertakings, and reduce asymmetries in bargaining power between small states and larger economic entities. Acting together, the Pacific Island states could take advantage of these possibilities. Integration through trade has already been discussed in Chapter 2, which suggests that regional cooperation in trade is best achieved by early integration in the APEC framework.

The predominant objective of economic cooperation is to raise incomes and provide employment. Within this broad objective, two specific categories of economic benefits can be identified. First, economic cooperation can provide member countries with access to broader markets. And second, the sharing of common services and their costs can reduce unit costs and eliminate unnecessary duplication of services.[1] The chapter discusses four areas of regional integration: (a) co-operation in trade and services within the APEC framework; (b) aviation and ocean transport; (c) natural resource management; and (d) co-operation in economic and social services, particularly in higher education and environmental management. It is evident, however, benefits from regional cooperation and integration will only accrue if the comparative advantage of cooperation is sizable, and the potential market increase substantial. Further, cooperation must function efficiently, with consensus building mechanisms able to achieve near-optimal economic solutions and not settle on the lowest common denominator, in order to avoid the degeneration of administration which would then add costs and delays in decision making.

Trade Cooperation

Scope for regional cooperation in trade amongst the Pacific Island nations is limited for a number of reasons. Imports are dominated by machinery, other capital goods and petroleum—most of which are not produced in the region. Likewise, exports are predominantly raw materials which are processed in distant industrialized nations. And finally, external trade policies tend to reflect major differences in the degree of fiscal dependence on import and export duties, with low tariffs prevailing in Kiribati, Marshall Islands and the Federated States of Micronesia, and moderate-to-high tariffs in Fiji, Tonga, Western Samoa and Solomon Islands.

There are, however, significant other constraints to pursuing trade cooperation within the region. First, the theory of integration suggests that benefits accrue when the trade patterns and commodities traded between countries are quite different. This condition is not met by the PMCs which, by and large produce and trade the same, or similar commodities. Thus, the potential benefits of integration are limited. Moreover, the experience of the South American countries from the 1970s suggests that regional trade accords which aim to promote goods produced within the region by limiting the entry of competing goods into these markets, only encourage inefficiency in production, thereby extend protection to the producing industries. Such policies entail a significant loss of welfare, with consumers bearing the brunt of this unintended protection.

Another factor which works against the PMCs is that benefits are maximized through regional integration in trade when the partner countries in question are dissimilar in size. Once again, the PMCs are more or less similar with respect to

[1] This chapter relies heavily on the comprehensive review of regional cooperation efforts contained in Uentabo Fakaofo Neemia, *Cooperation and Conflict: Costs, Benefits and National Interests in Pacific Regional Cooperation*, Institute of Pacific Studies, University of the South Pacific, 1986.

this attribute and so the potential gains are limited. This does, however, suggest that the PMCs need to look outward to improve their competitive positions through trade integration.

In the long term the PMCs should attempt to ally themselves in regional trading arrangements with larger, more dynamic economies than their own. In this respect, SPARTECA can be considered a first necessary step in the right direction. However, this must be considered as a stepping-stone to the next logical position which would be to join the APEC framework. Such an attempt at integration would be truly trade enhancing and would subject the PMCs to the competition necessary to increase efficiency. If direct entry into such an arrangement is obstacle-ridden, then the PMCs may want to consider piggy-backing into the APEC framework through their larger SPARTECA partners.

Given the difficulty of directly obtaining membership in a regional accord such as APEC, as well as the long-term nature of such an endeavor, there is, however, a good case for the PMCs to unilaterally adopt investment and trade liberalization measures as they are negotiated and agreed to within the APEC group. This would serve to increase the outward orientation and efficiency of the PMCs and could widen their duty free access to other markets. At the same time it would have the positive effect of promoting their case for membership in pacts such as APEC.

The main impediments to benefiting from intra-regional trade are those mentioned above which all point to the small size of the market as the limiting factor. This, in turn, suggested that the PMCs look outward in order to realize benefits from integration and cooperation in trade. At the same time it must be stressed that such cooperation must function efficiently in practice, leading to *best practice* decisions being taken. Otherwise rising administrative costs and inertia will derail such cooperation efforts and reduce the net benefits from integration significantly.

Coordinating Trade Administration. The quarantine, labeling, custom's codes, consumer protection and rules-of-origin procedures differ significantly among the Pacific Island states and in their major trading partners. The lack of uniform trade procedures adds to the costs of importing and exporting and, for fresh produce, the lack of uniform procedures serves to jeopardize access to major consumer markets.

The Forum Secretariat has reviewed the administrative aspects of market access[2] and has recommended, amongst others, that steps be taken to harmonize quarantine risk assessment, treatment and inspection procedures; standardize phytosanitary and veterinary certification; broaden the adoption of the harmonized system of tariff classification; standardize custom's documentation; centralize and make more transparent trade licensing; establish regional consumer protection, packaging and labeling legislation; and establish a uniform certificate of origin for all trade within the region. Such initiatives merit serious consideration.

There are other benefits that could accrue from coordinating trade policies. As in the case of the Caribbean states, the discipline of a common external tariff could serve to encourage more outward oriented and transparent trade regimes. In this sense, a multilateral trade policy approach could serve to enhance the capacity of each individual nation to respond to changing global trading conditions.

Cooperation in Aviation and Sea Transportation

Air and sea transportation link Pacific Island nations to the larger global markets. Distances are great and trade volumes tend to be small. These factors combine to raise transport and shipment costs. In addition, the operation of modern aviation and freight facilities is highly capital intensive, technologically complex and exhibits significant economies of scale and scope. All of these are factors that argue in favor of regional cooperation.

---

[2] See Development Strategies Consultants Pty Ltd, Review of Administrative Aspects of Market Access in the Region, Forum Secretariat, September 1993.

The PMCs have cooperated in establishing a common sea freight service and in load-sharing international flight segments. The high financial losses associated with operating independent national airlines, however, bears witness to the need to improve regional integration in operating international aviation services.

During the 1960s, an attempt was made to establish a regional international airline with Fiji (Fiji Airlines) as the hub. While shares of the airlines were distributed to different island governments, the airline was unable to adequately address the needs of the different island states. In the 1970s, national airlines were founded in Papua New Guinea (Air Niugini), Vanuatu (Air Vanuatu), Solomon Islands (Solomon Airlines), Tonga (Royal Tongan), Kiribati (Air Tungaru), New Caledonia (Air Caledonia International), Western Samoa (Polynesian Airlines), and Marshall Islands (Airline of the Marshall Islands). Many of these airlines have received grants in cash and kind from donors and governments, and practically all have operated with large losses.

In 1993, total losses from the region's air carriers were estimated to be of the order of US$60 million per annum. For some countries, these losses may have serious macroeconomic repercussions[3]. Conversely, after many years of losses and capital injections, Air Pacific, Air Vanuatu and Air Niugini have reported operating profits—all three having developed a diversified tourism, business travel and air cargo customer base. Fiji's national carrier, Air Pacific, envisions itself as the hub of the South Pacific in airline operations and has been one of the leading proponents of the *hubbing concept*. In 1985, Air Pacific entered into an alliance agreement with Qantas under which Air Pacific would coordinate global routes with Qantas. Qantas owns 10 percent of Air Pacific and is represented on its Board of Directors. The other shareholders of Air Pacific include the Governments of Western Samoa (5 percent), Tonga (5 percent) and Fiji (70 percent).

Largely in recognition of the critical financial situation of many of the smaller island airlines, attempts have already been made to rationalize services, through code-sharing different routes, wet-leasing planes and eliminating non-viable routes. As discussed in Chapter 3, given the precarious financial circumstances of the smaller airlines, new approaches to international aviation cooperation may need to be pursued.

One option would be to revive efforts made to establish a truly regional airline. This could be accomplished by merging existing national carriers into an expanded Air Pacific. The terms and conditions of such a merger would require extensive negotiations and would require some conversion of outstanding airline debt into equity. Once consolidated, Air Pacific should be granted the autonomy needed to conduct its operations as a commercial entity, while providing an assured level of international air access to the smaller regional states.

There are other options for improving regional air access that would benefit from collective action. Very few charter flight operators serve Pacific Island destinations, outside of Tahiti and New Caledonia. The PMCs have not actively attempted to encourage charter airlines because of the competition that this would bring to already financially ailing national carriers. The advantages of broadening air access by encouraging charter operations far outweighs the costs in market share to national carriers. In fact, the tourism industry in the Maldives, Gabon, the Gambia and the majority of small Caribbean nations rely primarily on air access through charter flight operations. A combined effort by the civil aviation authorities of the respective PMCs to promote charter airline operations, and to grant air access into the region on a non-reciprocal basis, would help to improve

[3] In 1993, operating losses of Solomon Airlines were in excess of US$10 million or close to one-fifth of public expenditures. Accumulated debts of Polynesian Air were in excess of US$20 million, with annual losses estimated in 1994 at close to WS$15 million per annum.

international air access and lower the cost of transacting business in the Pacific.[4]

Forum Shipping Lines. The Pacific Forum lines came into being in 1978 to provide regular sea freight services to all of the Forum Secretariat nations, including the provision of essential services on non-commercial routes. The Forum Lines is owned by the nations of the South Pacific Forum and leases boats from four of the member nations. The European Community provided an initial capital subsidy of 6 million ECU. Additional subsidies have been provided on a regular basis by the Governments of Australia and New Zealand. Financial problems have plagued the Forum Lines and have led to the elimination of operations on those routes with limited cargo. At the same time, on the higher volume routes (between Fiji, Japan and the Northern Pacific), there has been a significant increase in competition from commercial freighter services.

The chronic financial problems of the Forum Lines dictate the need to re-examine the direction and focus of the cargo service. As a *carrier of last resort,* there are numerous advantages to subsidizing cargo services. But on the more commercial routes, there is little justification for public sector support.

[4] Pacific Islands States have been reluctant to grant landing rights and fifth-freedom rights to nations that do not grant reciprocal treatment to their national carriers. This has hindered the development of charter operations from distant markets, as these nations generally do not have aviation agreements in place with the PMCs. The general principle in aviation negotiation should not be one of securing rights for national carriers but should be one of encouraging carriers to provide links between distant markets and the South Pacific. Accordingly, a policy of non-reciprocal airline market access should be considered. These efforts have been supported by the Oceanic Fisheries Program of the SPC, which is responsible for stock assessment and statistical information gathering.

Splitting the Forum Lines into distinct entities merits consideration. One would be responsible for the more commercial routes and would be operated as a fully commercial entity, without government subvention. The other would be given responsibility for servicing the freight routes to the small island states, which tend to be loss-leaders. Separating the commercial from the non-commercial services would provide greater transparency in apportioning the costs and benefits of providing regular freight services to the smallest Pacific states.

Cooperation in Resource Management

The economic fortunes of the PMCs are closely linked to the effective management of natural resources. Fragile ecologies, growing population pressures, mounting evidence of unsustainable rates of resource exploitation and rising demand for fisheries and forestry products suggests the need for careful management of the region's resources.

Cooperation in natural resource management has been largely limited to the exchange of scientific information. Each nation has tended to regulate the use and trade of natural resource products in an independent fashion. Due to unequal bargaining power and access to information, the PMCs have reached resource exploitation agreements that are too lax and difficult to enforce.

Fisheries. Within the exclusive economic zone of the Forum Island states lies more than half of the world's supply of canning-grade tuna. The distant water fishing resources of the member states are difficult to police and are exploited by vessels from more than 20 different nations. In recognition of the importance of the region's marine resources, and of the advantages to seeking common solutions to resource management, the Forum Fisheries Agency (FFA) was established in Honiara, Solomon Islands in 1979. The FFA has a professional staff of 25, and an annual budget of US$1.6 million. It has been instrumental in assisting member countries with management, licensing, monitoring, and surveillance of offshore tuna resources. It has been largely responsible for establishing, harmonizing and coordinating fisheries policies, particularly those pertaining to foreign fleet access to national waters, between it's member states. Consequently the fisheries sector provides the best example of successful regional cooperation in the Pacific.

Building upon the work conducted at the FFA, further efforts are required to monitor and assess the factors influencing fisheries resource levels (see Chapter 4). Collective initiatives are also needed to improve surveillance and conservation programs. These efforts will help ensure that the region's fisheries stocks are exploited in a sustainable manner.

A strong case can also be made for buttressing collective efforts to assign deep sea fishing rights to foreign vessels. With the exception of the multilateral fisheries agreement with the United States, which fixes and distributes the resource rent amongst the countries in which the fish were caught, other nations have entered into deep-sea resource use agreements on a bilateral (enterprise or country) basis.

The strategy of bilateralism may have reduced possible market returns to the PMCs. As noted in Chapter 4, the estimated value of the distant PMC catch is of the order of US$1.2 billion, while fees paid to island nations are of the order of US$56 million, or just over 4 percent of the value of the catch. There is considerable variation in access fees paid by the different fishing nations: the USA pays 10 percent of the value of the catch; Japan 5 percent; Taiwan 3.7 percent and Korea 2.2 percent. Under reporting is also an issue, and is estimated to have exceeded 50 percent of the 1992 Taiwanese and Korean catch from the South Pacific.

Shifting the basis of deep-sea fisheries agreements from bilateral to multilateral accords will provide PMCs the opportunity to reap significantly higher resource rents and will ease enforcement and resource conservation efforts. Negotiations are underway to develop a multilateral arrangement with the Government of Taiwan. By signaling the intention to shift fisheries agreements from bilateral arrangements to a common multilateral standard, as agreed at the 1994 Brisbane meeting, the Forum States would improve their negotiating position with foreign vessels and enhance their ability to fully enforce such agreements. In support of a stronger focus on multilateral agreement it will be important for Pacific Island countries to ensure that sound management principles are harmonized around the region, by providing legal backing through national legislation, and by incorporating these principles as conditions of access in new multilateral agreements.

Forestry. As seen in Chapter 5, forest products are a major source of export earnings in PNG, Solomon Islands, and Fiji. Over- exploitation of natural forests, under reporting of exports, and high profits accruing to logging firms, particularly in recent years, are problems common to several of the PMCs. Countries have tried to address these problems by developing forestry policies and by strengthening institutional capacity in forestry management. Still, forest resources are not managed in a sustainable and economic fashion.

With the increasing scarcity of natural forest products in world markets, there will be increasing pressure on PMCs to over-exploit fragile forest resources. Underscoring the urgency of improving forestry management, Pacific Island countries are exploring the feasibility of adopting a common code of conduct for logging operations in indigenous forests and to improve the monitoring of logging and timber exports.

The South Pacific Forestry Development Program is an important UNDP regional program, executed by FAO, which is aimed at improving coordination of activities within the sector and providing support to member countries. Key initiatives supported by the program include, the Regional Heads of Forestry Meeting held annually, the production of a regional newsletter entitled, *"Pacific Islands Forests and Trees"*, and publication of a *Directory of the Oceania Forest Sector*. This program has played a valuable role in fostering closer cooperation, coordination and collaboration among persons and agencies working in the forestry sector within the region.

Cooperation in Economic and Social Services: Higher Education and Environment

In an increasingly competitive global environment, the size, composition and productivity of the skilled labor force will become an increasingly important determinant of international competitiveness. The small numbers of graduates and the need for highly specialized training facilities suggests that there are significant benefits to be garnered from regional cooperation in higher education. The past efforts to support a regional University reflect an awareness of the benefits to be derived from regional cooperation in post-secondary education.

Higher Education. The University of the South Pacific (USP), was founded at Laucala Bay, Suva, on the site vacated by the Royal New Zealand Air Force in February 1970. The USP continues to occupy the main campus in Suva and has a smaller agricultural campus in Apia, Western Samoa. Special satellite units of the University are also located in Niue, the Cook Islands, Tuvalu, the Solomon Islands, Nauru, Tonga, Vanuatu and Kiribati. With its 350 professional staff, an annual budget of US$18 million and close to 2,000 students enrolled in tertiary training, USP is the single largest source of higher education for students in the region. Greater cooperation amongst the PMCs to resolve current problems affecting the USP is urgent, if the Pacific Island countries wish to benefit from a regional institution.

Demand for post-secondary training is forecast to rise rapidly over the coming decade. This is due to a combination of population increase, improved access to secondary education and a growing demand for students with post-secondary training to provide economic services within the region or abroad. As noted in Chapters 3, 4, and 5, more training in the field of tourism, fisheries, and forestry will be required. First and foremost, such training is most effectively carried out in collaboration with the respective industries.

The main regional post-secondary training challenge is to meet rising internal demand and improve the effectiveness of USP. To this end, the following initiatives merit consideration:

- tighten management and quality standards for both faculty and student bodies to match rising global tertiary training standards;

- shift the training focus from liberal arts and other forms of training from qualifying purely for public administration to technical sciences and business administration so that USP training will be more responsive to market forces;

- reallocate a major portion of donor support for tertiary training programs from high cost Rim country institutions to USP; and

- establish mechanisms to coordinate training offered in USP with the Institutes for Higher Education with those in PMCs and Rim countries.

Environment. A fragile environment is perhaps the most common feature the Pacific Island countries share because of their unique topographies. Managing the environment and environmental services through cooperative regional arrangements has the potential to generate significant benefits for two reasons. First, given the small physical size of the countries, cooperation in this area should allow countries to benefit from economies of scale. Second, given the weak human resource base in the region, sharing in such an area as this should contribute to institution-building. In recognition of this, the Pacific island countries established the South Pacific Regional Environmental Program (SPREP) in 1983.

Problems of coastal pollution and degradation are evident in all the PMCs with many common elements—urban encroachment on natural habitats, loss of mangrove areas and lagoon eutrophication. Damage to coral reefs due to pollution or coral blasting may have serious socio-economic consequences. This is due to the importance of reefs as centers of marine resources and their relation to the food-chain; and, to the important function that reefs serve by way of protecting low-lying-atolls and islands from the open ocean. Thus protection of coastal habitats is an essential function which could form one basis for regional cooperation on the environment.

The vulnerability of many of the Pacific Islands to natural phenomena, such as cyclones, flooding, etc., suggests another important area where the countries may benefit from a regional sharing arrangement. Thus, early warning systems and other elements of disaster preparation and response are issues which lend themselves to regional cooperation. Considerable cost savings may be realized by lowering the unit costs through sharing, given the high capital costs of some of these activities

Finally, a third area which may lend itself to regional efforts concerns marine conservation issues. Given its status as the largest ocean, the Pacific is host to a great diversity of marine life and habitats, and the scope for conservation is very large indeed. These potential conservation areas, however, are distributed without regard to national boundaries. Thus, the trans-boundary nature of the resource would necessitate multinational or regional efforts in the area of conservation.

SPREP, headquartered in Apia, was established to assist the countries of the region to maintain and improve the quality of the environment. It's mandate gives it an extremely broad coverage of environmental issues, both terrestrial and marine. To date, it has assisted many Pacific Islands with the preparation of their National Environmental Management Strategies, playing a largely coordinating role. It also conducts research in all pertinent environmental areas, relying heavily on a cooperative approach to project implementation.

Considerable scope exists for SPREP to undertake more initiatives at the regional level as discussed above. An area which should lend itself particularly well to this is the establishment and management of marine conservation areas. External funding is potentially available for such efforts—through, for example, the Global Environment Fund—and SPREP, with its technical expertise, is ideally placed to take advantage of such opportunities at the regional level. Finally, it can play a catalytic role in the region by actively disseminating information about environmental issues, actions and their outcomes in different Pacific Island countries.

NGOs can also play an important role in articulating and addressing environmental concerns. The Pacific Islands have a strong, and in some instances well-established record of NGO participation in environmental areas. These organizations can be an extremely cost-effective way of undertaking initiatives whether in surveys, research, implementation, or dissemination. For example, in the Solomon Islands NGOs have been extremely active in the past few years in the forestry area and are considered to have made a positive contribution. This has been done mainly through village-level education programs, designed and conducted by NGOs, on forestry conservation practices and the linkages of logging to degradation of terrestrial and marine habitats. Thus the PMCs should encourage these types of initiative, especially since they are in the long-term national interest and are usually cost-effective, relying on few public funds.

COUNTRY PROFILES

FIJI

Population: **759,000 (1993)**

GDP: **US$1,647 million (1993)**

GNP Per Capita: **US$2,130 (1993)**

Introduction

Fiji is endowed with a rich natural resource base, including abundant stocks of forests, minerals and fisheries resources. Despite remoteness, vulnerability to natural hazards and other natural handicaps, as a small island economy, Fiji ranks as one of the largest and most developed of the Pacific Island economies. Sugar and tourism have traditionally been the life-blood of the economy, with garments emerging as a significant new industry beginning in the late 1980s. It has a comparatively high level of human resource development, with an average life expectancy at birth of 72 years, an infant mortality rate of about 23 per thousand, and a literacy rate over 80 percent. Fiji has a standard of living of a lower-middle income developing country with a per capita income of US$2,130 (1993).

The upheavals associated with the events of 1987 represent an economic and political watershed for Fiji, with repercussions still evident. The economic recession that followed the political turmoil quickly eroded the limited gains in income that had been achieved over the previous decade, and much of Fiji's growth since 1987 has served primarily to recover the ground lost in that short period. The Government confronted the economic crisis by adopting an economic reform program that focused on restoring stability through prudent management of fiscal, monetary and exchange rate policies. While the initial economic response to the program was favorable (GDP grew by over 8 percent per year during 1989-90), the recovery was short-lived. Since then, economic performance has been disappointing, with real per capita output growth averaging only around 1 percent per annum during 1991-94.

Recent Economic Developments

Overall *GDP performance* has been somewhat stronger in the 1992-94 period than in previous years, with the major contribution occurring from agriculture. Sugar cane value added expanded by over 9 percent in 1992 and 1994, the two years in which GDP growth exceeded 2 percent. The slowdown in economic expansion in 1993 to under 2 percent in part reflects adverse weather conditions early in the year (Cyclone Kina) as well as industrial disputes in the sugar sector that depressed agricultural production. Non-sugar crops suffered a steep fall in value added, and subsistence agriculture registered a 3 percent decline. With the completion of the construction phase of major public investment projects, construction activity also declined sharply after rapid expansion in the previous two years, an adverse movement that was more than offset by strong growth in services, particularly tourist activity.

The most recent Government estimates show that GDP grew at 5.2 percent in 1994, led by a record sugar production (of 517,000 tons) and an increase in tourist arrivals (to 319,000), surpassing previous records of sugar production in 1986 and tourist arrivals in 1993. The growth is fairly broad-based, with all sectors expected to gain except wholesale and retail trade. Despite the record number of tourist arrivals, the services sector is growing more slowly than any other major sector.

FIJI: KEY ECONOMIC INDICATORS

	1990	1991	1992	1993
Real GDP growth (%)	4.7	0.6	3.1	1.9
Gross Investment/GDP (%)	17.5	13.4	13.1	15.1
Public/GDP (%)	10.4	6.7	6.9	7.2
Private/GDP (%)	7.1	6.7	6.2	6.3
Gross National Savings/GDP (%)	14.4	14.5	14.4	13.2
Consumer Inflation (%)	8.1	6.5	4.9	5.2
Broad Money (M3) Growth (%)	24.5	15.5	14.1	6.5
Government Revenues (% GDP) a/	30.4	29.7	28.8	29.5
Government Expenditures (% GDP)	30.1	31.2	32.0	33.4
Overall Balance (% GDP)	0.3	-1.5	-3.2	-3.9
Exports, fob (US$m)	467	427	417	422
Imports, fob (US$m)	-642	-549	-539	-653
Current Account (US$m) a/	-43	16	21	-32
(% of GDP)	-3.1	1.1	1.3	-2.0
Overall Balance (US$m)	37.5	8.3	53.1	-43.0
Gross Reserves (end period, US$m)	261	271	318	269
(months of imports,fob)	4.9	5.9	7.1	4.9
External Debt/GDP (%) b/	25.7	23.4	20.7	17.4
Debt Service Ratio (%) c/	11.5	9.2	7.6	6.6
Memo items:				
GDP (nominal, US$m)	1,390.6	1,479.7	1,592.6	1,647.0
Grants (US$m) : net official transfers	16.7	30.0	25.8	27.1

a/ Includes grants.
b/ Includes IMF obligations.
c/ In percent of exports of goods and services.
Sources: IMF Recent Economic Developments, 12/94 and Fiji: Restoring Growth in a Changing Global Environment, World Bank, 1/95.

During 1991-94, *formal sector employment growth* averaged 2 percent annually, indicative of the generally modest pace of economic activity. Formal (paid) agricultural employment has vacillated sharply, but this is relatively unimportant given that this sector accounts for only 2 percent of the total. Manufacturing employment has also been erratic, with a sharp drop in 1992, and an equally sharp increase in 1993 as new investment (particularly in garments) took place. In 1994, despite the expected moderate expansion in real income, total formal sector employment growth will be limited to around 1 percent, representing the creation of only around one thousand additional formal sector jobs in the Fijian economy. Formal sector unemployment rate is estimated to reach 6.0 percent in 1994, up from 5.4 percent in 1992. With nearly two-thirds of the labor force engaged in self-employed activities, primarily in the agricultural sector and in small-scale trade and distribution, this figure may underestimate the extent of unemployment, particularly for the 13,000 annual school leavers.

Investment rates in Fiji are low both by Asian and especially by Pacific Island standards. Over the past 15 years, gross domestic investment averaged 32 percent in East Asian and Pacific countries and 21 percent in low-income economies (excluding China and India). The average for Fiji over the same period was 21 percent of GDP, but this has fallen during the 1990s to less than 15 percent. At 12-13 percent of GDP, total fixed investment in Fiji is among the lowest in the Pacific Island economies. Public investment has been very low at around 7 percent of GDP in recent years, compared to much higher ratios in the 1970s generated by large infrastructure projects.

The introduction of the Tax Free Factory/Tax Free Zone scheme in 1989 generated significant foreign direct investment inflows, although private investment activity has still exhibited a steady downward trend in recent years: Private fixed investment fell from an average of 12 percent of GDP during 1980-86, to 6 percent in 1989 and remained stagnant at under 5 percent from 1992-94. Lack of financing does not appear to have been a serious constraint on investment: the national savings rate averaged a healthy 17 percent during 1980-94.

Since 1987, as part of the program of economic restructuring and financial stabilization, fiscal policy has aimed at reducing the overall size of the public sector and the size of the budget deficit so as to ensure the availability of resources for private sector growth. However, rapid expenditure expansions in the face of slower growing revenues have led to increasing fiscal imbalances in recent years. Budgetary targets have been exceeded as expenditure overruns have exerted pressure on the fiscal accounts. These spending overruns have resulted particularly from public sector salary and wage increases which, until the 1994 budget, have been consistently under-budgeted and have required supplementary appropriations. Expenditure control measures put in place in 1993 in an effort to contain expenditure growth have been relatively ineffective.

After averaging around 1 percent of GDP during 1989-91, the fiscal deficit widened to 3.2 percent in 1992. This deterioration stemmed partly from delayed implementation of the VAT, which had an adverse impact on revenues. Expenditures, on the other hand, grew more rapidly owing in part to generous public sector wage settlements. The higher overall deficit in 1993 (3.9 percent of GDP compared to a target of 2.5 percent) reflected revenue shortfalls related to adverse weather as the economy slowed much more than anticipated, and a decline in customs and excise receipts as a result of tariff reductions associated with trade liberalization. On the expenditure side, outlays on wages and salaries increased (by 5 percent), as did allocations for rehabilitation and relief operations following the cyclone. Sizable reallocations were made to the operating budget to finance cyclone relief operations, resulting in a drop in capital expenditures. Also contributing to expenditure pressures was increased military spending and additional on-lending provisions to public enterprises.

Current estimates suggest that the Government has achieved its 1994 Budget deficit target of 2.9 percent of GDP. The 1995 Budget projects a further modest reduction in the deficit to 2.5 percent. However, these figures were based on government plans to restrict wage pressures by placing public service wage settlements under control of the Counter-Inflation Act, rather than allow for arbitration. Since this proposal had been rejected by Cabinet, it was not clear whether the target of reducing the deficit to 2.5 percent for 1995 was feasible.

During the past several years the deficit has been financed from domestic sources, leading to a rise in domestic public debt outstanding. At the end of 1994, it is estimated that total outstanding government debt reached the equivalent of 42 percent of GDP, up slightly from 41 percent in 1992; but the composition has changed, with domestic debt now amounting to 34 percent of GDP, as compared to only 31 percent in 1992.

Monetary policy in recent years has focused on price stability and on managing the high build-up of liquidity in the banking system brought on in part by the low private sector demand for credit. The rapid growth in total liquidity during the past several years slowed to 3 percent at end-June 1994, down from 7 percent in 1993 and 25 percent in 1990. Moderation in excess liquidity was achieved primarily through substantial declines in net foreign assets. Domestic credit expansion has decelerated slowly since the rapid growth in 1990-91, dropping to only 10 percent for 1994. Public credit demand grew more rapidly than private credit for 1994; this lackluster private performance reflects the continued absence of private investment activity throughout the economy.

Interest rates have generally been on a declining trend over the recent period despite reduction in excess liquidity. At the end of June 1994, the weighted average lending rate of commercial banks stood at 11.5 percent, down from 12.4 percent in January 1993. The weighted average deposit rate on outstanding savings deposits showed a similar decline from 4.1 percent to 3.2 percent during the same period, leaving the intermediation spread virtually unchanged. Low inflationary pressures as well as the low Minimum Lending Rate of the Reserve Bank (currently 6 percent, down from 8 percent in November 1992) have also contributed to the declining interest rates.

Inflation. Despite the recent monetary expansions, *inflation* in Fiji has been moderate, indicative of the nation's prudent approach to monetary management. Consumer inflation fell from 8 percent in 1990 to around 5 percent during 1992-93, reflecting in part, low imported inflation from major trading partners. The 1993 rate would have been lower except for special factors, including the introduction of the value added tax in July 1992, weather-related shortages of some locally grown foodstuffs, and substantial increases in public housing rental rates in early 1993. Inflationary pressures have since abated, and the annual average inflation rate had fallen to 1.5 percent in 1994 and to a low of 0.7 percent in early 1995.

After registering a surplus of 1.3 percent of GDP in 1992, up from 1.1 percent in 1991, the external current account shifted into a deficit of 2.0 percent of GDP in 1993. The surplus in 1992 stemmed from a moderate decline in exports particularly garment exports (due to recessionary conditions in Australia and New Zealand) that was more than offset by strong growth in tourism-related receipts. Imports were stagnant, reflecting the cumulative effect of tight monetary policy, in particular credit restraint, that has been in effect since 1990. In 1993, the merchandise trade deficit widened substantially as food import demand responded to domestic production shortfalls, and higher demand for investment and other consumer goods followed the overall credit expansion in the latter half of the year. While garment exports recovered, and the services and transfers accounts improved (in part because of rising tourism earnings), these movements only partially offset the sizable trade deficit. In 1994, exports are estimated to have expanded fairly rapidly, reflecting moderate increases in the traditional exports of sugar, gold, timber and fish, the continued surge in tourism earnings, and the re-export of an aircraft leased in 1990. Imports would remain strong, again due in part to the import of an aircraft, but lag behind export growth. The consequent improvement in the trade deficit, coupled with strong tourism earnings would improve the 1994 current account deficit to 1 percent.

The (non-monetary) capital account has remained in surplus since 1992, an outcome attributable to movements in private capital, which has recorded net inflows in recent years, offsetting net outflows on official capital as public loan disbursements slowed and amortization payments (including prepayment) increased. The overall balance registered a surplus of US$53 million in 1992, causing gross official reserves to increase to over US$300 million (equivalent of 7 months of imports) by year-end, the highest level in several years. In 1993, reserves dropped to less than five months of import cover, as the overall balance shifted into a deficit owing to the current account imbalance, and a sharp decline in nonmonetary capital flows as prepayment of official capital was accelerated and commercial banks increased their holdings of foreign assets. The 1994 capital account should register a substantial surplus because of direct investment inflows to finance the aircraft import and a reduction in commercial banks net holdings of foreign assets which, together, more than offset net outflows on official and short-term capital. The overall balance should improve but remain in deficit, causing reserves to decline to the equivalent of 4.3 months of import payments.

In 1987, the Fiji dollar was devalued in two steps by 30 percent against the weighted basket of currencies to which it is pegged in an attempt to stem the surge in capital flight and remittances that took place following the coup. The resulting large depreciation in the real effective exchange rate strengthened Fiji's competitive position at a time when it was seeking to re-orient its economy towards production for export. In recent years, however, both the real and nominal effective rates have tended to drift upwards. During 1993, the nominal and real effective rates appreciated by some 6 and 3 percent respectively, and while 1994 witnessed some reversal of this trend, attention must be paid in the future to further drift which would erode the competitive gains achieved by the 1987 devaluation and undermine prospects for strong, export-led growth over the medium term.

Key Policy Issues

Resolving Policy Uncertainty. In the aftermath of 1987, two political issues continue to cast a long shadow over the economic environment. First is the issue of political rights. Second is the issue of the impending expiration of sugarcane land leases, which has further aggravated relations between ethnic groups. With political and property rights in question, economic reforms cannot take hold and entrepreneurs are reluctant to make long-term investment commitments.

Facing a Changing Global Economy. Historic changes in the global economic environment are underway that affect Fiji's current prospects and future opportunities:

- signing of the Uruguay Round Agreement, which could lead to a downward trend in sugar prices and a reduction in preferential market access to the European Union over time;
- increasing international competition in textile and garment industries as a consequence both of continued erosion of SPARTECA tariff preferences and eventual abolition of the distortionary MFA import quotas.

Restoring Investment. Both private and public investment are needed to restore Fiji to a sustained path of high economic growth and employment generation. Since 1990, both public and private investment have been on a flat or declining trend: fixed investment has dropped to only 12 percent of GDP, with private investment only 5 percent, the lowest in the region. The roots of the investment shortfall lie in domestic conditions, including: continuing political uncertainty; lack of confidence regarding the direction and continuity of public policy; and concerns over loss of competitiveness. As long as these macro concerns persist, narrow policy reforms directed at stimulating investment will have little impact, and Government should avoid introducing policies such as special tax holidays that further distort the incentive structure and generate little, if any, desirable new investment.

Promoting Public Sector Investment. The slippage in the budget deficit over the last several years is cause for concern primarily because *fiscal policy has been largely ineffective in promoting the government's broader development goals*. Fiji's deficit has been a "low-quality" deficit: rather than stemming from an active, targeted development strategy, it emerges from expenditure pressure. One corollary of this is public expenditure imbalance between recurrent and capital spending; at only 2 percent of GDP, Fiji's public investment is exceptionally low. The Public Sector Investment Program (PSIP) needs to reflect more directly a vision about the future needs of the economy, and the Government needs to commit itself to systematic public investment procedures, rather than allowing investment expenditure to be squeezed by an ever expanding recurrent cost budget.

Controlling Public Sector Wages. The dominant item in Government expenditures is the recurrent cost of the public sector wage bill. Two-thirds of discretionary recurrent expenditures is for direct wage and salary-related costs of the Public Service. Efforts to consolidate Fiji's fiscal structure must concentrate on efforts to reduce the size of the civil service, a need made more pressing by the leading role played by civil service wage and salary movements in the pattern of wage settlements in the private sector. Controlling civil service wage levels and the size of the public wage bill influences the overall competitiveness of the economy as well as fiscal and macroeconomic stability. The Government should adopt "affordability" as the primary criterion for determining civil service pay awards, and strive to lower the public wage bill from its current 14 percent of GDP.

Improving Fiscal Performance. A major restructuring of revenue sources has occurred over the last few years as Government has developed and implemented major tax reforms designed to simplify and modernize the tax system. The direct tax reforms have been relatively successful, in part because they built on an existing administrative structure. A new value added tax (VAT) was introduced to provide a non-distortionary source of indirect tax revenue and replace the customs duty, a series of sales taxes, and miscellaneous excise taxes. Difficulties have been encountered with implementation of the VAT, which need to be addressed in order to provide a stable non-distortionary tax base.

Trade Policy Reform. Considerable progress has been registered in reducing non-tariff barriers to trade and in reducing protective tariffs. Since 1990, average tariffs have fallen by more than a third in a wide range of product categories, many of which are key intermediate inputs that do not compete with domestic products. However, despite this progress, Fiji's import tariffs remain high, inspiring firms to seek import duty concessions and exemptions, and effective rates are well below nominal rates. The tariff burden is unevenly applied, revenues are lost, and the fiscal capacity to lower rates further is jeopardized. To improve revenue performance and reduce distortions, existing concessions should be documented, the discretionary authority of officials to grant special concessions revoked, and concessions for non-exporters phased out over a 2 to 3-year period.

Investment Incentives and Capital Markets. Initiatives to provide incentives to foreign and domestic investors have made some headway, although one result has been a proliferation of different investor incentive schemes that rely on discretionary administrative judgment, including some incentives (such as the 13-year tax holiday for export-oriented firms) which were introduced as emergency measures taken to restore investor confidence in the aftermath of political turmoil. The current preparation of a comprehensive Investment Act provides an opportunity to reassess investment approval procedures, and to provide a framework for more automatic provision of investor incentives and work permit approvals. As the Fijian economy becomes more outward-oriented, the Investment Act will need to rely more on market mechanisms to determine commercial viability, rather than administrative judgment, by streamlining the investment approval process, provide transparent criteria for determining eligibility for investment concessions, and elimination of many of the existing fiscal incentives.

Public Enterprise Reform and Privatization. In 1993, the Fiji government put forth a comprehensive public enterprise reform program emphasizing privatization and/or commercialization across a wide range of activities, but actual progress to date has been limited. There is an urgent need for Government to re-establish the credibility of the program and regain momentum, by accelerating contracting for specific professional services or use of outside management, and give high priority to plans to commercialize statutory bodies and government commercial activities, opening up to competition markets previously limited to SOEs, and stripping away the non-economic functions performed by some SOEs so that each enterprise can concentrate on its core business activities.

Land Tenure and the Renewal of Land Leases. More than any other issue, the lease renewal controversy symbolizes the economic, political and ethnic polarization that has emerged in Fiji over the last decade. The renewal question involves difficult issues of individual property rights, tenancy rights and obligations, and governmental authority. The most pressing need is to identify the means to achieve a broad-based settlement as soon as possible. Uncertainty created by the impending renewal is already affecting the economy—private banks are pulling back from lending to farmers whose leases are due to be renewed in the next several years. The current confrontational nature of land lease discussions in Fiji means that special efforts should be made to keep tensions from mounting unnecessarily.

Restructuring Sugar. The sugar industry is now at a crossroads, facing issues that need to be resolved to maintain its economic viability. The combination of changing world prospects for sugar and domestic uncertainties over renewal of land leases creates an explosive mixture. Given the importance of the sugar sector in Fiji's economy, either issue would pose a difficult challenge. Both of them occurring together complicates the policy issues substantially, and to some extent, limits the range of feasible policy choices. Stagnation in the sugar sector over the last fifteen years has shifted the industry from being a relatively low-cost producer to an average-to-high cost producer. The industry has become especially vulnerable to a reduction in the price received for exports to the European Union (EU). Although the immediate threat of sharply lower prices and exports to the EU appears to have been averted for now, eventual erosion in the above-market sugar price received by Fiji must be anticipated.

Industry. While trade measures undertaken during the period 1987-94 have begun to remove the cushion of trade protection from domestic industries, over the next decade, Fijian exporters must anticipate the steady erosion of existing preferential trade access for their products in global markets. Changes in global trading arrangements will have a powerful effect on the preferences that Fijian manufacturers enjoy, particularly those associated with the SPARTECA and GATT accords. For Fiji's relatively new garment industry, rationalization of world textiles trade will give Fiji the opportunity to increase market share and expand production, but only if it is able to compete on the basis of its own strengths, particularly the ability to field and respond to small orders relatively rapidly. The potential for expanding niche-oriented manufacturing and services is considerable, but there is little that the Government can do to directly promote these activities. The most effective form of public sector support for these potentially important industries is a competitive enterprise environment, improvements in economic infrastructure, and a sustained commitment to human resource development.

Tourism. Tourism is Fiji's single largest source of export earnings, accounting for about a quarter of national output, and providing around 18,000 jobs. Tourism remains an important area of future growth, and innovative efforts are underway to broaden the range of tourism services including movement into areas such as eco-tourism and cultural tourism. In order to improve the attractiveness of the Fiji tourist product, measures are needed to improve air access, stimulate the rationalization of visitor accommodations by focusing investment and development activities on new deluxe sites, and facilitating sale of mid-quality resorts to investors that can upgrade the properties to deluxe-premium standards or downgrade to tourist and budget standards.

Kiribati

Population: **76,000 (1993)**

GDP: **US$32 million (1993)**

GNP Per Capita: **US$710 (1993)**

Background

Kiribati consists of 33 atolls dispersed over a wide area of the Pacific Ocean. The country has vast marine resources with a large exclusive economic zone of 5 million square kms of the central Pacific Ocean, but limited land area composed of poor coralline soil. Agriculture and fisheries employ about half of the labor force and contribute approximately 25 percent of GDP. Service activities, dominated by public administration account for about one fourth of GDP. Manufacturing activities are limited. The urban population is highly dependent on imported food.

Recent Economic Developments

The sharp drop of 5 percent in real GDP in 1992 abated somewhat in 1993 to 3 percent, similar to the decline registered on average in the 1989 to 1990 period. Unfavorable weather conditions adversely affected copra output in 1993 and estimates for the commercial fishing and construction sectors were revised downwards for 1992 and 1993. The manufacturing sector remains small but some gains have been made in producing substitutes for some consumer imports.

Inflation in Kiribati has been relatively modest, averaging 5 percent per year since 1988. Price movements strongly reflect inflation in the main import source countries, especially Australia. Inflation in 1992 was 5.8 percent and remained at that level in 1993 following the weakness of the Australian dollar and an increase in import duties in January 1993.

Public finances have been managed prudently, with recurrent expenditure maintained within the bounds of domestic revenue and drawdowns of interest from the Revenue Equalization Reserve Fund (RERF). The interest from the RERF was equivalent to 30 percent of GDP in 1993. Current revenue declined in 1993, mainly because of a decline in non tax revenue from lower fishing royalties. With external development grants half of what they were in 1992, total revenue is estimated at 92 percent of GDP in 1993 as compared to 133 percent in 1992. Current expenditure in 1993 was estimated to be about the same in GDP terms as in the previous year, but development expenditure was substantially lower so that total expenditure was about 102 percent of GDP as compared to 122 percent in 1992. Hence the overall fiscal balance shifted from a surplus of about 12 percent of GDP in 1992 to a deficit of about 10 percent of GDP in 1993. Taking into account the reinvested RERF earnings, there was a fiscal surplus of nearly 9.2 percent of GDP in 1993, as compared with surpluses ranging from 32 percent to 18 percent of GDP in the previous three years.

The external accounts in Kiribati remained in a healthy position despite large and increasing trade deficits. Exports (mainly copra and marine products) have been declining in recent years whereas imports have risen steadily. The emergence of seaweed and aquarium fish as exports in recent years broadened the export base previously limited to copra and edible fish. Despite this development, exports remain only a small fraction of imports. The sustained strong performance of the services and income accounts has enabled not only these deficits to be covered but also external reserves to steadily expand. The main sources of these inflows are interest income on RERF investments, remittances from workers abroad, and official aid transfers. The current account balance (including official transfers) in 1993 registered a surplus of only 5.3 percent of GDP, a decrease from the previous year. External

KIRIBATI: KEY ECONOMIC INDICATORS

	1989	1990	1991	1992	1993
Real GDP Growth Rate (%)	-4.5	-1.5	1.9	-5.1	-2.8
Gross Investment/GDP (%)	26.3	24.9	23.5	21.7	n.a.
Public/GDP (%)	28.4	35.4	n.a.	n.a.	n.a.
Private/GDP (%)	-2.1	-10.5	n.a.	n.a.	n.a.
Consumer Inflation (%)	6.1	3.8	4.3	5.8	5.8
Government Revenues (% of GDP) a/	82.4	102.8	102.3	133.0	92.3
Government Expenditures (% of GDP)	83.4	104.0	95.8	121.5	102.3
Overall Balance (% of GDP)	-1.0	-1.2	6.5	11.5	-10.0
Exports, fob (US$m)	5.1	2.9	2.9	4.8	3.0
Imports, fob (US$m)	-22.6	-26.8	-25.9	-37.7	-27.8
Current Account (US$m)	4.9	4.2	10.3	5.5	1.7
(% of GDP)	14.8	12.5	28.9	16.1	5.3
Overall Balance (US$m)	7.7	7.6	11.7	14.4	2.3
Gross Reserves (in years of imports)	8.9	8.1	9.8	7.1	10.1
External Debt /GDP(%)	6.4	8.6	9.2	12.4	20.8
Debt Service Ratio (%) b/	2.4	0.9	0.7	1.0	1.2
Memo items:					
GDP (nominal, US$m)	33.2	33.6	35.7	33.9	32.1
Grants (US$m): net official transfers	14.3	20.4	18.5	24.6	13.7

a/ Includes grants.
b/ As a percentage of exports of goods and nonfactor services.
Source: IMF, Recent Economic Developments August 18,1993, World Bank, Economic Memorandum, Vol. 3, 1993; and Kiribati Statistics Office.

reserves increased in 1993 and were equivalent to about 10 years of imports.

Kiribati has no monetary authority and uses the Australian dollar as its currency. The only commercial bank, the Bank of Kiribati is jointly owned by the Government and an Australian bank. Due to a dearth of domestic investment opportunities, most financial institutions hold a significant amount of assets abroad.

The contribution of tourism to GDP remains small. The main factors constraining development of tourism are remoteness, infrequency of flights, limited infrastructure, and poor knowledge of Kiribati in the major markets of Japan and the United States. However, there has been some increase in tourist arrivals with the establishment of a regular flight from Honolulu, the reopening of Kanton airport, and the upgrading of Bonriki airport.

Key Policy Issues

Marine resources, remain a mainstay of the economy as fishing rights fees paid by foreign vessels provide important budgetary support and balance of payments support. In view of the recent rapid increase in tuna fishing in the region, it is generally agreed that there is an urgent need: (i) to define sustainable catch levels for all fisheries; (ii) for countries to work together to enhance monitoring to prevent illegal fishing; and (iii) to obtain fair prices for the fisheries resource.

Unemployment has become a serious problem in Kiribati, with the public sector, the dominant employer of the formal labor force, unable to meet the growing demands for jobs. This situation is expected to worsen unless effective measures are taken. A review, undertaken with the aim of reducing the size of the public sector and government expenditure on unproductive enterprises, identified 12 public enterprises, which could be privatized. In view of the shortage of local skills and finance, joint ventures with foreign investors are being encouraged to facilitate privatization.

Another area of concern for government is the development budget. The Government needs to assume greater control over priority setting. Public investment programming should reflect the long-term development objective of improving the quality of life for the people and providing alternative means of employment, as well as better utilization of donor funds. To ensure the sustainability of development expenditures and to preserve the integrity of the RERF, the Government needs to reinforce and maintain recent efforts to strengthen fiscal management.

Federated States of Micronesia

Population: 105,000 (1993)

GDP: US$194 million (1993)

GDP Per Capita: US$1,850 (1993)

Background

The Federated States of Micronesia (FSM) consists of four states that encompass 607 islands and atolls in the Northern Pacific. The country has a narrow productive base comprised primarily of subsistence farming (accounting for about 25 percent of GDP), reef and deep-sea fishing. Manufacturing and other industrial activities, such as utilities and construction, are a very small component of GDP. The dominant sector and the largest employer is the public sector, accounting for over 75 percent of GDP. The economy remains highly dependent on external assistance, nearly all of which is provided by the United States through the Compact Agreement. The major element of this assistance is a block grant of US$60 million annually for the first 5 years beginning in 1986, US$51 million for the next 5 years, and US$40 million for the last 5 years. Consumption is high and met mainly by imports. Significant macroeconomic imbalances exist, on the external side, with imports exceeding exports by a factor of five and on the internal side where the budget deficit (before grants) exceeds 50 percent of GDP.

Recent Economic Developments

Output is estimated to have grown by 5 percent in real terms in 1993, after having stagnated in the period 1990-92. Most of this increase came from increased activity in fishing and the completion of several large capital projects.

Tuna is the country's richest natural resource, and substantial stocks of skipjack, yellow fin and bigeye tuna are found in the exclusive economic zone (EEZ). In 1992, the value of fish exports more than doubled, from US$9 million to US$20 million. Revenue from fishing rights fees charged to foreign vessels that fish in the EEZ rose from US$8 million in 1988 to US$17.6 million in 1993, reflecting mainly an enormous influx of foreign fishing vessels. This has resulted in an increase in informal sector activity and all five (national and state) governments provide expanded dock services to foreign fleets so as to generate additional income and local employment.

In agriculture, production of the traditional export crop, copra, has steadily declined in recent years from the 1979 peak of 8,500 metric tons to 200 metric tons in 1992, recovering partially in 1993. This steady decline in production is a result of low world prices, aging trees, and alternative opportunities for farmers. Pepper, the other major agricultural crop, recovered partially in 1992/93 after production had declined severely in 1991 as the result of a typhoon. However, income from this source remains low because of depressed world prices.

Manufacturing activity in FSM remains small and concentrated on food processing, with the exception of two garment firms. There was some new activity in 1993, with the Pohnpei Government opening a fish processing plant, which will operate at fifty percent of its capacity by mid-1994, and a state cooperative to process and sell lower quality pepper. Garment and button production expanded from $1.5 million in 1990 to $2.2 million in 1992.

The estimated number of tourists increased from 22,000 in 1988 to over 30,000 in 1993, yet further development continues to be hindered by a lack of direct air service and quality accommodation.

FSM: KEY ECONOMIC INDICATORS

	1988/89	1989/90	1990/91	1991/92	1992/93
Real GDP Growth Rate (%)	-1.7	-2.7	4.3	-1.2	5.2
Consumer Inflation (%)	4.5	3.5	4.0	5.0	6.0
Government Revenues (% of GDP)[a/]	103.2	105.8	101.0	91.0	84.3
Government Expenditures (% of GDP)	91.6	103.7	106.3	91.4	94.4
Overall Balance (% of GDP)	11.6	2.1	-5.3	-0.4	-10.1
Exports, fob (US$m)	2.5	4.6	10.8	21.0	25.6
Imports,fob (US$m)	-84.9	-107.6	-133.6	-114.6	-148.1
Current Account (US$m)	43.5	28.6	-2.0	7.6	-20.8
(% of GDP)	28.4	18.5	-1.2	4.4	-10.7
Overall Balance (US$m)	11.8	16.9	59.4	-5.3	-15.3
Gross Reserves (end period, US$m)	103.3	120.2	179.6	174.3	159.0
External Debt/GDP (%)	n.a.	9.5	58.6	67.8	70.4
Debt Service Ratio (%)[b/]	n.a.	n.a.	8.3	35.4	26.1
Memo items:					
GDP (nominal, US$m)	153.3	154.7	167.8	174.1	194.2
Grants(US$m): net official transfers	118.9	124.7	121.9	104.2	108.9

a/ Includes grants.
b/ As a percentage of goods and nonfactor services.
Source: IMF, 1994.

Systematic price information is not available; therefore, no consumer price index or GDP deflator is calculated in the country. Hence, prices are estimated based on trends in the United States and the Marshall Islands. Based on such estimates, prices seem to have risen at 5-6 percent annually, which is faster than in the United States, mainly due to limited competition in wholesale and retail trade at a time of increasing demand, weather-related factors, and public sector tariff increases.

The overall consolidated fiscal position of the Government weakened further in 1992/93 to a deficit greater than 10 percent of GDP. Both current and capital expenditure increased in all the states with total expenditure equivalent to 94 percent of GDP in 1992/93. Tax revenue remained more or less constant, with income tax levied only on wages and salaries at a relatively low rate and because of large scale avoidance of import and sales tax. However, there was a substantial increase in non-tax revenue in 1993, mainly because of an increase in fishing rights fees.

The role of monetary policy is limited due to use of the U.S. dollar as legal tender. The locally operated Bank of the Federated States of Micronesia has expanded operations substantially though limiting itself to consumer and short-term commercial loans. Interest rate spreads have increased, as banks charge the maximum legal rate for loans, while deposit rates have fallen in line with US rates. As of 1994, commercial banks are allowed to charge 4 percent, rather than the previous 2 percent above the US prime rate for commercial loans.

Corresponding to the weakening fiscal position, the external position has been deteriorating for the last 3-4 years, reflecting increasing trade and service account deficits and declining official transfers, the latter due to the phase-down of U.S. grants. Exports of fish, and some manufactured products rose sharply, but were only a small proportion of imports. The composition and direction of trade changed significantly. In 1993, fish exports comprised 80 percent of total exports, compared with 15 percent of the total in 1988. Direction of exports also changed significantly, with the share of total exports to Japan increasing to 80 percent in 1993 compared with 20 percent in 1989. At the same time, exports to the United States have declined. Increased public and private consumption and large capital projects led to a sharp increase in imports. A sharp increase in earnings from fishing licensing fees and tourism was more than offset by a sharp rise in freight and insurance payments and interest payments on public sector debt. Official transfers declined, reflecting the first phase-down in Compact funding.

Key Policy Issues

One of the main challenges facing the Government is to reduce its dependence on U.S. assistance as this declines in the next few years and to find sustainable alternative sources of financing.

The Government is aware of the need to focus on fiscal discipline and longer term development issues. With an excessively large public sector, public enterprises not covering costs, and with inadequate infrastructure to promote private investment and growth, public sector reform should constitute a vital part of the adjustment process. The size of the public sector needs to be reduced not only by limiting the range of its functions but also by increasing the efficiency of what remains. Relatively high wages undermine competitiveness. The major adjustments, will need to be in public sector expenditure, with a substantial reduction in the level of personnel expenditures and transfers to public enterprises. Also any program of public sector restructuring and possible downsizing must be complemented by improvements in the environment facing the private sector.

In the fisheries sector, the issue of increased fishing fleets is of concern both from the environmental standpoint of damage to the nearshore environment and the sustainability of the resource. There are good prospects for development in several sectors, specifically, fisheries, agriculture, and tourism. The achievement of significant results in these sectors over the next few years will require not only well targeted investment in these areas but also the building up of a supportive infrastructure.

MARSHALL ISLANDS

Population: **51,000 (1993)**

GDP: **US$85 million (1993)**

GDP Per Capita: **US$1,670 (1993)**

Background

The Republic of the Marshall Islands (RMI) was part of the Trust Territory of the Pacific administered by the United States (US) from 1945 to 1986. In 1986, under the terms of the Compact of Free Association, the US formally relinquished its trusteeship and the RMI assumed self-governing status. Under the terms of the Compact, the US provides substantial annual economic assistance to the RMI, principally through a series of grants to Government. The Compact grants provide a total of about US$53 million for each of the first 5 years, declining to about US$49 million for the next 5 years, and then to about US$46 million for the last 5 years. Over the 15 years during which the Compact is in effect, the RMI will receive an estimated total of US$1 billion, adjusted for inflation.

The country has a narrow productive base consisting primarily of coconut harvesting and processing, subsistence farming and deep sea fishing. As a small island economy, economic growth is constrained by the dispersal of the atolls, shortages of skilled labor, high wages and remoteness from markets.

Recent Economic Developments

After stagnating in 1990/91-1991/92, partly due to adverse weather, economic growth recovered in 1992/93 with real output recording a modest 2.5 percent increase. This improvement was largely due to increased activity in the copra sector in response to price incentives provided by Government, and to increased foreign investment in fisheries. Although economic expansion was expected to continue into the 1993/94 fiscal year, the pace was expected to slow to 2 percent as growth in copra output stagnates because of anticipated declines in international prices.

Inflation at the consumer level, which had increased sharply from under 1 percent in 1989/90 to over 10 percent in 1991/92, moderated to 5 percent in 1992/93, because of an improved domestic supply situation. Consumer inflation is estimated to have remained low at nearly 3 percent during 1993/94. After registering a surplus of 2 percent of GDP in 1989/90, the overall fiscal balance, inclusive of grants, shifted into a deficit of 25 percent of GDP in 1991/92, reflecting mainly a slowdown in revenue growth, declining grant aid and rapidly increasing current expenditure. While the budget of 1992/93 envisaged a reduction in the fiscal deficit to 10 percent of GDP because of anticipated increases in import duties, lower subsidies and a cut in capital expenditures, the fiscal situation deteriorated further, resulting in a budget deficit of over 17 percent of GDP. Contributing to the poor fiscal performance were expenditure overruns on purchases of goods and services, increased subsidy to Air Marshall Islands and poor revenue performance. The deficits were financed by grants primarily from the Compact, and external commercial borrowing against future Compact assistance. A marked improvement in the budgetary outcome for 1993/94 was expected as major expenditure reductions are anticipated.

MARSHALL ISLANDS: KEY ECONOMIC INDICATORS

	1989/90	1990/91	1991/92	1992/93	1993/94 Est.
Real GDP growth (%)	3.2	0.1	0.1	2.5	2.0
Consumer Inflation (%)	0.7	4.0	10.3	5.0	2.8
Gross Investment/GDP (%)	42.3	33.1	43.3	n.a.	n.a.
Government Revenues (% GDP)	110.7	96.0	87.3	78.4	74.2
Government Expenditures (% GDP)	108.6	104.5	112.2	95.6	83.5
Overall Balance (% GDP)	2.1	-8.5	-24.9	-17.2	-9.3
Exports, fob (US$m)	2.7	8.8	9.6	9.5	4.7
Imports, cif (US$m)	-63.7	-56.2	-77.0	-75.0	-60.6
Current Account (US$m)	2.4	1.3	-26.9	-21.9	-5.4
(% of GDP)	3.5	1.8	-33.9	-25.7	-6.0
Overall Balance (US$m)	-5.1	30.7	-17.5	-3.1	-19.6
External Debt/GDP (%)	106.2	146.1	157.1	182.2	152.1
Debt Service/Exports (%)	44.7	38.7	55.1	51.9	57.3
Memo items:					
GDP (nominal, US$m)	69.0	71.8	79.3	85.3	89.3
Grants (US$m): net official transfers	62.5	51.4	53.3	49.4	49.0

Source: IMF, 1994.

The external current account which had recorded surpluses after grants, up to 1990/91, swung into a substantial deficit averaging nearly 34 percent of GDP in 1991/92 and nearly 26 percent in 1992/93. This reflected primarily increased merchandise trade deficits, a deteriorating services account and reduced external grants. While total exports, comprising mainly coconut oil and fish, amounted to only 11 percent of GDP in 1992/93, imports were the equivalent of 88 percent of GDP because of increased public and private demand. The growing deficits on the services account reflected, in part, higher interest payments on public sector debt.

The capital account, excluding private sector capital transactions, has registered moderate surpluses because of public sector borrowing, mainly against future Compact receipts, to finance infrastructure and fisheries projects. International reserves represented by central government holdings of financial assets abroad have declined since 1990/91 as substantial fiscal deficits necessitated their draw down.

Reflecting increasing government borrowings in recent years as noted above, external public debt outstanding rose sharply to US$156 million (182 percent of GDP) in 1992/93, from US$73 million (106 percent of GDP) in 1989/90. The external debt service ratio increased from 45 percent to 52 percent of exports of goods and services during the same period.

The Government recognizes the need for adjustment in light of declining Compact assistance. Consequently, high priority has been attached to strengthening the export sector through expanding and diversifying the productive base.

The Government has announced its intention to progressively reduce the size of the civil service and the public sector wage and salary bill.

The Government is also committed to substantially reducing subsidies and transfers to public enterprises in the 1994/95 fiscal year. There are plans to privatize enterprises, where feasible and to commercialize operations of certain remaining state owned enterprises.

To support expansion of the productive base, including manufacturing and the tourist sector, there is a need for adequate infrastructure and services. The investment program would need to focus on public infrastructure to support private sector activity, particularly in fishing and agriculture, where the country has potential for export growth and import substitution.

Key Policy Issues

Fiscal Discipline. As Compact assistance is scheduled to be phased out, there is a need for Government to undertake major fiscal adjustment. This will require, inter alia, increased domestic resource mobilization and reduced public expenditures to curb consumption and lessen dependence on imports.

Public Enterprise Reform. Continued budgetary support to public enterprises in the form of subsidies and transfers has contributed to fiscal pressures in recent years. Reducing and eliminating the dependence of public enterprises on the budget will significantly help redress the fiscal imbalances. For the national airline, in particular, measures to reduce losses would include terminating unprofitable routes, and merging with or establishing a regional carrier. According to recent reports the losses of Air Marshall Islands declined significantly from US$9 million in 1990/91 to US$4 million in 1992/93.

Limiting Public Borrowing. The high share of debt service payments in current expenditures is of particular concern. Government needs to curtail further borrowing against future Compact flows.

SOLOMON ISLANDS

Population: **354,000 (1993)**

GDP: **US$245 million (1993)**

GNP Per Capita: **US$740 (1993)**

Background

Development performance in the Solomon Islands, which became independent in 1978, is influenced by its size and geography. First, it is a small country, with a population of 354,000 and a GDP of around US$245 million (1993). Second, it is archipelagic in nature, comprising six main islands and many smaller ones extending over almost 1300 kilometers of ocean; this feature makes it difficult to develop a domestic market and increases the unit costs of providing basic public services. Third, it is remote from major external markets, being over 2000 km away from Australia, the closest large economy.

Economic activity is dominated by export-oriented production involving tree crop plantations, commercial fishing, and logging; a large public services sector; and a subsistence agricultural sector that provides the main source of livelihood for over 80 percent of the population. There has been little structural transformation of the economy in the past decade. The manufacturing sector remains minuscule, contributing less than 4 percent of GDP. Exploitation of natural resources has been rapid, but the benefits have largely accrued to foreign investors. The economy is quite open, with exports (of fish, timber, copra, palm oil and cocoa) and imports (consumer goods and light machinery) being equivalent to 42 and 55 percent of GDP, respectively. Consequently, economic performance is strongly influenced by changes in the external terms of trade and the availability of foreign exchange.

Recent Economic Developments

Economic activity during 1993 was dominated by developments in the forestry sector. Due to a rise in the world price, timber production increased rapidly in late 1992 to unsustainable levels and was the main factor behind the GDP increase of 10.5 percent. Although the rate of logging has been escalating since 1992, it has not been able to maintain such a high GDP growth rate. GDP growth for 1994 was expected to be a more modest 4 percent. The principal productive sectors are agriculture, forestry and fisheries and copra. Services comprise about 10 percent of GDP and manufacturing which is confined to small-scale activities, about 1 percent. The subsistence or non-monetary economy in the Solomon Islands is still important with much of the population participating in both the monetary and subsistence economies. Although no firm estimates are available, it is believed that the subsistence sector constitutes about 20-40 percent of GDP.

Increased logging revenues, combined with expenditure restraint, narrowed the budget deficit to about 23 percent of GDP in 1992 and 1993. As the development budget is largely aid-driven, the budget for current expenditure is the principal source of discretionary spending with over 40 percent of this allocated to wages and salaries.

The Government resorted to domestic borrowing to sustain the fiscal imbalances of 1991-93. This was done through the banking sector and contributed to a sharp rise in the money supply, and increased aggregate demand pressures which in turn resulted in higher inflation, averaging in excess of 10 percent per year over 1992-93.

SOLOMON ISLANDS: KEY ECONOMIC INDICATORS

	1990	1991	1992	1993
Real GDP growth (%)	1.0	1.7	10.5	0.9
Gross Investment/GDP (%)	29.1	28.1	n.a.	n.a.
Public/GDP (%)	13.9	14.3	n.a.	n.a.
Private/GDP (%)	15.2	13.8	n.a.	n.a.
Consumer Inflation (%)	8.6	15.2	13.1	9.3
Total Liquidity (M3) Growth (%)	11.5	22.1	26.0	14.5
Government Revenues (% GDP) a/	29.2	27.9	31.2	26.1
Government Expenditures (% GDP)	58.8	60.1	53.9	49.0
Overall Balance (% GDP) a/	-29.6	-32.2	-22.7	-22.8
Exports, fob (US$m)	70.2	84.7	103.8	131.7
Imports, cif (US$m)	-92.8	-110.4	-104.9	-144.5
Current Account (US$m) a/	-62.5	-70.6	-37.4	-51.7
(% of GDP)	-37.1	-37.9	-17.9	-21.1
Overall Balance (US$m)	-7.2	-6.3	15.9	-3.0
Gross Reserves (end period, US$m)	17.6	10.1	23.9	21.1
(months of imports)	1.4	0.7	1.8	1.2
External Debt (MLT)/GDP (%)	94.1	90.4	109.9	78.1
Debt Service Ratio (%) b/	10.7	11.4	13.4	23.0
Memo items:				
GDP (nominal, US$m)	168.8	186.4	209.0	245.0
Grants (US$m): net official transfers	33.2	36.3	36.7	37.8

a/ Excludes grants.
b/ In percent of exports of goods and nonfactor services.
Sources: IMF, Recent Economic Developments, 3/94 and IMF Briefing Paper 6/94.

The current account balance which had been recording deficits of 30-40 percent of GDP each year, improved considerably in 1992 to about 18 percent of GDP mainly on account of the increase in log exports. Despite continued high export growth from the increase in logging, the current account balance deteriorated to about 21 percent of GDP in 1993 due mainly to a surge in imports and a decline in the fish catch. Official reserves which were at one point in 1991 down to the equivalent of less than two weeks import coverage, increased sharply in 1992 to nearly two months of imports. The expansion of imports in 1993 reduced the level of reserves to just over one month of imports but these have since recovered somewhat.

The relatively low levels of external borrowing combined with the sharp rise in GDP during the past year, and a one-time lumping of amortization payments, led to a reduction in the debt burden from 110 percent of GDP in 1992 to about 78 percent of GDP in 1993. The ratio of debt service to exports of goods and non-factor services did not show a similar improvement in 1993, instead rising sharply to 23 percent from 13 percent the previous year. This was due to the increased amortization payments, and the debt service ratio is estimated to decline back to its 1992 trend, thereafter.

Key Policy Issues

Fiscal Discipline. Attention to fiscal imbalance is a priority in returning the Solomon Islands to a sustainable pattern of growth and development. Attaining a sustainable fiscal balance will require expenditure restructuring, combining: (i) containment of the wage/salary bill by nominal wage restraint and targeted reductions in government employment of urban-based administrators; (ii) reductions in transfer payments to public enterprises and provincial governments; and (iii) additional aid financing in forms which help meet recurrent expenditure obligations. In addition, the composition of expenditure growth needs to be changed in favor of operations and maintenance and higher capital expenditures (particularly in the social sectors). Expenditure restructuring can help to raise trend growth in the economy. There is a good opportunity to make progress along these lines in the present environment of strong revenue growth arising from favorable terms of trade developments.

Forest Management. Another priority is to curtail the present excessive and unsustainable rate of timber harvesting. Around 700,000 cubic meters of logs were harvested in 1994 even though the sustainable rate is estimated to be only 290,000 cubic meters per annum. The rate of timber harvest has increased sharply early in 1995, with 100,000 cubic meters approved for export in February, 1995. At this rate of extraction, the commercial forest resources of the Solomon Islands will be exhausted within eight to ten years. In this sense, therefore, the Solomon Islands is rapidly depleting its "capital" whereas, for sustainability it should seek to live off the "interest". Policies which could set forest management on a sustainable track include: (i) negotiation with existing license holders to reduce the annual cut to a sustainable level; (ii) collection of higher export taxes to extract a greater proportion of the economic rent going to loggers and to reduce the incentives to log; (iii) improvements in the monitoring of log harvesting techniques and outputs and (iv) greater involvement of landowners in the sustainable management of forests.

Private Sector Development. The establishment of an enabling environment for private sector development is the core of a reform program. Under the present policy stance, domestic borrowing by the government is expensive and crowding-out private investment, adversely affecting both business confidence and the rate of growth of private investment. Domestic debt servicing obligations will remain a source of pressure on the budget for several years to come and could affect spending priorities. Moreover, human resource development is suffering because of the large share of resources going into the wage bill and subsidies and transfers to money-losing public enterprises. Sustained stabilization policies, restructuring of public expenditures, privatization of public enterprises, strengthening of the financial sector, reform of investment incentives and procedures and creative solutions to greater access to land constitute key elements to bring about the expansion of the private sector.

TONGA

Population: **98,000 (1993)**

GDP: **US$145 million (1993)**

GNP Per Capita: **US$1,530 (1993)**

Background

With a per capita income of US$1,610 in 1993, the Kingdom of Tonga ranks among the lower-middle income group of developing nations. However, social indicators reflect living conditions more akin to those prevailing in upper income nations due in part to the high level of investment in human resources. Agriculture and fisheries are the main economic activities, accounting for 50 percent of employment, 40 percent of national income, and approximately 80 percent of export earnings. In recent years, rapid expansion of squash and, to a limited extent, vanilla exports, have offset declining traditional exports of bananas and coconuts.

Emigration has played an important role in shaping economic activity. Nearly 45,000 ethnic Tongans are estimated to be residing abroad, with the majority in New Zealand, Australia and the USA. Overseas migrants come disproportionately from the highly educated segment of the population and the productive age group. Cash remittances from overseas residents are estimated to be about T$40 million per annum, or equivalent to 20 percent of nominal GDP. Although cash remittances have fallen off in recent years, there has been an upsurge in the provision of remittances in kind--mostly consumer durables and light consumer goods--which has substantially augmented private consumption levels.

Tonga has received substantial levels of official assistance on a per capita basis. For example during 1988/89-1992/93, external grants and official loan disbursements averaged US$18 million and US$3 million, respectively (or equivalent to US$233 per capita per annum). Such flows have supported development of a broad base of economic infrastructure and human resource services. Aid flows have also contributed to the buildup of a large public sector and to wage pressures in the formal sector. While aid to Tonga has focused on new investment in infrastructure and services, there has been relatively little support provided to the recurrent costs of managing and maintaining public services.

After nearly 150 years of monarchy, Tonga's first political party was formed in early August, 1994 by commoner politicians campaigning for democracy. The Tongan Democratic Party aims to promote democratic principles, and introduce constitutional changes and reforms whereby Parliament would elect the Government, rather than be appointed by the King.

Recent Economic Developments

Following stagnation in the late 1980s, the Tongan economy picked up moderately in the early 1990s, with real output growth averaging 3.5 percent annually during 1990/91-1992/93, albeit with considerable yearly variation. Economic growth over the period was fueled by strong agricultural performance, as squash production and exports boomed. The improved economic performance benefited from economic policies initiated during the latter part of the 1980s. These included domestic policies aimed at promoting a more efficient private sector by reducing government regulations and price support for copra, then the major export crop, and some incentives and subsidies offered to new manufacturing and agricultural activities. Fiscal policy was generally restrictive, as continued high levels of foreign aid

TONGA: KEY ECONOMIC INDICATORS

	1989/90	1990/91	1991/92	1992/93	1993/94 Est.
Real GDP growth (%)	-2.0	6.4	0.3	3.7	4.7
Gross Investment/GDP (%)	22.1	28.3	24.4	n.a.	n.a.
Public/GDP (%)	22.9	18.5	13.6	n.a.	n.a.
Private/GDP (%)	-0.8	9.8	10.8	n.a.	n.a.
Consumer Inflation (%)	5.6	13.3	8.7	3.0	2.4
Broad Money (M2) Growth (%)	7.1	9.1	22.6	-4.7	10.9
Government Revenues (% GDP) a/	39.8	36.1	37.4	42.3	41.2
Government Expenditures (% GDP)	46.0	40.8	41.0	42.1	39.8
Overall Balance (US$m) a/	-6.2	-4.7	-3.6	0.2	1.4
Exports, fob (US$m)	9.0	10.6	16.6	11.9	20.3
Imports, fob (US$m)	-49.4	-51.4	-48.4	-50.7	-57.8
Current Account (US$m) a/	12.5	-2.4	3.3	3.0	-0.6
(% of GDP)	11.0	-1.7	2.4	2.0	-0.4
Overall Balance (US$m)	-2.5	-1.7	0.5	3.8	-6.0
Gross Reserves (end period, US$m)	26.5	25.9	29.7	35.6	31.5
(months of imports) b/	5.0	4.4	5.8	6.8	5.2
External Debt/GDP (%)	40.0	33.7	35.8	35.2	31.8
Debt Service Ratio (%) c/	2.4	3.1	3.0	4.4	3.0
Memo items:					
GDP (nominal, US$m)	113.0	135.5	140.1	145.0	151.9
Grants (US$m): net official transfers	17.2	11.8	17.5	19.6	20.3

a/ Includes grants. b/ In months of non-aid imports of goods and services.
c/ In percent of private current account receipts.
Source: IMF Staff Report, April 1995.

funded much of the public sector investment program.

Domestic wage pressures, imported inflation, and public sector led monetary expansion contributed to high inflation during the early 1990s. Consumer inflation, which had averaged 4-5 percent at the end of the 1980s, surged to over 13 percent in 1990/91, reflecting mainly a 35 percent civil service wage and salary increase, higher oil prices and increases in indirect tax rates, as well as adverse domestic supply conditions. With inflationary pressures easing in the economies of major trading partners--Australia and New Zealand--and considerable improvement in domestic food supplies, inflation dropped significantly to 3 percent in 1992/93, down from nearly 9 percent in the 1991/92 fiscal year. The moderate growth in wages since the large civil servant salary increases in 1989/90-1990/91 has also contributed to the improved price performance in recent years.

After an expansionary fiscal stance in 1989/90, stemming mainly from the large civil service salary increase and an expansion of outlays on locally financed projects, budgetary policies have subsequently been tightened. The overall fiscal balance, which had recorded a deficit of over 6 percent of GDP in 1989/90, improved steadily through 1991/92, and in 1992/93 registered a slight surplus. Contributing to the improved fiscal performance since 1990/91 was a steady reduction in current expenditures, supported in 1992/93 by strong revenue performance-- resulting from several tax measures and efforts to collect tax arrears, and a large increase in external grants. Reflecting the improved budgetary performance the Government maintained large net positive balances with the banking system.

During 1989/90 to 1991/92, broad money growth averaged about 13 percent per year fueled primarily by a surge in domestic credit as net credit to government soared in the face of limited expansion in credit to the private sector. In 1992/93, the pace of broad money dipped downward, reflecting a sharp fall in net credit to the Government and the private sector that was only partially offset by a large increase in international reserves.

Despite the rapid monetary expansions, interest rates in Tonga have remained relatively stable in nominal terms since the late 1980s. Interest rate policy in recent years has focused on maintaining deposit rates which are positive in real terms. Following the complete elimination of interest rate restrictions in July 1991, the National Reserve Bank of Tonga (NRBT) has influenced interest rates paid by the Bank of Tonga (BOT), the sole commercial bank until late 1993, through the setting of the interest rate on time deposits at the NRBT, and more recently, on central bank notes. The BOT's short-term deposit rate which had remained at 6.5 to 7.5 percent declined in mid-1992 to 4.25 percent in line with a general fall in international interest rates. Despite the decline in deposit rates, lending rates remained fairly constant up until early 1993, resulting in the widening of BOT's spread as the Bank sought to recover some of the costs associated with the loan losses sustained in the late 1980s. In early 1993, the interest rate on new investment loans was reduced but the spread remained high because of fixed rates on existing loans and the limited opportunities for refinancing.

The external accounts registered overall surpluses during the early 1990s, except for a small deficit in 1990/91, allowing a build-up of external reserves at comfortable levels. At end 1992/93, gross official reserves peaked at US$36 million (equivalent to 6.8 months of imports), up from US$26 million (4.4 months of imports) at the end of fiscal year 1990/91. Underlying this performance was a fairly stable trade deficit which, together with moderate net outflows on the services account, was generally offset by increasing net inflows on the transfers' accounts. Private and official transfer receipts have continued to be high in recent years. The current account which had recorded a huge surplus in 1989/90 but a marginal deficit in the subsequent year, shifted back into surplus in 1991/92. The capital account registered a small surplus in 1990/91 and 1992/93, mainly as a result of official external borrowing.

Over the past three years, official external debt, almost exclusively on concessional terms, has remained relatively stable at about 35 percent of GDP. Reflecting the concessional nature of debt outstanding, debt service obligations have been low, averaging around 3.2 percent of current account receipts in recent years.

Key Policy Issues

Structural Reforms. Tonga's policies of courting private investment by maintaining a fully convertible currency and through provision of tax incentives, protective trade policies, and minimal regulation have been less successful than anticipated. This is partly due to structural deficiencies and continued public sector domination of key areas of the economy. Structural policy reforms can make an important contribution to improving the incentives environment for private sector development.

Public Sector Reform. Tonga faces the challenge of transforming a public sector dominated economy into a more dynamic market-based economy. There is scope for improving incentives for private sector development through tariff reform, provision of adequate infrastructure and broadening of financial markets.

Export Diversification. Continued reliance on a narrow range of income generating activities increases the economy's vulnerability to terms of trade and other external shocks. This underscores the need to intensify current efforts at diversification.

Competitiveness. Declining economy-wide competitiveness in Tonga since 1989 remains a concern. To correct this, Government needs to control budgetary expenditures, strengthen tax administration, reduce tax exemptions and resist any large, general wage increases.

Vanuatu

Population: **161,000 (1993)**

GDP: **US$186 million (1993)**

GNP Per Capita: **US$1,230 (1993)**

Background

The Vanuatu economy is dual in nature with about 80 percent of the population engaged in subsistence or small scale agriculture, primarily copra, cocoa and beef production. The formal economy is dominated by services, including government, tourism and an offshore finance center. Vanuatu faces a variety of geographical constraints to economic development including vulnerability to external shocks, remoteness from major markets and large distances from constituent islands. While poverty is limited, development has been focused on urban centers--particularly Port Vila, resulting in increasing regional income inequality and growing rural-urban migration. Vanuatu has good economic potential in agriculture, forestry and tourism. External aid has been generous by international standards, yet economic growth has been slow and uneven.

Recent Economic Developments

The Vanuatu economy rebounded in 1993, with a growth rate of 4.4 percent after virtually having stagnated in 1992. The performance of the agricultural sector, which accounts for 25 percent of the GDP, showed a strong recovery with a growth rate of 7.5 percent. The total production of copra, the main agricultural product, increased by 3.1 percent in 1993. Other agricultural commodities, such as beef, timber, cocoa, and kava, showed a much stronger performance. A new development was the increased production of squash for exports from 500 tons in 1992 to 1500 tons in 1993. World prices for squash were very favorable and increased about 240 percent in 1993.

Fishing is a major subsistence activity in Vanuatu. The manufacturing sector is small, and inward oriented, accounting for about 7 percent of GDP. The sector has been mostly stagnant owing to an uncertain political climate, protectionist policies (which reserve certain activities for ni-Vanuatu) restricting foreign investment, difficulties faced by local businessmen in raising capital, and the relaxation of certain import restrictions, which may have discouraged private investment.

The services sector accounts for two thirds of GDP. Growth in trade, hotels and restaurants has been weak. The tourism industry picked up in 1993 with visitor levels reaching 44,000 and was estimated to increase to 47,000 in 1994. The Government is giving special attention to the development of tourism, and a master plan has been outlined. However, infrastructural constraints such as inadequate accommodation capacity, limited air accessibility, lack of adequate infrastructure for travel within the country, and absence of systematic training for ni-Vanuatu seem to have caused the industry to plateau. In support of tourism development, the Government had embarked upon a program to rehabilitate the airports at Port Vila and at Espiritu Santo, with an estimated cost of US$15 million, but has recently limited the project to the latter airport at a cost of US$9 million.

Price movements in Vanuatu, as in most of the other PMCs have been modest, mainly influenced by price movements in the main import source country (Australia), the exchange rate, and import tariffs. Inflation in 1992-93 averaged about 3.4 percent with almost 60 percent of the consumer price index consisting of imported goods.

VANUATU: KEY ECONOMIC INDICATORS

	1989	1990	1991	1992	1993
Real GDP Growth Rate (%)	4.5	5.2	6.5	0.6	4.4
Gross Investment/GDP (%)	37.2	43.6	n.a.	n.a.	n.a.
Public/GDP (%)	23.9	19.1	n.a.	n.a.	n.a.
Private/GDP (%)	13.3	24.5	n.a.	n.a.	n.a.
Consumer Inflation (%)	6.9	5.2	5.6	5.1	1.7
Broad Money(M2)Growth (%)	35.8	11.4	23.8	-0.7	10.4
Government Revenues (% of GDP) a/	47.3	45.6	37.6	36.5	34.7
Government Expenditures (% of GDP)	52.1	54.1	43.7	39.0	37.3
Overall Balance (% of GDP)	-4.8	-8.5	-6.1	-2.5	-2.6
Exports, fob (US$m)	21.9	18.8	18.2	23.7	22.7
Imports, fob (US$m)	-59.3	-79.2	-66.5	-67.3	-72.7
Current Account (US$m) a/	11.0	4..3	-0.6	5.2	-11.2
(% of GDP)	7.8	2.8	0.3	2.8	-6.0
Overall Balance (US$m)	-4.2	1.1	2.2	2.4	3.7
Gross Reserves (end period, US$m)	36.2	37.3	39.5	41.8	45.5
(months of imports)	7.6	5.9	7.6	8.0	8.1
External Debt/GDP (%)	14.8	20.0	21.1	20.9	20.5
Debt Service Ratio (%) b/	2.0	2.2	1.4	1.5	1.9
Memo items:					
GDP (nominal, US$m)	140.9	152.9	180.3	187.9	186.0
Grants (US$m): net official transfers	31.8	29.8	35.5	36.2	35.3

a/ Includes grants.
b/ In terms of exports of goods, services, and private transfers.
Source: IMF Recent Economic Developments, February 1995.

Government budgetary operations in recent years have been conservative with the main aim being to balance the recurrent budget. A small surplus in the recurrent budget was achieved in 1993. The overall fiscal deficit after having declined partially in 1992 widened marginally in 1993 to 2.6 percent of GDP. The budget for 1994 retained a commitment to balance the recurrent budget. Expenditure estimates for 1994 indicated an increase of 10 percent in salaries and allowances, to be financed by efficiency savings through civil service reform. Initial steps in this direction are yet to be taken. However, as a result of the public servants' strike in 1993, there has already been a 20 percent reduction of staff.

The domestic tax base is very narrow with tax receipts about 75 percent of total revenue, of which virtually all came from indirect taxes such as customs duties (which are very high in the range of 40 to 80 percent). There are no direct taxes on personal and company incomes other than business license fees. The Government is aware that such a system will not last and is keen to broaden the tax base rather than increase overall tax relative to GDP. It may also introduce a personal income tax, although this has always faced opposition from the representatives of the offshore finance center. Some measures have been taken to broaden the tax base, including a turnover tax of 4 percent on wholesale and retail trade. The Government is also considering the lowering of import tariffs.

On the expenditure side, current expenditures were higher in 1993 due to reduction in fees for education and health. Most of the capital budget is financed by donors, and the Government is keen to set up a formal development budget.

On the external front, Vanuatu has normally recorded large merchandise trade deficits. The principal export is copra, returns from which have been unstable because of volume and export price fluctuations. Other exports are nearly all agricultural products, such as beef, kava, coffee, timber, and more recently squash. Trade data for 1993 indicate that total export receipts were slightly lower than in 1992. Lower earnings from copra, were offset by a sharp rise in returns from exports of beef, timber, and squash. Imports in 1993 are estimated to be about 8 percent higher than in 1992, resulting in a trade deficit of around 27 percent of GDP. The other main sources of foreign exchange receipts are tourism, and official and foreign investment, especially reinvested earnings, which together with official transfers have usually resulted in a sizable balance of payments surplus.

Key Issues

Civil Service Reform. The Government is committed to balancing the recurrent budget, hence reducing recurrent expenditure of which an average of 45-50 percent is spent on wages and salaries. The special Restructuring Commission recommended that the civil service be cut by 20 percent. The Government has decided to implement a 17 percent increase in nominal wages spread over a four year period. A 10 percent increase was given in 1994 and the balance will be provided later. As a result of the civil servants' strike from November, 1993 to March, 1994 there has already been some reduction in the size of the civil service, affecting services in education, agriculture and health.

Forestry Sector. During the past two years, Vanuatu has faced severe logging pressures which could have resulted in the entire country being logged out in less than five years. Licenses granted had allowed an annual cut of 290,000 cu meters compared to a sustainable rate of about 52,000 cu meters. This situation may have been brought under control through a ban on log exports imposed in June 1994 with the aim of limiting the export of raw logs.

Investment Program. The Government has stressed that priorities for the 1994-95 budget are in the areas of health, education, rural water supply, and the upgrading of two airports in Port Vila and Espiritu Santo. Financing for the upgrading of the airports was sought on commercial terms. This will put additional pressure on the fiscal balance, unless other items of expenditure are cut to reduce the fiscal deficit and the decision to limit rehabilitation to the latter airport is strictly adhered to.

Western Samoa

Population: **167,000 (1993)**

GDP: **US$122 million (1993)**

GNP Per Capita: **US$950 (1993)**

Background

Western Samoa comprises two main islands, Upolu and Savai'i, and seven small islands. Economic activity is largely based on agriculture (mainly coconuts, taro, bananas, and subsistence crops). The small manufacturing sector is oriented towards the processing of agricultural products. The majority of the population is engaged in the informal subsistence area and about one third of employment is in the government sector.

Recent Economic Developments

Economic growth in 1993 was positive and real GDP is estimated to have increased by about 5.3 percent, after a cumulative decline of over 12 percent in the period 1990-92. Growth was led by a strong recovery in agricultural production, especially taro, in the first half of 1993, and by a rebound in the service industry, led by tourism.

However, in the latter part of 1993, the expansion in agricultural production was brought to a halt, as a result of a leaf blight affecting the taro crop. In the absence of effective control measures, taro production has been reduced from the second largest agricultural product in the country to almost negligible levels. It is estimated that the supplies available at the Apia market in April 1994 were less than half of that available in the same months in 1993. The other major agricultural crop, coconut is recovering from cyclone damage. Some replanting has taken place and the trees were expected to mature by 1995. In 1993/94, coconut and banana production experienced some positive growth.

The manufacturing sector is small, primarily limited to the processing of agricultural products. The opening of an export-oriented automotive wiring assembly-plant in 1992 resulted in some export diversification. Production from this plant has increased rapidly and, in 1993, accounted for an estimated 18.5 percent of the total value of manufacturing production, or 3.5 percent of GDP.

Total manufacturing output declined by about 3.5 percent in 1993, reflecting shortages of locally grown copra and coconut for processing. Coconut cream production fell by 22 percent in 1993 as a result of the closure of one of the three factories, and for the others, imported copra is being used for production. The performance of other industries, such as beer, cigarettes, etc. in 1993 has been mixed.

Tourist arrivals rebounded in 1993, increasing by 24 percent. Gross earnings from tourism were WS$35.4 million in the first nine months of 1993. Although the Government is committed to the development of the tourism sector, the lack of appropriate accommodation for tourists from the main source markets (such as Japan) acts as a major constraint.

Inflation performance in recent years has been strongly influenced by the impact of external shocks on the economy, influenced by two major cyclones in 1990 and 1991. The annual average inflation rate fell from 8.5 percent in 1992 to 1.7 percent in 1993, mainly as a result of improved domestic production and a tightening of monetary policy. However, by late 1993 prices came under renewed pressure owing partly to shortages due to the impact of taro leaf blight. The CPI increased by a further 17 percent in the first four months of 1994, reflecting the combined effect of the 10 percent value added goods and services tax (introduced on January 1, 1994), further declines in taro supplies and increases in the prices of certain essential items.

WESTERN SAMOA: KEY ECONOMIC INDICATORS

	1989	1990	1991	1992	1993
Real GDP Growth Rate (%)	1.9	-9.4	-1.9	-1.3	5.3
Gross Investment/GDP (%)	26.4	34.4	40.5	42.0	n.a.
Public/GDP (%)	21.6	31.1	36.0	36.6	n.a.
Private/GDP (%)	4.8	3.3	4.5	5.4	n.a.
Consumer Inflation (%)	6.5	15.2	-1.3	8.5	1.7
Broad Money(M2)Growth (%)	16.7	19.2	-1.9	0.8	-0.7
Government Revenues (% of GDP) a/	57.4	64.8	61.5	65.6	69.0
Government Expenditures (% of GDP)	55.1	69.7	63.9	83.2	90.9
Overall Balance (% of GDP)	2.3	-4.9	-2.4	-17.6	-21.9
Exports, fob (US$m)	12.9	8.9	6.5	5.8	6.4
Imports, fob (US$m)	-75.5	-80.6	-94.0	-110.1	-102.7
Current Account (US$m) a/	15.1	13.4	-29.9	-24.7	-33.9
(% of GDP)	13.0	11.8	-26.3	-20.8	-28.0
Overall Balance (US$m)	14.4	16.3	1.4	-8.2	-8.1
Gross Reserves (end period, US$m)	55.2	69.0	67.9	57.6	48.9
(months of imports)	7.6	8.7	7.2	5.3	4.6
External Debt/GDP (%)	66.3	82.7	101.2	110.9	118.0
Debt Service Ratio (%) b/	7.8	6.0	6.8	5.7	5.2
Memo items:					
GDP (nominal, US$m)	116.2	113.6	113.7	118.8	122.0
Grants (US$m): net official transfers	16.7	18.8	9.3	19.2	18.3

a/ Includes grants.
b/ In terms of exports of goods, services, and private transfers.
Source: IMF Recent Economic Developments, 10/94.

In the case of fiscal policy, total expenditure has been rising with most of this spending attributable to cyclone rehabilitation programs. Recurrent expenditures have also been on the rise, reflecting the increases in government departments and continuing high levels of public sector wages and salaries. However, despite significant increases in government revenue, overall fiscal balance moved from a moderate balance in 1989 to a deficit of 22 percent of GDP in 1993, largely due to the final stages of cyclone rehabilitation expenditure. In 1993/94 with completion of cyclone rehabilitation and the scaling down of expenditures on other infrastructure projects, the overall budget deficit of the central government is estimated to have declined.

As for monetary policy, growth in bank credit to the private sector slowed down in 1993, though total domestic credit (as a percent of broad money) accelerated from 8.3 percent in 1992 to 13.5 percent in 1993, mainly due to a rapid draw down of government deposits with the banking sector.

The external position of Western Samoa has been deteriorating since the early 1990s. The value of merchandise exports fell by more than half between 1989 and 1993, with the traditional exports of cocoa, coconut products and timber virtually eliminated as a result of the cyclone. Imports for reconstruction rose rapidly over this period. The current account balance deteriorated from a surplus in 1990 to a deficit of 28 percent of

GDP in 1993, despite substantial increases in remittances, a strong growth in earnings from export processing and tourism activities, and a recovery in agricultural production in the first half of the year. Exports of Yazaki wiring harness factory, which are not included in merchandise exports, have been increasing consistently In 1992, Yazakis' gross exports were US$24 million and it contributed US$2 million to service receipts as its net value added.

Key Policy Issues:

The short-term prospects for the economy remain difficult, with the continued spread of taro blight, real GDP is estimated to have declined in 1994, and exports fell further in 1994. The annual average inflation rate is estimated to have reached 18 percent, reflecting shortages in the economy. Given the huge macroeconomic imbalances, large balance of payments deficit, low level of international reserves and narrow production base, the economy remains vulnerable to external shocks. The levels of the central government budget deficit and spending have been high and at unsustainable levels. According to the 1994/95 budget, the Government expects a significant reduction in the deficit, owing to (i) a reduction in development expenditures and (ii) a shift in funding from domestic sources and foreign concessional loans to external grants.

The greatest risk to the fiscal outlook is posed by the state-owned Polynesian Airlines. Since it first leased a long range aircraft in mid-1993 for services to North America, the airline has incurred large losses and liabilities, which have accumulated to about WS$45 million (about US$18 million) or about 23 percent of central government revenue. The Government made unanticipated capital transfers of WS$8.8 million in 1992/93-1993/94 and has guaranteed a large proportion of the company's non operating debt, contracted on commercial terms. It is imperative that the size of the fleet and the operations of the airline be drastically reduced, and efficiently managed. The Government has taken some initial steps in this direction. But the main challenge will be to meet the new debt service obligations through expenditure cuts in other areas, and sale of government assets.

BIBLIOGRAPHY

General

Asia Productivity Organization. *APO Study Mission on Agricultural Extension.* 1988.

Bear, Marshall, and M. Tiller. *Microenterprise Development in the Outer Islands of Fiji: The Rural Area Appropriate Technology Unit Project.*

Browne C., and D. A. Scott. *Economic Development in Seven Pacific Island Countries.* International Monetary Fund, Washington, D.C. 1989.

de Melo, J. *The Macroeconomic Effects of Foreign Aid: Issues and Evidence.* World Bank Discussion Paper No. DRD 300, 1987.

Development Strategies Consultants Pty Ltd. *Review of Administrative Aspects of Market Access in the Region.* Forum Secretariat, September, 1993.

Duncan, I., and others. *Dismantling the Barriers: Tariff Policy in New Zealand.* Wellington, NZIER, 1992.

Edwards, S. *Real Exchange Rate Misalignment in Developing Countries: Analytical Issues and Empirical Evidence.* CPD Discussion Paper No. 1985-43,1985.

Government of Fiji. *Medium-Term Strategy for the Garment Export Industry of Fiji.* Suva, 1994.

Nagasaka, T. *Globalization of Japanese Corporations and Their Changing Role in Asia. - Pacific Development.* In Evolution of Asia-Pacific Economics: International Trade and Direct Investment. Ed. I. Yamagazawa and F. Lo. Asian and Pacific Development Centre, Kuala Lumpur, 1993.

Neemia, Uentable Fakaofo. *Cooperation and Conflict: Costs, Benefits and National Interests in Pacific Regional Cooperation.* Institute of Pacific Studies, University of the South Pacific, 1986.

Pacific Islands Review. *Australia Agrees to SPARTECA Changes.* September, 1994.

Pacific Islands Review. *The Shackles of SPARTECA.* June, 1994.

Price Waterhouse. *Review of the Foreign Investment Climate in South Pacific Forum Countries.* South Pacific Forum, Suva, 1994.

Singh, M. *Sugar: the Challenge.* The Pacific Islands Review, July, 1994.

Thistlethwatie, R., Volaw, Gregory and SPREP. *Environment and Development: A Pacific Island Perspective.* 1992.

Van Wijnbergen, S. *Aid, Export Promotion and The Real Exchange Rate: An African Dilemma.* CPD Working Paper No. 1985-54, World Bank, 1985.

UNDP/NACA. *UNDP/NACA Technical Programme of Assistance to Developing Countries in Asia-Pacific Aimed at Developing Agriculture on a Sustainable and Environmentally Sound Basis.* 1992.

UNDP. *Development Cooperation, Fiji, Kiribati, Nauru, Solomon Islands, Tonga, Federated States of Micronesia, Marshall Islands, Palau, Tuvalu, Vanuatu and Pacific Regional Programmes, Suva, Fiji, 1985-86.* 1988.

U.S. General Accounting Office, Report by the Comptroller General of the United States. *The Challenge of Enhancing Micronesian Self-Sufficiency.* Washington, D.C ,1983.

World Bank. *Building on the Uruguay Round: East Asian Leadership in Liberalization.* A Discussion Paper, 1994.

--. *Caribbean Region: Coping With Changes in the External Environment.* April, 1994.

--. *Fiji: Sugar Sector Study.* August, 1994.

--. *Global Economic Prospects and the Developing Countries.* various issues.

--. *Health Priorities and Options in the World Bank's Pacific Member Countries.* 1994.

--. *Identifying South Pacific Project Opportunities.* Gemini Consultants/IFC, September, 1993.

--. *Managing Urban Environmental Sanitation Services in Selected Pacific Island Countries.* February 1995.

--. *Market Outlook for Major Primary Commodities: Volume II, Agricultural Products, Fertilizers, and Tropical Timber.* October, 1992.

--. *Market Outlook for Major Primary Commodities: Volume I, Energy Materials and Minerals.* February, 1994.

--. *Pacific Island Economies: Towards Efficient and Sustainable Growth* (in Nine Volumes). 1993.

--. *Pacific Island Economies: Towards Higher Growth in the 1990s.* 1991.

Tourism

Annals of Tourism Research. *The Political Economy of Tourism in the Third World.* Volume 9, 1982.

Briguglio, L. *Tourism Impact on the Environment of Small Islands with Special Reference to Malta.* University of Newcastle, Occasional Paper in Economic Development No. 46, Newcastle, 1992.

Dwyer, L. and P. Forsyth. *The Case for Tourism Promotion: An Economic Analysis.* Australian National University, Centre for Economic Policy Research, Discussion Paper No. 265, Canberra, 1992.

Hagan and Mooney. *Input-Output Multipliers in a Small Open Economy: An Application to Tourism.* Economic and Social Review, Vol. 14, No. 4, Dublin, 1983.

Keith-Reid, R. *Investment-the $10,000m Target.* Islands Business, Suva, December, 1985.

Tabor, Steven. *Issues in Tourism in the South Pacific.* mimeo., Amsterdam, 1992.

Tisdell, C.A. *Tourism, the Environment, International Trade and Public Economics.* ASEAN-Australia Economic Papers No. 6, Kuala Lumpur and Canberra, 1984.

--. *Tourism, the Environment and Profit.* Economic Analysis and Policy, Vol. 17, No. 1, Brisbane, 1987.

--. *Economic Management of Tourism Based on Natural Sites: Volume, Pricing, Site Allocation and Competition with Science for Sites.* University of Newcastle, Department of Economics, Occasional Paper No. 160, Newcastle, 1989.

Tourism Council of the South Pacific. *South Pacific Regional Tourism Statistics, 1992.* Suva, 1993.

World Bank. *Mauritius: Expanding Horizons.* Report No. MAR-11010, Washington D.C. 1992.

--. *Pacific Island Transport Sector Study* (in seven volumes), Report No. 10543-EAP, March 1993.

--. *Tourism in Small Island Economies: A Research Proposal.* 1993.

Fisheries

Adams, and others. *Pilot Survey of the Status of Trochus and Beche-de-Mer Resources in the Western Province of the Solomon Islands With Options for Management.* South Pacific Commission (SPC), Inshore Fisheries Research Project. Draft, June/July 1992.

Adams, T. *Resource Aspects of the Fiji Beche-de-Mer Industry.* SPC Beche-de-Mer Information Bulletin No. 4, July, 1992.

Asian Development Bank. *Fisheries Development Project Appraisal.* Document No. LAP MAR 24261, Marshall Islands, September, 1991.

Asian Development Bank. *Economic Report on the Republic of the Marshall Islands.* Document No. ECR MAR 91006, 56-57, March, 1991.

Bell, Lui A.J, and Moses Amos. *Fisheries Resources Profiles, Republic of Vanuatu.* Forum Fisheries Agency Report 93/49, Honiara, 1993.

Bell, Lui A.J., Ulunga Fa'anunu, and Taniela Koloa. *Fisheries Resource Profiles: Kingdom of Tonga.* Forum Fisheries Agency Report 94/5, Honiara, 1994.

Conand, Chantal. *Recent Evolution of Hong Kong and Singapore Sea Cucumber Markets.* Beche-de-Mer Information Bulletin #5, SPC, August, 1993.

Coreoli, Martin. *Pearl Production and Marketing in French Polynesia.* SPC Pearl Oyster Info Bulletin #3, SPC, July, 1991.

Coreoli, Martin. *The Cultivated Pearl Market in Tahiti.* SPC Pearl Oyster Information Bulletin #6, SPC, May, 1993.

Crossland, J., and P.W. Philipson. *The Rural Fishing Enterprise Project in Solomon Islands: Fish Market and Marketing Study.* Report prepared for the Commission of the European Communities, Honiara, 1993.

Dalzell and Adams. *The Present Status of Coastal Fisheries Production in South Pacific Islands.* Inshore Fisheries Research Project Meeting Report, SPC/Fisheries 25, WP8, South Pacific Commission Fisheries Programme, February, 1994.

Dalzell and Preston. *Deep-Slope Fishery Resources of the South Pacific.* Inshore Fisheries Research Project, South Pacific Commission, Technical Document No. 2. 1992.

David, G. *Le Marche des Produits de la Peche a Vanuatu.* Institut Francais de Recherche Scientifique Pour le Developpement en Cooperation (ORSTOM) Notes et Documents d'Oceanographie No. 18., June, 1988.

David, G. and E. Cillaurren. *National Fisheries Development Policy for Coastal Waters, Small-Scale Village Fishing and Food Self-Reliance in Vanuatu.* Man and Culture in Oceania, 8:35-38, 1992.

Dixon, Y. *Coastal Resources in Kosrae: An Undeveloped Economic Resource.* Kosrae Island Resource Management Plan (Volume II), Collected Papers, 1989.

Doulman, D. *Community-Based Fishery Management-Towards the Restoration of Traditional Practices in the South Pacific.* Marine Policy: 108-117. March, 1993.

Eaton, Peter. *Land Tenure and Conservation: Protected Areas in the South Pacific.* SPREP/Topic Review 17, South Pacific Commission, Noumea, New Caledonia.,1985.

Food and Agriculture Organization (FAO), United Nations. *Food Balance Sheets, 1984-86 Average.* Rome, 1991.

--. *Food Composition Tables.* Rome, 1954.

--. 1972. *Food Composition Table for Use in East Asia.* U.S. Department of Health, Education and Welfare; Nutrition Program, Center for Disease Control and Food Policy and Nutrition Division of Food and Agriculture Organization of the United Nations, December, 1988.

--. Agrostat Database. various years.

Fao, Bernard. *Information on Trochus Fisheries in the South Pacific.* Trochus Information Bulletin No. 1, SPC, July, 1992.

Fassier, Richard C. *Pearl Culture Development, A Proposal for a South Pacific Pearl Conference.* Pearl Oyster Information Bulletin #5, SPC, September, 1992.

Fiji Republic Gazette. *Laws of Fiji.* Chapter 158, Fisheries, Fisheries Act (Amendment) Decree 1991.

Financial Times. *Fijians Get Taste for Fish Farming in Village Ponds.* Monday, December 30, 1991.

Floyd, Jesse M. *The Federated States of Micronesia and The Republic of the Marshall Islands: Fisheries Sector Profiles.* Report prepared for the International Bank for Reconstruction and Development by Development Alternatives, Inc., Bethesda, Maryland, 1992.

Forum Fisheries Agency. *Nearshore Marine Resource Management.* Pacific Island Outreach Workshop, July,1994.

Gillett, Robert, and P. Hürrell. *Catching On: Tonga's Healthy Trade in Snapper.* Island Business Pacific, August, 1993.

Gillett, Robert. *Pacific Islands Trochus Introductions.* SPC Trochus Information Bulletin No. 2, South Pacific Commission, September, 1993.

Gordon, H.S. *An Economic Approach to the Optimum Utilisation of Fishery Resources.* Journal of Fisheries Research Board of Canada, 10:442-457, 1953.

Gordon, H.S. *The Economic Theory of the Common Property Resource: The Fishery.* The Journal of Political Economy, 62:124-142, 1954.

Government of Kiribati. *Kiribati 7th National Development Plan. 1992-95.*

Hampton, J. *Status of Tuna Stocks in the SPC Area: A Summary Report for 1993.* South Pacific Commission, Noumea, 1993.

Holthus, Paul. *Coastal Resource Use in Pacific Islands: Gathering Information for Planning from Traditional Resource Users.* Tropical Coastal Area Management, April/August, 1990.

--.*Coastal and Marine Environments of Pacific Islands: Ecosystem Classification, Ecological Assessment, and Traditional Knowledge for Coastal Management.* In Small Island Oceanography, Coastal and Estuarine Studies. 1994.

Hviding, Edvard, and Graham Baines. *Community-based Fisheries Management, Tradition and the Challenges of Development in Marovo, Solomon Islands.* Development and Change, Vol. 25:13-39, 1994.

IKA Corporation. *IKA Annual Report. 1991,* Suva..

Indonesia Department of Fisheries (IDOF). *International Trade Statistics of Fisheries Commodities.* 1993.

Integrated Marine Management, Ltd. *Kiribati Marine Resources Sector Study.* July, 1993.

Johannes, R.E. *Government-Supported, Village-Based Management of Marine Resources in Vanuatu.* FFA Report #94/2, Forum Fisheries Agency, Honiara, 1994.

Kenneth, and Dorostay. *Hard Choices in Fisheries Development Policies: The Case of the Village Fisheries Development Programme in Vanuatu.* CNAA Master of Science Thesis, Portsmouth Polytechnic, UK, 1990/91.

Kriz, A. *Marketing of South Pacific Seafood: A Case Study of Sea Cucumber.* FFA Report No. 94/11, Forum Fisheries Ageney, May, 1994.

Lawson, T. (ed.). *South Pacific Commission Tuna Fishery Yearbook 1993.* SPC. Noumea, 1994.

Leary, Tanya (ed.). *Rapid Ecological Survey of the Arnavon Islands.* The Nature Conservancy, Honiara, 1993.

Leary, Tanya and Sango Mahanty. *Consultative Workshops and Household Surveys: Kia Community; Resource Users of the Arnavon Islands.* The Nature Conservancy and Solomon Islands Environment and Conservation Division, December, 1993.

Les Nouvelles de Tahiti. *Quality is the Key to Success of Our Black Pearl Industry.* SPC Oyster Information Bulletin No. 5, SPC, September, 1992.

Lodge, Michael. *Minimum Terms and Conditions of Access - Responsible Fisheries Management Measures in the South Pacific Region.* Marine Policy: 277-305, 1992.

MacAlister and Partners. *Urban Fish Marketing in Vanuatu.* Final Report, Port Vila, August , 1992.

Marine Science and Resources Investigation (MSRI). *A Study of the Economic and Social Costs of Under Pricing of Resource Rent and Under Reporting of Tuna Fish Catches in the South Pacific.* Final Draft Report Prepared for the Australian International Development Assistance Bureau by Marine Science and Resource Investigations Pty. Ltd., September 30, 1994.

McElroy, S. *The Japanese Pearl Market.* SPC Pearl Oyster Info Bulletin No. 2, SPC, November, 1990.

Micronesian Maritime Authority. *1993 Annual Report.* Federated States of Micronesia..

Ministry of Primary Industries, Fisheries Dept. *Fisheries Division Annual Report.* (Various years). Suva, Fiji.

Mueller, P. *An Overview of Living and Non-Living Marine Resources.* In Marine Resources and Development. Ed. G. South. University of the South Pacific Library, pp. 2-33, 1993.

Mulipola, Atonio. *Current Status of Beche-de-Mer Resource and Exploitation in Western Samoa.* Western Samoa Fisheries Division, Apia, June, 1994.

--. *The 1992 Report on Inshore Fisheries Commercial Landings at the Apia Fish Market.* Western Samoa Fisheries Division, Apia, 1993.

--. *Summary of Programmes Implemented by the Research Section in 92/93 Period.* Western Samoa Fisheries Division, Apia, 1994.

Naidu, S. and others. *Water Quality Studies on Selected South Pacific Lagoons.* UNEP Regional Seas Reports and Studies No, 136, SPREP Reports/Studies No. 49, 1991.

Nash, W. *Drop in Price Observed for the Trochus Shell Between Mid-1991 and Mid-1992.* Trochus Information Bulletin No. 1, SPC, July, 1992.

Nash, W. *Trochus.* pp. 451-495 in Wright and Hill (eds), Nearshore Marine Resources of the South Pacific, Institute of Pacific Studies, Suva, Forum Fisheries Agency and International Centre for Ocean Development, Canada, 1993.

Nguyen-Khoa. *Efficience et Impacts Halieutique, Economique, et Social des DCP dans les Societes Insulaires.* ORSTOM , Port Villa, June, 1993.

Owen, A. and D. Troedson. *Modelling Tuna Prices in Japan: A Vector Autoregressive Approach.* In H. Campbell and A. Owen. *The Economics of Papua New Guinea Tuna Fisheries.* Australian Centre for International Agricultural Research, Canberra ,1994.

Pacific Fishing Company Ltd. *Thirtieth Annual Report.* Suva, 1992.

Preston, and Tanaka. *A Review of the Potential of Aquaculture as a Tool for Inshore Marine Invertebrate Resource Enhancement and Management in the Pacific Islands.* SPC/Fisheries 22/ IP.5, August 5, 1990.

Preston. *Study of the Aitutaki Trochus Fishery.* SPC Trochus Information Bulletin No. 1, South Pacific Commission, 1992.

Republic of the Marshall Islands, Office of Planning and Statistics. *Second Five-Year Development Plan, 1991/92-95/96.* Majuro, 1991.

Richards, A. *Live Fish Export Fisheries in Papua New Guinea: Current Status and Future Prospects* (Abridged). FFA Report No. 93/10, Forum Fisheries Agency, 1993.

Richards, A., and others. *Fiji Fisheries Resources Profiles.* Third Draft 09/06/94. Forum Fisheries Agency Report No. 94/4, Honiara, 1994.

Richards, A.H., L.J. and J.D. Bell. *Fisheries Resources and Management in the Solomon Islands,* Forum Fisheries Agency and International Centre for Living Aquatic Resources Management, Solomon Islands, Undated.

Sasabule, John A. *Fish Marketing and Distribution: A Case Study of Rural Fishermen in Western Province, Solomon Islands.* Gizo, Western Province, Solomon Islands, June ,1991.

Schaefer, M. *Some Considerations of the Population Dynamics and Economics in Relation to the Management of Commercial Marine Fisheries.* Journal of Fisheries Research Board of Canada, 14:669-681, 1957.

Skewes. *Marine Resources Profiles: Solomon Islands.* FFA Report 90/61, Forum Fisheries Agency, Honiara, 1990.

Smith, Andrew J. *Federated States of Micronesia: Marine Resources Profiles.* FFA Report No. 92/17, Forum Fisheries Agency, Honiara, 1992.

Smith, Andrew J. *Republic of the Marshall Islands: Marine Resources Profiles.* Draft report prepared for the South Pacific Forum Fisheries Agency (FFA) at the request of the Marshall Islands Marine Resources Authority, Forum Fisheries Agency, Honiara, July, 1992.

Solomon Islands Fisheries Department. Miscellaneous fisheries statistics (unpublished). Undated.

Solomon Islands Gazette. *The Fisheries (Amendment) Regulations, Honiara. 1993.*

South Pacific Commission. *Non-Reporting and Under-Reporting of Catches by Western Pacific Purse Seiners in Data Collected by Coastal States.* Working Paper 6, Tuna and Billfish Assessment Programme, Noumea, New Caledonia, 1992.

South Pacific Commission. *South Pacific Economies: Statistical Summary.* No. 13. Noumea, New Caledonia, 1993.

South Pacific Commission. *An Assessment of the Skipjack and Baitfish Resources of Northern Mariana Islands, Guam, Palau, Federated States of Micronesia, and Marshall Islands.* Skipjack Survey and Assessment Programme Final Country Report No. 18, 1984, Noumea, New Caledonia, Cited in Smith, A., *Republic of the Marshall Islands: Marine Resources Profiles.* Honiara, July, 1992.

South Pacific Commission. *Tuna Fishery Yearbook.* Noumea, New Caledonia, 1993.

South Pacific Commission. *Collaboration in Pacific Island Pearl Oyster Resource Development.* 24th Regional Technical Meeting on Fisheries, Working Paper No. 8, SPC Pearl Oyster Infomation Bulletin #7, SPC, February, 1994.

Systems Science Consultants. *The Development Study on Improvement of Nationwide Fish Marketing System in Solomon Islands.* Technical Assistance Report prepared for Japan International Cooperation Agency (JICA), System Science, Consultants Inc., Solomon Islands, 1994.

Tonga Ministry of Fisheries. *Report of the Minister of Fisheries for the Year 1993.* Tongatapu, 1994.

Troedson, D., and G. Waugh. *Rent Generation and Sustainable Yield in the PNG Tuna Fishery.* In The Economics of Papua New Guinea Tuna Fisheries. Ed. A. Owen and H. Campbell. Australian Centre for International Agricultural Research, Canberra. 1994:11-123.

USDA. *Composition of Foods: Raw, Processed, Prepared.* Agriculture Handbook No. 8, Agricultural Research Service, United States Department of Agriculture.

USITC. *Tuna: Competitive Conditions Affecting the U.S. and European Tuna Industries in Domestic and Foreign Markets.* USITC Publication 2339, United States International Trade Commission, Washington, D.C., 1990.

Uwate, R. *Japanese Aid and Access Fees to FFA Member Countries.* FFA Report 89/37, Forum Fisheries Agency, Honiara, 1989.

Vanuatu Department of Agriculture. *1993 Agricultural Census Report.* Memo from Director of Agriculture to Director of Fisheries, July 1, 1994.

Vanuatu Fisheries Department. *Vanuatu Draft Fisheries Bill.* Unpublished manuscript,1994.

Vanuatu Fisheries Department. Miscellaneous fisheries statistics (unpublished).

Vanuatu Fisheries Department. *Coastal Fisheries in Vanuatu: Present Situation, Trends and Recommendations.* Undated.

Watts, W. *The Crisis in Fiji's Deep-Sea Fishing Industry.* A Submission to Government, Report with Proposals and Recommendations Commissioned by the Full Membership of the Fiji Deep Sea Fisherman's Association. August, 1991.

Waugh, G. *The Collection of Rent in the South Pacific Tuna Fisheries.* Islands/Australia Working Paper No. 87/3. National Centre for Development Studies, Australian National University, Canberra, 1987.

Waugh, G. *The Development of Fisheries in the South Pacific Region with Reference to Fiji, Solomon Islands, Vanuatu, Western Samoa and Tonga.* Islands/Australia Working Paper No. 86/2. National Centre for Development Studies, Australian National University, Canberra, 1986.

Western Samoa Department of Trade, Commerce and Industry. *General Price Order 1994 No. 4, Upolu and Savaii.* Effective April 1, 1994, Apia.

Western Samoa Fisheries Division. *Annual Fisheries Reports 1988-91.* Apia.

Western Samoa Fisheries Division. National Fisheries Legislation. Draft. Undated.

Wright, A. and L. Hill (eds). Nearshore Marine Resources of the South Pacific. Institute of Pacific Studies, Suva, Forum Fisheries Agency, Honiara; International Centre for Ocean Development, Canada, 1993.

Zann. *The Inshore Resources of Upolu, Western Samoa, Coastal Inventory and Fisheries Database.* FAO/UNDP Field Report No. 5, 1991.

Forestry

Australian International Development Assistance Bureau (AIDAB). *Assessment of Commercially Sustainable Utilization of Forest Resources in Fiji - Economic Impact of Development Options.* 1993.

--. *Reassessment of Sustainable Yield for the Forests of Vanuatu.* 1994.

--. *Australian Development Cooperation in the Forest Sector of the South Pacific, Policy, Practice and Prospects.* 1994.

--. *Environments of Vanuatu: Classification and ATLAS of Natural Resources of Vanuatu and their Current Use as Determined from VANRIS.* 1992.

--. *Fiji Forest Resource Tactical Planning and Environmental Protection Project: Draft Project Implementation Document.* 1994.

Asia Money. *Supplement to Asia Money: Fiji.* 1993.

Baisyet, P.M.,and Malaki Iakapo. *Peoples Participation and Conflict Resolution in Watershed Management.* Paper Presented to 1994 Pacific Heads of Forestry Meeting, 1994.

Byron, N., and Waugh, G. *Forestry and Fisheries in the Asian Pacific Region, Issues in Natural Resource Management.* Asian-Pacific Economic Literature, Volume 2, March 1988.

Cassells, D.S., M. Bonnell, D.A. Gilmour and P. S. Valentine. *Conservation of Australia's Tropical Rainforests - Local Realities and Global Responsibilities* in Proceedings of the Ecological Society of Australia. Vol. 15. 1988.

Cassells, D.S. *Sustainable Forest Management - Some Myths, Misinterpretations, Misconceptions and Miscalculations.* Paper presented to the IUCN General Assembly Workshop. January, 1995.

Coopers and Lybrand, Honiara. *A Report on Timber Processing in the Solomon Islands and Strategies to Achieve a Profitable Industry Through Sustainable Production Levels.* Solomon Islands Forest Industries Association, November 1993.

Counterpart Foundation Inc. *1993-94 Program Summary and Annual Report.* 1994.

Dahl, L. Arthur. Oceania's Most Pressing Environmental Concerns. In AMBIO. Vol. XIII, No. 5-6, 1984.

Douglas, J. *Revenue Generation and Sustainable Forest Management.* Draft Working Paper. The World Bank, 1994.

Duncan, R. *Melanesian Forestry Sector Study.* Draft Report. National Centre for Development Studies, Australian National University, July 1994.

European Union. *Overall Summary of the Mid-term Review of the Forestry Development Project, Santo Industrial Forest Plantations Project.* Vanuatu, 1993.

Food & Agriculture Organization (FAO). *Report on the In-session Seminar on Forestry Investment in the Asia Pacific.* 1994.

FAO/United Nations Development Programme (UNDP). *PFF for Proposed Solomon Islands Natural Forest Management and Utilization Project. Status Report.* Fiji, 1994.

FAO/UNDP; Byron, Chang and Newell. *Report of Review Mission on Staffing and Training Needs and Facilities in South Pacific.* SPFDP, 1992.

Flenley, J.R. and King, S.M. *Late Quaternary Pollen Records from Easter Island.* Nature. 307: 47-50

Fiji Pine Limited. *A Government Project in Partnership with Landowners.* 1994.

--. *Annual Report, 1992.* 1992.

--. *Six Year Summary of Financial Plantation.* Wood Supply and Employment Data (1985-1990), 1990.

--. *Wood Supply Records 1990-1993 (by product type).* 1994.

Fingleton, J.S. *Resolving Conflicts Between Custom and Official Forestry Law in the South-Western Pacific.* Unisylva 175 Vol. 44, 1993.

Foundation for the Peoples of the South Pacific (FSP)/United States Department of Agriculture (USDA) Forest Service. *Programmatic Environmental Assessment; Sustainable Forestry Program for PNG, Solomons and Vanuatu.* 1993.

Fry, K., and N. Devoe. *FSP's Experience with Portable Sawmills in Melanesia. FSP*, Pacific Heads of Forestry Meeting, 1992.

German Bundestag (ed.). *Protecting the Tropical Forests: A High-Priority International Task; Second Report of the Enquete-Commission*, Preventive Measures to Protect the Earth's Atmosphere, of the 11th German Bundestag. Bonn, 1990.

Govt. of Fiji and The World Conservation Union (IUCN). *National Environment Strategy. Draft Report.* 1993.

Govt. of Fiji, Dept. Of Energy. *Carbon Farming-Growing Trees in Rural Areas of Fiji.* Discussion Paper. 1993.

Govt. of Fiji, Forestry Dept. *1992 Annual Report.* 1993.

Govt. of Fiji, Native Land Trust Board (NLTB). *Newsletter on Royalty/Rent Incomes.* Vanua, December, 1990.

Govt. of Fiji. *Environment Fiji: The National State of the Environment Report*, 1992.

Govt. of Vanuatu. *National Conservation Strategy.* 1993.

--. *Third National Development Plan (1992-1996*). 1992.

Govt. of Western Samoa. *Public Sector Investment Program (1992/93 to 1994/95).* 1992.

--. *Seventh Development Plan 1992-94.* 1992.

--. *Status of the Forestry Development Project After Cyclones.* 1994.

Govt. of Western Samoa and Govt. of New Zealand. *Western Samoa Forestry Policy Review - 3 Volumes, Forest Policy Statement; Forestry Situation, Outlook and Strategy; Implementation.* 1994.

Groome Poyry and Fiji Forest Industries (FFI). *A Reconciliation of the Forest Resources of Fiji.* 1991.

Iakopo, Malaki (Forest Dept). *Western Samoa - A Country Report*, 1994.

International Monetary Fund (IMF). *Fiji-Briefing Paper for 1993 Article IV, Consultation.* 1993.

--. *Vanuatu - Staff Report for 1993, Article IV, Consultation.* 1994.

--. *Western Samoa - Recent Economic Developments.* 1993.

Institute of Pacific Isles Forestry. *Forestry in the South Pacific: Regional Needs and Recommendations.* 1990.

Institute of Pacific Isles Forestry. *Progress Reports to Cooperators on Selected Activities* (October 1993). 1993.

ITTO. *Guidelines for the Sustainable Management of Tropical Natural Forests.* ITTO Development Series Number 1, International Tropical Timber Organisation, Yokohama, Japan. 1991.

--. Criteria for the Measurement of Sustainable Forest Management. ITTO Policy Development Series Number 3, International Tropical Timber Organisation, Yokohama, Japan. 1992.

--. *Analysis of Macroeconomic Trends in the Supply and Demand of Sustainably Produced Tropical Timber from the Asia Pacific Region.* 1994.

IUCN. *Environmental Law in Vanuatu - Description and Evaluation.* 1991.

--. *Draft Guidelines for the Ecological Sustainability of Non-Consumptive and Consumptive Uses of Wild Species.* IUCN - The World Conservation Union, Gland, Switzerland. 1992

Jiko, L.R., and J. Devletter. *Natural Forest Management Pilot Project - A Program of Applied Research in Fiji*, 1994.

Kilman, W., German Technical Cooperation, and Forest Research Institute of Malaysia (GTZ, FRIM). *Report on Fact Finding Mission on Coconut Palm Wood Marketing in Fiji and Tonga.* 1994.

Koffa, S.N. *Land Tenure: Its Impacts of Forest Land Use in Western Samoa and the Solomon Islands.* Canopy International 3rd Quarter 1994.

Lees, A. and B. Evans. *Helping Conservation Pay; Village Micro Enterprise Development in the Solomon Islands.* Fifth South Pacific Conference on Nature Conservation and Protected Areas, Tonga, October 1993.

Martell F. *Western Samoa Plantation Timber: Report on Royalty Rate Adjustment.* 1990.

Martell, F., and A. Fyffe. *Forest Resources of Western Samoa and Proposed Utilization Strategy*, Department of Agriculture, Forestry Division, Government of Western Samoa, 1990.

Mussong, M. (GTZ). *Prestudy for an Economic Evaluation of Different Logging Intensities in the Natural Forest Management Pilot Project.* 1993.

Mussong, M. *Fijian Land Owner Tree Selection System (FTS), Fiji German Forestry Project. Technical Report No. 15*, 1992.

New Zealand Ministry of External Relations and Trade. *A Review of NZ ODA Assistance to Fiji Hardwood Program.* 1992.

New Zealand Tropical Timber Group. *Towards Sustainably Managed Forests: Tropical Eco-Timber from Melanesia - A Trial Program.* 1994.

Pacific Islands Business. *The Logging Boss Who Has a Plan for Sustainable Development.* August, 1994.

Poore, D. , P. Burgess, J. Palmer, S. Rietbergen and T. Synnott. *No Timber Without Trees - Sustainability in the Tropical Forest.* Earthscan Publications. London. 1989.

Poore, D. *The Sustainable Management of Tropical Forests: The issues.* in S. Rietbergen (ed) The Earthscan Reader in Tropical Forestry. Earthscan Publications. London. 1993.

Rao, Y.S. *Forestry Research in Asia and Pacific; Focus on FORSPA.* Unisylva No. 177 Vol. 45, 1994.

Rosaman, G. (Green Peace). *New Zealand Imported Tropical Timber Group: The Timber Trade and Conservation NGOs Working Together.* 1994.

Sedjo and othe ... *ces of Domestic Forest Land Use Policy.* Resources

Sedjo and othe ... *Market.* Resources for the Future. 1994.

SPREP. *Trans ... he Role of Sediments as Pollutants in the South Pac*

Submission b ... *Development of the Forest Resources of Vanuatu.*

Tacconi, L., a ... *Erromango Kauri Protected Area.* Univ. of NSW, I ... Forest Conservation Research Report No. 5, 1994.

Tacconi, L. *A ... ion and Trade in Vanuatu.* Sandalwood Workshop

Tacconi, L. *R ...* . Draft, Department of Forests, Vanuatu, October 7

Takeuchi, K. ... rnational Economic Development. World Bank. 19

Tang, Pinso a ... *s.* Sabah Foundation. 1988.

Thaman, R.R. *Agro Deforestation and Neglected Trees: Threat to Well Being of Pacific Societies.* 1989.

--. *Land, Plant, Animals and People: Community-Based Biodiversity Conservation as a Basis for Ecological, Cultural and Economic Survival in the Pacific Islands.* 1993.

--. *Pacific Islands Agro Forestry: An Endangered Science.* 1992.

Thaman, R.R., and Whistler, UNDP/FAO South Pacific Forestry Development Program (SPFDP). *Strategies for Protection and Planting of Trees: A Preliminary Report of a Review of Uses, Husbandry and Performance of Trees in Forestry/Agroforestry Systems in Samoa, Tonga, Kiribati and Tuvalu.* 1993.

Tuinivanua, O. *Potential Functions for Fiji's Forests.* 1994.

United Kingdom, Overseas Development Assistance (ODA). *Britain's Aid to Fiji.* 1994.

United Nations Commission on Trade and Development (UNCTAD). *Project Report on Forestry Development.* 1993.

UNDP/FAO SPFDP. *Pacific Islands Forests and Trees* (SPFDP Newsletters 1993-94; 6 Issues). 1993.

--. *Heads of Forestry Meeting - Proceedings.* 1991, 1992, 1993 and 1994.

--. *Overall Regional Program Outlines for Regional Forestry Program.* Pacific Island Countries Development Partners' Meeting, March 1992, Suva, Fiji, 1992.

--. *Proceedings of Heads of Forestry Meeting.* Sept. 1992, Apia, W.Samoa, 1992.

--. *Status of Recommendations of 1993: Heads of Forestry Meeting.* 1994.

UNDP, Fiji Forest Department and SPFDP. *RAS/92/361: Draft Report of the Evaluation Mission.* Aug, 1994.

Ward, J. and Associates. Japanese Market for Tropical Timber: An Assessment for the ITTO. 1990.

Wilson, L.A. *Timber Industry in Perpetuity: Sustainable Yield Forest Management (Draft) Land Use Planning Including Forests.* 1994.

World Bank. *Market Prospects for Forest Products from Pacific Islands - Vols. 1 and 2.* Washington, D.C., 1990.

--. *Strategy for Forest Sector Development in Asia.* Report No. WTP-0182, Washington, D.C., 1992.

--. *Price Prospects for Major Primary Commodities, Vol II: Agricultural Products, Fertilizers and Tropical Timber.* 1992,1993 and 1994.

World Wide Fund for Nature (WWF), South Pacific Program. *Melanesian Forest Conservation Review.* December, 1993.

Wyatt, Stephen. *From Rough Sawn to High Quality in Vanuatu - Using Chainsaw Mills to Export Timber Doors.* Pacific Forest and Trees, 1994.

Yabaki, K.T. *Peoples Participation and Conflict Resolution in Fiji's Pine Industry.Paper for 1994 Heads of Forestry Meeting.* 1994.

Working Papers

Blakeney, Kelso J., and Irene Davies. *The Pacific Islands: Forestry Sector Profiles.* Draft Working Paper , The World Bank, Washington, D.C., 1994.

Bettencourt, S., J. Floyd, and E. Loayza. *Fisheries Sector Profiles.* Draft Working Paper, The World Bank, Washington, D.C., 1994.

Bettencourt, S., *Estimating the Value of Subsistence Fisheries.* Draft Working Paper, The World Bank, Washington, D.C., 1994.

Iqbal, Farrukh, and Thorsten Block. *The Determinants of Growth in Pacific Island Member Countries.* Draft Working Paper, The World Bank, Washington, D.C., 1994.

Tabor, Steven. *The Changing Global Setting.* Draft Working Paper, The Netherlands, 1994.

Tabor, Steven. *External Shocks and Policy Performance Measures: Methodology and Results.* Draft Working Paper, The Netherlands, 1994.

Waugh, G. S. *Rent and Development Issues in the Pacific Islands Tuna Fishery.* Draft Working Paper, University of New South Wales, Sydney, 1994.

Distributors of World Bank Publications

Prices and credit terms vary from country to country. Consult your local distributor before placing an order.

ALBANIA
Adrion Ltd.
Perlat Rexhepi Str.
Pall. 9, Shk. 1, Ap. 4
Tirana
Tel: (42) 274 19; 221 72
Fax: (42) 274 19

ARGENTINA
Oficina del Libro Internacional
Av. Cordoba 1877
1120 Buenos Aires
Tel: (1) 815-8156
Fax: (1) 815-8354

AUSTRALIA, FIJI, PAPUA NEW GUINEA, SOLOMON ISLANDS, VANUATU, AND WESTERN SAMOA
D.A. Information Services
648 Whitehorse Road
Mitcham 3132
Victoria
Tel: (61) 3 9210 7777
Fax: (61) 3 9210 7788
URL: http:www.dadirect.com.au

AUSTRIA
Gerold and Co.
Graben 31
A-1011 Wien
Tel: (1) 533-50-14-0
Fax: (1) 512-47-31-29

BANGLADESH
Micro Industries Development Assistance Society (MIDAS)
House 5, Road 16
Dhanmondi R/Area
Dhaka 1209
Tel: (2) 326427
Fax: (2) 811188

BELGIUM
Jean De Lannoy
Av. du Roi 202
1060 Brussels
Tel: (2) 538-5169
Fax: (2) 538-0841

BRAZIL
Publicacões Tecnicas Internacionals Ltda.
Rua Peixoto Gomide, 209
01409 Sao Paulo, SP.
Tel: (11) 259-6644
Fax: (11) 258-6990

CANADA
Renouf Publishing Co. Ltd.
1294 Algoma Road
Ottawa, Ontario K1B 3W8
Tel: 613-741-4333
Fax: 613-741-5439

CHINA
China Financial & Economic Publishing House
8, Da Fo Si Dong Jie
Beijing
Tel: (1) 333-8257
Fax: (1) 401-7365

COLOMBIA
Infoenlace Ltda.
Apartado Aereo 34270
Bogotá D.E.
Tel: (1) 285-2798
Fax: (1) 285-2798

COTE D'IVOIRE
Centre d'Edition et de Diffusion Africaines (CEDA)
04 B.P. 541
Abidjan 04 Plateau
Tel: 225-24-6510
Fax: 225-25-0567

CYPRUS
Center of Applied Research
Cyprus College
6, Diogenes Street, Engomi
P.O. Box 2006
Nicosia
Tel: 244-1730
Fax: 246-2051

CZECH REPUBLIC
National Information Center
prodejna, Konviktska 5
CS – 113 57 Prague 1
Tel: (2) 2422-9433
Fax: (2) 2422-1484
URL: http://www.nis.cz/

DENMARK
SamfundsLitteratur
Rosenoerns Allé 11
DK-1970 Frederiksberg C
Tel: (31)-351942
Fax: (31)-357822

ECUADOR
Facultad Latinoamericana de Ciencias Sociales
FLASCO-SEDE Ecuador
Calle Ulpiano Paez 118
y Av. Patria
Quito, Ecuador
Tel: (2) 542 714; 542 716; 528 200
Fax: (2) 566 139

EGYPT, ARAB REPUBLIC OF
Al Ahram
Al Galaa Street
Cairo
Tel: (2) 578-6083
Fax: (2) 578-6833

The Middle East Observer
41, Sherif Street
Cairo
Tel: (2) 393-9732
Fax: (2) 393-9732

FINLAND
Akateeminen Kirjakauppa
P.O. Box 23
FIN-00371 Helsinki
Tel: (0) 12141
Fax: (0) 121-4441
URL: http://booknet.cultnet.fi/aka/

FRANCE
World Bank Publications
66, avenue d'Iéna
75116 Paris
Tel: (1) 40-69-30-55
Fax: (1) 40-69-30-68

GERMANY
UNO-Verlag
Poppelsdorfer Allee 55
53115 Bonn
Tel: (228) 212940
Fax: (228) 217492

GREECE
Papasotiriou S.A.
35, Stournara Str.
106 82 Athens
Tel: (1) 364-1826
Fax: (1) 364-8254

HONG KONG, MACAO
Asia 2000 Ltd.
Sales & Circulation Department
Seabird House, unit 1101-02
22-28 Wyndham Street, Central
Hong Kong
Tel: 852 2530-1409
Fax: 852 2526-1107
URL: http://www.sales@asia2000.com.hk

HUNGARY
Foundation for Market Economy
Dombovari Ut 17-19
H-1117 Budapest
Tel: 36 1 204 2951 or 36 1 204 2948
Fax: 36 1 204 2953

INDIA
Allied Publishers Ltd.
751 Mount Road
Madras - 600 002
Tel: (44) 852-3938
Fax: (44) 852-0649

INDONESIA
Pt. Indira Limited
Jalan Borobudur 20
P.O. Box 181
Jakarta 10320
Tel: (21) 390-4290
Fax: (21) 421-4289

IRAN
Kowkab Publishers
P.O. Box 19575-511
Tehran
Tel: (21) 258-3723
Fax: 98 (21) 258-3723

Ketab Sara Co. Publishers
Khaled Eslamboli Ave.,
6th Street
Kusheh Delafrooz No. 8
Tehran
Tel: 8717819 or 8716104
Fax: 8862479

IRELAND
Government Supplies Agency
Oifig an tSoláthair
4-5 Harcourt Road
Dublin 2
Tel: (1) 461-3111
Fax: (1) 475-2670

ISRAEL
Yozmot Literature Ltd.
P.O. Box 56055
Tel Aviv 61560
Tel: (3) 5285-397
Fax: (3) 5285-397

R.O.Y. International
PO Box 13056
Tel Aviv 61130
Tel: (3) 5461423
Fax: (3) 5461442

Palestinian Authority/Middle East
Index Information Services
P.O.B. 19502 Jerusalem
Tel: (2) 271219

ITALY
Licosa Commissionaria Sansoni SPA
Via Duca Di Calabria, 1/1
Casella Postale 552
50125 Firenze
Tel: (55) 645-415
Fax: (55) 641-257

JAMAICA
Ian Randle Publishers Ltd.
206 Old Hope Road
Kingston 6
Tel: 809-927-2085
Fax: 809-977-0243

JAPAN
Eastern Book Service
Hongo 3-Chome,
Bunkyo-ku 113
Tokyo
Tel: (03) 3818-0861
Fax: (03) 3818-0864
URL: http://www.bekkoame.or.jp/-svt-ebs

KENYA
Africa Book Service (E.A.) Ltd.
Quaran House, Mfangano Street
P.O. Box 45245
Nairobi
Tel: (2) 23641
Fax: (2) 330272

KOREA, REPUBLIC OF
Daejon Trading Co. Ltd.
P.O. Box 34
Yeoeida
Seoul
Tel: (2) 785-1631/4
Fax: (2) 784-0315

MALAYSIA
University of Malaya Cooperative Bookshop, Limited
P.O. Box 1127
Jalan Pantai Baru
59700 Kuala Lumpur
Tel: (3) 756-5000
Fax: (3) 755-4424

MEXICO
INFOTEC
Apartado Postal 22-860
14060 Tlalpan,
Mexico D.F.
Tel: (5) 606-0011
Fax: (5) 606-0386

NETHERLANDS
De Lindeboom/InOr-Publikaties
P.O. Box 202
7480 AE Haaksbergen

NEW ZEALAND
EBSCO NZ Ltd.
Private Mail Bag 99914
New Market
Auckland
Tel: (9) 524-8119
Fax: (9) 524-8067

NIGERIA
University Press Limited
Three Crowns Building Jericho
Private Mail Bag 5095
Ibadan
Tel: (22) 41-1356
Fax: (22) 41-2056

NORWAY
Narvesen Information Center
Book Department
P.O. Box 6125 Etterstad
N-0602 Oslo 6
Tel: (22) 57-3300
Fax: (22) 68-1901

PAKISTAN
Mirza Book Agency
65, Shahrah-e-Quaid-e-Azam
P.O. Box No. 729
Lahore 54000
Tel: (42) 7353601
Fax: (42) 7585283

Oxford University Press
5 Bangalore Town
Sharae Faisal
PO Box 13033
Karachi-75350
Tel: (21) 446307
Fax: (21) 454-7640

PERU
Editorial Desarrollo SA
Apartado 3824
Lima 1
Tel: (14) 285380
Fax: (14) 286628

PHILIPPINES
International Booksource Center Inc.
Suite 720, Cityland 10
Condominium Tower 2
H.V dela Costa, corner
Valero St.
Makati, Metro Manila
Tel: (2) 817-9676
Fax: (2) 817-1741

POLAND
International Publishing Service
Ul. Piekna 31/37
00-577 Warzawa
Tel: (2) 628-6089
Fax: (2) 621-7255

PORTUGAL
Livraria Portugal
Rua Do Carmo 70-74
1200 Lisbon
Tel: (1) 347-4982
Fax: (1) 347-0264

ROMANIA
Compani De Librarii Bucuresti S.A.
Str. Lipscani no. 26, sector 3
Bucharest
Tel: (1) 613 9645
Fax: (1) 312 4000

RUSSIAN FEDERATION
Isdatelstvo <Ves Mir>
9a, Lolpachnii pereulok
Moscow 101831
Tel: (95) 917 87 49
Fax: (95) 917 92 59

SAUDI ARABIA, QATAR
Jarir Book Store
P.O. Box 3196
Riyadh 11471
Tel: (1) 477-3140
Fax: (1) 477-2940

SINGAPORE, TAIWAN, MYANMAR, BRUNEI
Asahgate Publishing Asia Pacific Pte. Ltd.
41 Kallang Pudding Road #04-03
Golden Wheel Building
Singapore 349316
Tel: (65) 741-5166
Fax: (65) 742-9356

SLOVAK REPUBLIC
Slovart G.T.G. Ltd.
Krupinska 4
PO Box 152
852 99 Bratislava 5
Tel: (7) 839472
Fax: (7) 839485

SOUTH AFRICA, BOTSWANA
For single titles:
Oxford University Press Southern Africa
P.O. Box 1141
Cape Town 8000
Tel: (21) 45-7266
Fax: (21) 45-7265

For subscription orders:
International Subscription Service
P.O. Box 41095
Craighall
Johannesburg 2024
Tel: (11) 880-1448
Fax: (11) 880-6248

SPAIN
Mundi-Prensa Libros, S.A.
Castello 37
28001 Madrid
Tel: (1) 431-3399
Fax: (1) 575-3998
http://www.tsai.es/mprensa

Libreria Internacional AEDOS
Consell de Cent, 391
08009 Barcelona
Tel: (3) 488-3009
Fax: (3) 487-7659

SRI LANKA, THE MALDIVES
Lake House Bookshop
P.O. Box 244
100, Sir Chittampalam A. Gardiner Mawatha
Colombo 2
Tel: (1) 32105
Fax: (1) 432104

SWEDEN
Fritzes Customer Service
Regeringsgaton 12
S-106 47 Stockholm
Tel: (8) 690 90 90
Fax: (8) 21 47 77

Wennergren-Williams AB
P. O. Box 1305
S-171 25 Solna
Tel: (8) 705-97-50
Fax: (8) 27-00-71

SWITZERLAND
Librairie Payot
Service Institutionnel
Côtes-de-Montbenon 30
1002 Lausanne
Tel: (021)-320-2511
Fax: (021)-320-2514

Van Diermen Editions Technique
Ch. de Lacuez 41
CH1807 Blonay
Tel: (021) 943 2673
Fax: (021) 943 3605

TANZANIA
Oxford University Press
Maktaba Street
PO Box 5299
Dar es Salaam
Tel: (51) 29209
Fax (51) 46822

THAILAND
Central Books Distribution
306 Silom Road
Bangkok
Tel: (2) 235-5400
Fax: (2) 237-8321

TRINIDAD & TOBAGO, JAMAICA
Systematics Studies Unit
#9 Watts Street
Curepe
Trinidad, West Indies
Tel: 809-662-5654
Fax: 809-662-5654

UGANDA
Gustro Ltd.
Madhvani Building
PO Box 9997
Plot 16/4 Jinja Rd.
Kampala
Tel/Fax: (41) 254763

UNITED KINGDOM
Microinfo Ltd.
P.O. Box 3
Alton, Hampshire GU34 2PG
England
Tel: (1420) 86848
Fax: (1420) 89889

ZAMBIA
University Bookshop
Great East Road Campus
P.O. Box 32379
Lusaka
Tel: (1) 213221 Ext. 482

ZIMBABWE
Longman Zimbabwe (Pte.)Ltd.
Tourle Road, Ardbennie
P.O. Box ST125
Southerton
Harare
Tel: (4) 662711
Fax: (4) 662716